CULTURAL POLITICS

# Poetry, language
# and politics

# CULTURAL POLITICS
general editors Jonathan Dollimore and Alan Sinfield

# Poetry, language
# and politics

John Barrell

MANCHESTER UNIVERSITY PRESS

distributed exclusively in the USA and Canada by ST. MARTIN'S PRESS, New York

Published by Manchester University Press,
Oxford Road, Manchester M13 9PL, UK
Distributed exclusively in the USA and Canada
by St. Martin's Press, Inc.,
Room 400, 175 Fifth Avenue, New York, NY 10010, USA

British Library cataloguing in publication data
  Barrell, John
    Poetry, language and politics.—(Cultural
    politics).
    1. English poetry—History and criticism
    2. Politics and literature
    I. Title  II. Series
    821'.009        PR508.H5

Library of Congress cataloging in publication data applied for

ISBN 0–7190–2441–2 hardback
    0–7190–2442–0 paperback

Photoset in Linotron Joanna by
Northern Photototypesetting Co, Bolton

Printed in Great Britain
by Hartnolls (1985) Limited, Bodmin, Cornwall

# Contents

For
TOM  AND  VAL  RAWORTH

    give me
    he said
    an old map
    some bones
    anything
    touched by the subject
    i shall
    be in my segments

# Foreword: **Cultural politics**

The break-up of consensus in British political life during the 1970s was accompanied by the break-up of traditional assumptions about the values and goals of literary culture. Initially at specialised conferences and in committed journals, but increasingly in the mainstream of intellectual life, literary texts have been related to the new and challenging discourses of Marxism, feminism, structuralism, psychoanalysis and poststructuralism, and juxtaposed with work not customarily accorded literary or artistic standing. Once more, in the tradition of Shelley, Arnold, Eliot, Leavis and Williams, though often in terms very different from theirs, culture is at the centre of important intellectual debates.

Some recent developments offer a significant alternative to traditional practice; others are little more than realignments of familiar positions. But our belief is that a combination of historical and cultural context, theoretical method, political commitment and textual analysis offers the strongest challenge and has already contributed substantial work. We call this *cultural materialism*.

There are (at least) two ways of using the word 'culture'. The evaluative use has been more common when we are thinking about 'the arts' and 'literature': to be 'cultured' is to be the possessor of superior values and a refined sensibility, both of which are manifested through a positive and fulfilling engagement with 'good' literature, art, music and so on. The analytic one is used in the social sciences and especially anthropology: it seeks to describe the whole system of significations by which a society or a section of it understands itself and its relations with the world. Cultural materialism draws upon the latter, analytic sense, and therefore studies 'high' culture alongside work in popular culture, in other media and from subordinated groups.

'Materialism' is opposed to 'idealism': it insists that culture does not (cannot) transcend the material forces and relations of production. Culture is not simply a reflection of the economic and political system, but nor can it be independent of it. Cultural materialism therefore sees texts as inseparable from the conditions of their production and reception in history; and as involved, necessarily in the making of cultural meanings which are always, finally, political meanings. Hence the series title: Cultural Politics.

Finally, cultural materialism does not pretend to political neutrality. It does not, like much established literary criticism, attempt to mystify its perspective as the natural or obvious interpretation of an allegedly given textual fact. On the contrary, it registers its commitment to the transformation of a social order that exploits people on grounds of race, gender, sexuality and class.

Jonathan Dollimore
Alan Sinfield
University of Sussex

# Preface

'The bourgeois novel is comfortably established as a genre produced by and about a particular class,' wrote Cora Kaplan in 1976, but 'oddly we still seem to expect poetry to produce universal meanings.'[1] Even more oddly, this still seemed true – true at least of the experience of poetry most students of English are offered at university – when Kaplan's essay was reprinted, ten years later. This book, a collection of five essays on poetry from Shakespeare to Wordsworth, is an attempt to argue that much of the poetry in the canon of English literature can also be read as writing produced by and about a particular class and gender, and that it will produce 'universal meanings' only for those who define the universal in the image of that class and gender. It tries to argue this by means of a close reading of the poems it discusses, and in doing so, it attempts a criticism of a more traditional practice of close reading – still, it seems to me, the dominant one in English universities, though in slow decline – by which students are still taught to look for universal meanings in poetry.

There are five people in particular who have influenced the way this book has been written. A series of conversations with Matthew Barrell, who persuaded me the book was worth writing, renewed my interest in questions of grammar at a time when it was flagging. I do not imagine that Donald Davie will like these essays, but I hope he will acknowledge a number of them as bastard offspring of his own teaching. Chris Prendergast discussed the essay on Milton with me at such length and in such detail that he became in effect its co-author, and his comments on my essay on Wordsworth were invaluable. Jacqueline Rose read and commented with immense thoughtfulness on the first, second, and final essays, and took so much trouble over my draft of the introduction that I am almost inclined to hold her responsible for its remaining shortcomings. Most of all, Harriet Guest not only encouraged the project throughout and discussed with me drafts of most of the essays, but is the co-author of the essay on Pope, and contributed to it whatever resolution it arrives at of the problems it addresses.

My thanks also to Jonathan Dollimore and Alan Sinfield, who commissioned the book; to the publisher's anonymous readers, for their suggestions and advice; to John Banks, for editing the manuscript; and to him and others on the staff of Manchester University Press who contributed to the production of the book.

A longer version of the essay on Pope first appeared, as 'On the use of Contradiction: Economics and Morality in the Eighteenth-Century Long Poem', in The New Eighteenth Century, eds. Laura Brown and Felicity Nussbaum (New York and London: Methuen, 1987). A few pages of the essay on Thomson and Clare originally appeared, in rather different form, in The John Clare Society Journal, 1983.

## Note

1 Cora Kaplan, 'Language and Gender', in her book Sea Changes: Culture and Feminism (London: Verso, 1986), p. 69.

# Introduction

What is is that makes the study of English literature a 'discipline'? The most usual answer to that question, over the last half-century or so, has begun by claiming that students of English literature acquire a specific skill, with its own rules and procedures: the skill of close critical reading, or 'practical criticism'. The notion that to grasp the meaning of a text it is necessary to pay close attention to the detail of its articulation is not, of course, unique to the study of English – it is no less crucial to the study of philosophy. But for the student of philosophy, the practice of close critical reading has been performed with a rather different end in view. It has been undertaken in order to arrive at the fullest possible understanding of the argument of a philosophical text, how it holds together, where it falls apart. The close reading undertaken by students of English has been predicated on a different notion of how a text has meaning, or, more usually, on the belief that a 'literary' text has meaning of a different kind from the meaning of other types of texts.

The meaning of a literary text, according to the advocate of practical criticism, is not to be looked for, primarily, in the argument it develops; a literary text is not primarily concerned to develop an argument. It is concerned to represent an 'experience', actual or fictional – a complex of event, feeling, perception, reflection. It does not represent this experience by any simple process of narration or description of the kind that can be summarised or paraphrased in words other than the words of the text, as the argument of a work of philosophy can be. A literary text, and pre-eminently a poem, employs all the resources of language – imagery and other figurative devices, ambiguity, the patterning of sound by rhythm, rhyme, alliteration and so on – in such a way as makes them the signifiers of that experience as much as is its merely paraphrasable meaning. Its meaning is to be discovered no more in what it says than in how it says it, and a competent close reading will be one which describes the text so as to show that the 'what' and 'how' are inseparable, and cannot be conceived of in isolation from each other; or, if they can, that is an indication that the text is 'flawed', that it fails to be fully 'literary'. Thus practical criticism is more than merely a skill: to read a text well is to arrive at a statement of its value. Just as, in the work itself, form and content are inseparable, so in a properly critical close reading, to describe a text is also to evaluate it.

Implicit, and sometimes explicit, in these notions of close reading and of the literary – and I am concerned in what follows with practical criticism not as an articulated approach or method, but as, precisely, a *practice*, developed in practical teaching situations – is the belief that language is thoroughly referential: words have meaning because they refer to something, the world and our experience of it, that is beyond and prior to language. The world we experience is not understood as constructed by language; it is already there, and words name it, describe it, more or less accurately. This belief seems to make it possible to speak not only of the value of a text, but of its truth to experience, either to what might be an 'actual' experience represented in the text, or to the fictional experience it represents, whose validity is dependent on its being somehow like actual experience, and so 'rooted' in it. There is of course an evident difficulty in making this kind of judgment, for we can have access to the experience the text refers to only through the text itself, so that it must somehow be claimed that the words of a text can do two things at once. On the one hand, they represent, with more or less success, an experience of the world, whether actual or rooted in the actual; on the other, they enable us first to intuit the 'real' nature of the experience, and then to judge the adequacy of the representation to the reality.

The question of how words can do both these things is answered, or managed rather, by understanding the relations of the real and the representation in the same terms as the relations of form and content are understood. That is to say, insofar as it seems possible to claim of a text that its meaning inheres indivisibly in its form *and* content, it is assumed that the text is an indivisible whole in which the representation of an experience is fully adequate to the reality of it; insofar as the text fails to embody its content fully in its form, the representation is inadequate to the reality. Thus to judge the text's 'truth to experience' is, after all, the same thing as to judge its value. The 'real', ostensibly outside the text and enabling us to evaluate the text's truth, is in fact located, though this is not acknowledged, only inside the text, as a product of the internal relations of form and content.

To make this location of the real within the text more secure and also more invisible, it has been necessary to insist that close critical reading should not be unduly concerned to understand the literary text in relation to the specific historical moment of its production. The meaning of a text, and still less its value, does not depend to any important extent on anything 'external' to it: on when it was written, for example, or whom it addressed, or on what was the function of any particular literary activity – writing epic poems, reading novels – at any particular period or for any particular kind of reader. The meaning of individual words, it is acknowledged, might change with time, and the competent practical critic will need to be aware of semantic changes. A thorough acquaintance with the literary tradition is also necessary, to enable a reader to judge how far a text is held within, and how far it transcends, the conventions of literary expression, and to judge also the degree of 'influence' one writer has over another. Such issues have a bearing on the originality, and so on the 'authenticity' of the text; on whether it is a 'firsthand' account of experience. But otherwise, the process of judging truth and value is a process to be conducted with reference only to the text itself, which contains almost all the information necessary to enable that judgment to be made. If a literary text is true and valuable, it has always been so, and always will be. Its qualities inhere within its language, within the relation between its form and content.

Now it goes without saying that there are a number of works of literature which have almost consistently been found of value since the time they were produced. But the criteria in terms of which they have been found valuable have certainly changed a good deal through history, and they did not usually bear much similarity to the criteria of value embodied in twentieth-century practical criticism. This seems to suggest that earlier readers of different periods may have had different notions of what literary texts meant and how they meant – different from each other, and different from critics of this century. To say that a text has always been regarded as valuable is not therefore in itself to say anything specific about the intrinsic nature of the text or of its language. Furthermore, practical criticism often attributes a permanent value to texts which have previously been largely ignored, and denies such value to texts which have hitherto enjoyed almost continual esteem. Issues like these might have led advocates of the practice to reflect on the historically-specific nature of the practice itself – to ask what it is about their own historical situation that has encouraged them to develop the specific criteria of value embodied in practical criticism.

If they have not done so, this is because to acknowledge that those criteria are historically-specific would of course be to acknowledge that

the critical judgments they produce are equally so. They have chosen
instead to assume the universality of those judgments by assuming a
notion of what it is to be 'fully human', a notion in which the idea of the
'fully literary' is metaphysically and morally grounded. To be fully human
is to take on a universal identity, and a permanent one which has not
changed throughout the whole of history, and it is to our 'full humanity'
that literary texts are claimed to be primarily addressed. If a truthful and
valuable work of literature has only occasionally been valued in the past,
that is because contingent cultural factors have usually made its potential
audience unreceptive to the particular kind of address it makes to that
humanity. No such merely contingent factors, however, prevent
competent modern readers from appreciating the universal and permanent value of works of literature, and for two reasons. They assume,
though without quite saying so, that they have a critical method which
makes the intrinsic qualities of a text entirely visible, and that, by virtue of
this method, they are able to discover exactly what it means to be fully
human; they have found a method of distinguishing the essential from
the merely contingent. They can thus lay claim even to the gift of proph-
ecy, for their understanding of why certain texts have 'survived' from the
past enables them to predict which will survive into the future. It is, in the
last analysis, on these beliefs and assumptions that the authority of
practical criticism is based.

So what version of full humanity is produced by this notion of close
critical reading? We can begin to answer this question by pointing out
that the refusal of the historically-specific nature of the writing of literary
texts, and of the method and criteria by which they are now to be read
and judged, is also a refusal of the political. Competent readers are those
who recognise that their political affiliations, and more generally their
shifting political situations as defined in particular by class and gender,
are somehow contingent to their identity as readers. How could it be
otherwise? For if each separate reader approaches a literary text from
within her or his own political situation and allegiancies, each will focus
on different features of the text as important ('what it means for me'), and
all will arrive at different judgments of its truth and value. Their different
interpretations and judgments will not speak simply of the text itself, for
they will not be based simply on the text's intrinsic qualities.

A similar notion of competence, as something above and beyond the
political, is applied to writers. The definition of what is properly a literary
text, and the belief in the pre-eminent value of literary over other kinds of
texts, are based in part on the claim that the former aim at the resolution

of conflicting constructions of experience, or, where that is impossible – some oppositions, it is acknowledged, are irresoluble – at the balance of opposing constructions. These notions of resolution and balance also in part account for the high valuation accorded to instances of ambiguity by practical criticism, for the ambiguous word or construction has seemed to be the epitome of an idea of literary expression as the resolution or balance of oppositions, one which cannot unambiguously be attributed either to the area of form or to that of content. And in a more general sense, the indivisibility of form and content in a literary text, and that associated idea of balance, have been taken as signs of the text's 'control' over the oppositions it thus resolves. Conversely, when an imbalance of form and content is detected, this is a sign of the writer's failure of control (often described as a failure of 'maturity') which is in turn the sign of a failure to subordinate her or his particular situation (gender and class specific, defined by a personal psychological history) to the universal and transcendent position of the fully human.

The judgment that a text fails to achieve a properly literary matching of form and content seems to be based on the feeling that the content has been bent to fit the form, or that the form has been wrenched out of shape to fit the content. But it is hard to know on what such feelings would be based, because, rather as in the question of the adequacy of representation to reality, we would have to believe we can intuit what the content would have been before it was embodied in the text, or what the form was that has been distorted to fit the content. In practice, an unfavourable judgment of the text as 'unbalanced' tends to mean one of two things: that the content is too urgent, emotional, partisan, 'raw', to find adequate embodiment in literary form; or the form is too limp, or too mechanically unresponsive to the energy or subtlety of the content to embody it adequately. A properly balanced text, on the other hand, should be, it emerges, a place rather like a court of law or a dinner-table, where voices should never be raised above a certain register, and where no utterance should be diffident or repetitious. The balance that the text should achieve, which was originally validated and witnessed by the matching of form and content, returns now as what validates and bears witness to that matching.

This notion of balance, as something which proceeds from a position beyond the political, is in fact a thoroughly political notion. That position, a middle point between and above all merely partial and particular situations, bears a close resemblance to a certain ideal construction of the situation of the middle-class – neither aristocratic nor vulgar, neither reactionary nor progressive. And similarly, the balance and resolution which literary texts seek to achieve bear a close resemblance to the political balance which, in England especially, was both cause and effect of the increasing power of the middle class, and which has made the notion of 'balance' itself a term of value with a crucial function in middle-class ideology, underwriting the political authority of 'consensus', or the 'middle ground', by representing as irrational extremism whatever cannot, or whatever refuses to be, gathered into the middle ground. If working-class writers fail to manifest the control necessary to the production of a properly literary text – if the 'tone' of their writings is 'awkward' or 'strident', and so apparently betrays their failure fully to have internalised the linguistic manners of the middle class – then this is evidently the result of their failure to transcend their particular class situation. If middle-class writers fail to exhibit control, this is also the result of a failure to transcend the circumstances of their lives, but their membership of a particular class is not among these.

The universal, the fully human position, from which properly literary texts, and properly literary criticism, can be produced, is also a masculine position. Masculinity cannot of course serve the mediating function between two given opposites that can be served by the position of the middle-class between the aristocratic and the vulgar. So in this case one half of the opposition is elevated into the neutral and therefore, by implication, the 'balanced' position; and the notion that men are generally more 'balanced' than women has no doubt helped to construct the competent writer and reader as masculine. Thus if women writers speak with an uncontrolled 'shrillness' of tone, for example, this is the sign of a failure to transcend their femininity – but no male writer ever lost control of his text through a failure to transcend his masculinity.

In short, the ideology of control, of balance, of unity, primarily as these are believed to be evinced by the mutual inherence of form and content, and the identification of these with the essential and the universal – both require that working-class writers and readers alike, and female writers and readers, should regard their class and gender as contingent to, as irrelevant to, their identity as writers and readers. The evidence of their success in doing so will be that the texts and the readings they produce will not be distinguishable from those ideally produced by middle-class men. Such men, whatever individual disabilities they might have to overcome to occupy the position from which creative or critical activity – properly impersonal, literary, and universal – can proceed, are handicapped by no such generic disabilities as class and gender. We can become competent close readers, according to these critical principles or assumptions, only insofar as we can identify with a 'universal' identity which turns out to be a thoroughly particular and specific identity, masculine, middle-class, and suspicious equally of reaction and of progress.

## II

The sketch I have offered of what I believe to be the politics of traditional practical criticism, as it was taught to me and as it has been taught for decades in English universities, is no more than that – a sketch, and an inadequate one, of the ethos of an institutionalised classroom practice. It is not offered as an account of practical criticism as it was differently defined and instantiated by its most influential exponents, I. A. Richards, for example, or Empson, or Leavis, or (in its American manifestation as the 'new criticism') Cleanth Brooks. And even as a sketch of a teaching practice, it leaves out much that would need to be included in a more worked-up account. It ignores the detail of different practices within the general one. It makes connections between the various assumptions that underlie that general practice in a way that its most committed practitioners would certainly contest, and in doing so it attributes a theoretical, if not a very logical, coherence to a practice which is self-consciously untheoretical and antitheoretical. And because the politics of that practice, and the notion of what it is to be human that lies concealed within it, is never very fully articulated by its practitioners, practical criticism has always been able to remain a very broad church, and it would be hard to find an actual, individual teacher whose practice has ever fully matched the account I have offered.

Indeed, the practice has in the last twenty years or so been adopted or adapted by many who would certainly deny that they endorse the political assumptions on which it is based. It is possible, for example, to read works of literature in the way I have described, and to believe oneself to be a Marxist, or a feminist; though it would be hard to produce a coherent account of how that is possible. Such developments are probably best understood in terms of what has been a widespread decline in the confidence with which practical criticism has been taught, under pressure from competing and more theoretical accounts of how texts can be read. That decline has been dramatic enough to tempt me to rewrite my account of the politics of practical criticism in the past tense. But it is a decline which, because of the resistance to theory that is, I have suggested, a defining characteristic of what has always been anxious to represent itself as a critical practice, has led to no examination of its ideological assumptions among those who still choose to teach within its terms.

If it has become possible, however, in recent years, to attempt to identify something of the covert politics of practical criticism, this is the result of the questioning of that practice that has been undertaken partly, though by no means exclusively, by marxist and feminist critics who are prepared to subject the practices of writing and reading to a more theoretical scrutiny. Once again, this introduction can attempt to offer no more than a brief sketch of a complex issue, but I can begin to suggest what is at stake in this questioning by saying something about how that notion of full humanity that I discussed in the previous section has been put in question. Some recent critics have denied that there are any qualities that we can identify in human beings that are universal, unchanging, and so that constitute a deep ground of identity among all of us. The qualities that human beings express are entirely culturally con- structed, and furthermore they are constructed within language.

And it has also been claimed, by some recent critics, that it is possible to understand different utterances in terms of the different 'discourses' they employ. This notion of 'discourse', like practical criticism, argues that the content of an utterance, and its form, are indivisible. But they are so, not in terms of some matching of form and content which is uniquely characteristic of a certain kind of utterance, a literary text, but because sequences of ideas are always linked together within specific rhetorical structures or discourses, which have their own rules of procedure and embody their own representations of reality. The discourse within which we make an utterance determines to a large extent the nature of the connections that we can make between ideas; it determines, for example, what can stand as the cause of an effect, and what can be claimed to be the effect of a given cause. Thus it determines what can be said within it, about, for example, what it is to be human, or the nature of social experience. Practical criticism is therefore a discourse; and my critique of it has been cast within a discourse of 'materialism', a discourse defined in part by its hostility to the notion that there can be any universal and authoritative account of what it is to be human, or at least to any available account of what that might be.

Though it is possible to move from using one discourse to using another – we shall see examples of that happening and of how it might happen in the essays that follow – it is never possible to speak or write except in discourse; and because all discourses embody an account of reality, they all produce a position from which that account is assembled. Whenever we speak or write we are adopting, whether we know it or not, a specific discourse, one that we feel is more or less appropriate to the topic we are addressing and the situation in which our utterance is being made. All our utterances are therefore political utterances, in the widest sense of being attempts to claim for ourselves particular positions in language, which represent us as the subjects of knowledge, and represent the world as we, and as those whose interests we assume we share, claim to see it. And thus they represent other people and other groups as the objects of our knowledge, and as occupying positions that we define for them.

It is not necessary to believe that there is no such thing as an 'essential human nature' (and I don't see how the assertion that there is not can be proved or refuted) to agree that it is difficult to find any historical example of the attempt to define what it is to be human which has not served, or cannot be read as having served, to represent and enforce the power of a specific political interest. All such definitions seem to have the effect of representing different groups of people – people of different classes, of different races, of different genders, of different sexual preferences – as more or less fully human than others, and so to attribute authority to the utterances and practices of some at the expense of others. We have seen how practical criticism does exactly that: it announces that certain aspects of our complex identities have to be shrugged off if we are to read a literary text properly; we have to endorse and identify with a kind of position that may actually be oppressive to us in order to become competent critics, and it argues, always implicitly and sometimes explicitly, that in doing so we become more human and so better humans.

If we want to resist that oppression, it is necessary to refuse the discourse in which it is embodied, and the demands it makes, and to deny that there is any one position, from which all 'literary' texts can be read, which is more or less proper or competent than another. To say this, however, is not to endorse the equal validity of that infinite number of readings which might proceed from purely personal interests – 'what this means for me' – since to read from a position which is entirely concerned with the personal history of one's own life, conceived of as merely personal, is simply to challenge an organised and institutional form of political power by a statement of personal disaffection. To resist in a way that has a chance of effecting a political challenge to practical criticism and to the interests whose power it serves, it is necessary to identify the available positions from which an effective challenge can be made, which means to read from those generic positions which practical criticism seems to deny: the positions of an oppressed class, an oppressed gender, an oppressed race. And it is necessary to identify which of those positions it is appropriate to adopt in relation to each individual text we read. For any one discourse, and especially one claiming a general dominance, will invoke (if only by negation) those other positions which it seeks to exclude and oppress, and so will identify the terms on which another reading can potentially be made, one which can then challenge the dominance of the first.

From the claim that all utterances are actually or potentially political utterances, and from the refusal to accept the version of 'full humanity' defined by the reading-practice I described at the beginning of this introduction, it seems to follow that the very definition of the 'literary text' as defined by practical criticism is open to question. We have already seen how the notion that the fully literary text aims at the resolution or balance of oppositions may be identified as a notion proceeding from a specific, and therefore partial and political position. We also saw how the indivisibility of form and content within the text was represented as a sign that this aim had been achieved. The concept of discourse offers us one way of arguing that form and content are always, in some sense, indivisible: that it may be no mark of a literary text, but that it is true of any utterance, that it means as much in terms of what it says as of how it says it. And if we believe this is true, then we would need to be wary of attributing value to texts on the grounds that they achieve an indivisibility between the two, for we may be saying simply that we value the kind of indivisibility that we believe is unique to 'literary' texts.

But once the notion of balance has been put in question, it becomes hard to see how a literary text can exhibit a particular kind of relation between form and content, or why it should be valued for doing so. All utterances exhibit a particular rhetorical relation between their form and their content, whether balanced or not. And we can never say of any text that it has failed to exhibit such a relation, because to do so is to claim, as we have already seen, that we can intuit something about its form or content that no utterance of itself enables us to intuit.

This questioning of the notions of balance, and of a specifically 'literary' relation between form and content, can also be used to question the claim that a literary text does not present an argument, but represents an experience. This may be the case with some literary texts, though by no means with all of them, and even then the notion can be maintained only so long as we define argument in a particularly narrow way. If we adhere to a notion of utterance as discourse, then all texts are concerned to represent a certain account of the world and therefore to endorse or to correct or to contradict other accounts, and in that sense, all texts are arguments. But even in terms of a narrower definition of argument, it is manifestly true that many if not all of the poems, for example, that I discuss in this book do develop arguments, though no advocate of practical criticism would dispute that they are also literary texts. In fact, what seems to be meant by the claim that it is a characteristic of literary texts that they do not develop arguments is that they are a special kind of text which, when they are argumentative, do not require us to respond to their arguments in terms of assent or dissent. They represent arguments as experiences; as instantiations of what is is like to hold certain positions and beliefs.

But once again there seems to be nothing intrinsic to literary texts which obliges us to regard the arguments they develop in this way. Nor does there seem to be anything intrinsic to other kinds of texts that obliges us to regard them differently. It seems finally that the literary text, as constituted by practical criticism, has been constituted as such not by the kind of attention that it demands, and so by its intrinsic nature, but by the kind of attention that certain critics have chosen to bring to bear on it. To say this is another way of saying that certain texts have been defined as literary in a way that has had the effect of defining a kind of utterance which can be used at once to instantiate a political view of the world and to claim that this view is above the political; and that a particular reading-practice, a particular discourse, has been invented in terms of which that claim can be made. If we question the discourse, we are free to question also the objects it defines, and, along with the literary text, we are free to question the notion of 'full humanity' which validates the claim that such a text, because it is 'universal', is therefore not political.

## III

I have already suggested that in order to question this claim, it is necessary to try to read from within the positions of those whom the ideology of practical criticism denies to be fully human. In this book I shall often, though not always, adopt a further reading-strategy – to refuse to consider the literary text in that isolation from history which enables the qualities attributed to it by practical criticism to be represented as universal and permanent qualities. That is to say, I shall sometimes make an attempt to describe what the texts I discuss might have meant to certain kinds of readers at the time when they were written, or at some later time not our own. The point of doing this is to suggest that their intrinsic meanings and qualities, as these would be defined by the adherents of the reading-practice I am trying to criticise, might not have been the meanings and qualities that they would have been thought to have in the past. In that way I shall be trying to question the claims that they are and always have been examples of a particular kind of text, and that they demand, and always have done, a particular kind of attention.

The attempt made in this book to read poems by returning them to the historical moment at which they were written is not undertaken in the hope of recovering the 'real' experiences to which they refer, and with the aim of comparing representations with the reality they represent. For all we can hope to recover of the past is other representations of it: other texts, other discourses, or other examples of the discourses embodied in the text we are examining. But if we can compare a poem, as a discursive account of reality, with other such contemporary accounts, we can begin to understand it, precisely, as discourse, as the embodiment of a partial view of the world in competition with other partial views; as political, and not as universal. And if we then compare the poem that is produced by this way of reading, with the poem as it has been represented by the reading-practice I have been attempting to criticise in this introduction, we can arrive at a clearer understanding of how that reading-practice operates to substitute what it believes to be universal meanings for the political meanings we believe that we have discovered.

This is what I have attempted to do in my first essay, on Shakespeare's twenty-ninth sonnet. I read this poem not as an account of a generalised and universal statement about a universal human emotion – depression, or disappointment – but as a statement about the specific and historical problem of literary patronage and what is suffered by one who is denied the support of a patron. I attempt to identify the discourse of patronage in which this statement is embodied, and I argue that, in its final lines, the text tries but fails to move within the orbit of another discourse, or even to find a language which would not be discursive at all, which would escape the limitations which the discursive nature of language imposes on all our utterances. But I also try to show how some modern editions of the poem have concealed the presence of the discourse of patronage in the poem, or represented it as contingent to its universal meaning, and that one way they have done this is by repunctuating the original text so as to propose a new sentence-structure for the poem, and so a new relation of form and content, and therefore a new content – a content which is allegedly universal, but which is in fact enclosed within a specifically post-romantic and liberal ideology.

The second essay discusses some sonnets by Milton, and attempts to show that they propose – this is hardly surprising – an account of gender-difference which attributes value only to the masculine, and attributes value to women only insofar as they agree to accept a masculine definition of the virtues and vices of femininity. But more importantly, the essay tries to show that this account is not simply reinforced by, it is embodied within the sentence-structure of these sonnets, which attempts to manage our response in such a way as to oblige us to acknowledge that masculine subjects exhibit a consistency of character, a continuity of their identity through the vicissitudes of circumstance, of a kind that can operate as a power to subordinate circumstances to their own will. The essay then turns to examine the gendered account of sentence-structure which Coleridge developed in his reflections on seventeenth-century writing, and it attempts to show that his acknowledgement of a belief in the gendered nature of particular kinds of sentence-structure placed him in a critical dilemma. For he saw that a writer who, by favouring a particular kind of syntax, produced an identifiably masculine account of reality, could not easily be claimed as a universal writer. But he was also troubled that a writer as valued as Shakespeare should seem to demonstrate properties of language which, according to his account, were identified as feminine. The attempt to deal with this problem may have been what led to Coleridge's producing an account of the universality of Shakespeare as dependent on the androgynous nature of his mind. But the danger this involved, of attributing value to what he identified as feminine, led him also to conceive of Shakespeare's androgyny as somehow masculine, as consisting in a power – to resolve or to balance oppositions – which no woman could be imagined to possess.

The third essay, written with Harriet Guest, considers a passage from Pope's 'Epistle to Bathurst'. It tries to identify and to examine two different discourses the poem employs in its attempt to construct an account of economic morality appropriate to emergent capitalism. It argues that though these discourses conflict with and even contradict each other, the different versions of moral behaviour that each proposed were equally of service to the interests of emergent capitalism, and both needed to be enunciated to construct a defence which would be able to answer different kinds of objection to capitalist economic activity. We then attempt to discuss how these contradictory discourses could be knotted together in such a way as to conceal the contradiction between them; and we argue that the long poem in the eighteenth century was conceived of by literary critics as a kind of text which was hospitable to contradiction because it was hospitable to a variety of subject-matter. By developing an account of the skill by which various topics could be linked into one long poem, eighteenth-century critics were also describing the means by which contradictory discourses could be linked together, but one which, by focusing attention on the skill, diverted it from the examination of contradiction. And we further argue that the eighteenth-century habit of reading long poems piecemeal, as collections of separate paragraphs, also worked to divert attention from the contradictions between the discourses.

The fourth essay, on the representation of landscapes and places in the poetry of James Thomson and John Clare, is a reworking of a topic I have written about before. It focuses again on sentence-structure, this time in relation to the issue of class rather than gender, but, like the essay on Milton, it argues that a certain kind of syntax, as used by Thomson, can be read as an attempt to represent a continuous and transcendent identity, now attributed to a certain kind of observer of landscape – an identity which, by its ability to organise the objects in a landscape and to compose them into an aesthetic whole, represents itself as 'fully human' in the sense of being fully differentiated from the objects of its perception. This ability, and this full humanity, is claimed by the polite culture of the eighteenth and early nineteenth centuries to be something that the vulgar do not possess, and the essay argues that, indeed, the vulgar may have had no occasion to define their humanity in such terms, for they were terms on which was founded an exploitative relation to nature and to the working class alike. In the poems by Clare that I discuss, I argue that the sentence-structure proposes a different account of identity, as something *constituted* by one's different perceptions rather than as *transcendent* and so as unchanged by them, and I argue that its very success in doing this could work only to confirm for the polite their estimate of the failure of the vulgar to be fully human.

The final poem I discuss, Wordsworth's 'Tintern Abbey', is a poem which makes the issue of language its own central concern. I take as my starting-point Donald Davie's remarkable characterisation of the abstract language of *The Prelude* as non-referential, as a collection of signifiers which signify only in terms of the relations proposed among them by syntax, and I attempt to argue that this notion of how abstract words have meaning can be understood as a particularly eighteenth-century notion, and as related to a particular problem in eighteenth-century empiricist conceptions of language and of human development. In such conceptions, meaning is always conceived of as referential: words mean by reference to things or ideas of things; but though it may be easy to argue that this is true of words which name the immediate objects of sensation, it is very hard to argue that it is true of abstract nouns. At the same time, however, the ability to use a highly abstract vocabulary is regarded as the sign of an identity which is, once again, fully differentiated from the objects of sensation, and so as fully human. It is an ability which had generally been denied to the vulgar, to children, and to women, though that denial is of course in Wordsworth's writings ambiguously questioned and confirmed.

Out of these conceptions were generated two conflicting desires: to demonstrate how abstract words refer to the results of complex operations performed on the objects of sense, and are in some way founded on these objects; but also to insist on that abstract language as entirely sundered from sense, so as to confirm a clear division between those who are, and who are not fully human – between, for example, men and women. In 'Tintern Abbey', I argue, Dorothy Wordsworth is used in an attempt to fulfil both these desires. On the one hand, the process by which it is imagined she will mature, and in maturing will pass naturally from using a concrete to an abstract language, seems to guarantee that the passage Wordworth himself has made from youth to maturity, from sense to intellect, is a continuous and a natural passage which guarantees that his abstract language has meaning, has reference. On the other, Dorothy's present lack of an intellectual identity, fully differentiated from the objects of sensation, is used to confirm the absolute difference between them. But in this case, her achievement of a differentiated and intellectual identity will threaten his, and will threaten the notions of gender on which the difference between them is founded. Thus the poem has to allow that Dorothy will grow up, and also to wish that her maturity will be deferred; to grant her the potential to become fully human, and to pray that she will not become so.

I have discussed no poems by women writers, and this may appear as a glaring omission in a book which attempts among other things to show how some of the poems it considers are written from a masculine position, which represents women as irrational and therefore as inferior beings. I cannot wholly justify this omission, but I can try to explain it. I could not think of a way of writing about women's poetry which would not have reproduced many of the problems about the relations of form and content in poetic language which I have tried to talk about in this book. For it has been the strength of one kind of feminist criticism to concentrate on women's poetry, primarily at the level of content, in order to instantiate women's experience of patriarchy; and it seems impossible to discuss form in women's poetry without reference to some presupposed, even if somewhere destabilised, notion of the woman's voice. The available notions of gender-difference, in particular as regards language, have either been defined by masculine subjects, or seem to rely on a notion of the *essentially* female which reinforces some traditional accounts of gender-division, and can easily lead back to another claim to be able to distinguish what constitutes our full human-ity, and what is contingent to it. I was anxious not to fall into the trap of identifying a characteristically feminine language either in terms of a masculine stereotype, or as a language which women can speak or write by virtue of being women. This leaves me in an impasse which reflects a structural as well as a political problem for feminist criticism, one which it did not seem appropriate for me to try – even if I could have tried – to resolve.

## IV

In conclusion, I want to emphasise that this is intended as a critical, not as an exemplary, book. My aim has been to criticise what I see as an institutionalised and an oppressive reading-practice, though one whose authority is in decline, and I have tried to do this by trying to show that the poems I discuss can be read, and read closely, from some other position than that prescribed to the reader by the discourse of practical criticism. But I do not think of the book as providing examples of how the close reading of poetry should be undertaken. I advertise no alterna-tive method because I have no method to advertise. Though the texts I discuss seem to me to raise similar issues, they also seem to raise very different issues, and to be accessible by different routes; but I do not claim, in the case of any of the poems I discuss, that the approach I have taken is the only approach that a critic hostile to the ideology inscribed within practical criticism can take, or should take. It is in that critical hostility itself that any unity my readings exhibit is founded.

And there is another reason why I can claim no exemplary status for my readings of poetry. At the end of the first section of this introduction, I argued that the position of competence prescribed by the discourse of practical criticism was one whose authority was based on the claim to be the universal position from which any reading of poetry should proceed. Since I believe that there is no such universal position, and that any claim that there is should be resisted, any claim I might want to make for the exemplary status of the positions from which my readings should proceed would have to be, at the least, subjected to careful scrutiny. But I also argued that the 'universal' position defined by practical criticism was in fact one which attempted to characterise the competent reader as 'masculine, middle-class, and suspicious equally of reaction and of progress'. I am male and middle-class, and the positions I adopt as a reader no doubt remain as much constructed by masculine and middle-class discourses as they have been reconstructed by my opposition to them. I can believe that in my criticism I attempt to identify and distance myself from what I have argued is oppressive, but I am equally sure that there is much in my readings that remains complicit with what I have claimed to oppose. There is too much at stake, too much power at stake, for me to be able or even in some sense to wish to be able to identify how far what I do is an attempt to disarm, and how far it is an attempt to re-empower, my own masculinity and my class-identity. And something similar would need to be said about my racial identity and sexual preference, if this were a book in which such issues were raised (for the competent reader defined by practical criticism is also certainly white and heterosexual). Any implicit definition this book may offer, of what is reaction and what is progress, should also therefore be subjected to careful scrutiny. And so should this paragraph, which may be an attempt to invite criticism of my readings, or to disarm it.

# 1

# Editing out: the discourse of patronage and Shakespeare's twenty-ninth sonnet

## I

The only edition of Shakespeare's sonnets to be published in his lifetime is the quarto volume of 1609, printed by George Eld for Thomas Thorpe. In his own, enormous edition of the sonnets, first published in 1977, Stephen Booth prints a facsimile of each poem as it appears in the quarto, and on the opposite page a repunctuated version of the poem, with the spelling modernised (*Shakespeare's Sonnets*, edited with analytic commentary by Stephen Booth (New Haven and London: Yale University Press, 1977); page-numbers in brackets in this essay refer to the third edition, 1980). His purpose in producing his own versions of the sonnets is explained at length in the course of his preface and commentary, and I will consider what he has to say about this in some detail later in this essay. For the moment I shall quote only a few of the remarks he offers by way of explanation. 'My primary purpose', he writes, '. . . is to provide a text that will give a modern reader as much as I can resurrect of a Renaissance reader's experience of the 1609 Quarto; it is, after all, the sonnets we have and not some hypothetical originals that we value.' For 'the effects of almost four centuries are such that a modern reader faced with the Quarto text sees something that is effectively very different from what a seventeenth-century reader saw' (ix). As Booth points out, 'the spelling and punctuation of the 1609 Quarto are not necessarily or even probably Shakespeare's own', but 'probably result from a printer's whims, errors, or idiosyncrasies' (xiii–xv). And even if they were Shakespeare's, Booth argues, 'it would not matter much', for to modern readers, at least if they are not in the habit of reading renaissance texts in renaissance editions or in facsimiles, the original spelling may have a misleading quaintness. Furthermore, the function of punctuation, and the value of punctuation-marks, have changed considerably since 1609,

so that 'modern readers, accustomed to logically . . . directive punctuation' may well be 'inclined to misinterpret' poems if they are not aware
of this (ix).

Booth also attempts, in his commentary, to provide a full gloss on all
the words in the sonnets which seem to him ambiguous or which in the
Renaissance had meanings now unfamiliar to the modern reader. For
'once an editor has told him about the connotative and denotative
significance of some of Shakespeare's words and phrases, a modern
reader can read Shakespeare's sonnets and respond to them very much
as a seventeenth-century reader would. He enjoys them and, I think,
misses very little, if any, of their greatness and beauty' (xii). Booth's
purpose in doing this is not to enable us to arrive at a more correct
interpretation of the poems. On the contrary, one of his purposes in writing
his commentary, he explains, is 'to advertise a criticism that does not try
to say how a work should be read or should have been read in the past
but instead concerns itself with how the work is read, how it probably
was read, and why'. He believes that 'every impression that a poem
evokes in the majority of its modern readers and can be demonstrated as
a probable response in the majority of the poet's contemporaries is and
was a part of that poem and cannot be argued away' (508). The aim of the
glosses is to reopen poems that have been prematurely closed by interpretation, and by treating impressions of meaning which are surplus to
that interpretation as disposable.

Booth's hostility to the idea that poems have correct interpretations is
a part of his desire 'to recommend an unmediated analysis of works of
art': by 'unmediated' he seems to mean 'ideologically unmediated' (515,
513; my emphasis). But when he invites us to regard it as a matter of fact
that the sonnets are characterised by 'greatness and beauty'; when we
read that 'all of us were brought up on the idea that what poets say is
sublime – takes us beyond reason', and that Booth's commentary 'tries to
describe the physics by which we get there' (x); and when we are told
that it is this complexity which gives the sonnets their 'magic' (xiii) –
when we are told all this, we are forcibly reminded that what is ideology
to one person is nature to another. We may suspect that Booth's confidence, that he can offer something near to an unmediated account of the
sonnets, proceeds from an equal confidence that a belief 'all of us were
brought up on' is outside the realm of ideology – is simply true.

It seems from Booth's explanation of his commentary that impressions of meaning available to a modern reader, but not (by reason of
changes in the meanings of words) to a renaissance reader, are not as

much a part of the poem as the impressions available to them both. I agree with him; though it seems to me that in doing so I am indulging what he might call an 'ideological' predisposition to try to understand poems in relation to the historical moment of their production. It is less clear whether Booth believes that the opposite of his contention would also be true: that impressions available to the renaissance reader, but no longer to the modern reader, are equally less valid than those perceptible to both. Booth would no doubt argue that the completeness of his commentary is an attempt to ensure that this issue doesn't arise: the glosses try to give the modern reader access to all the meanings a renaissance reader might have experienced. But meaning, of course, is not just a function of semantics – it is a product also (as Booth himself is at pains to point out) of syntax; and if the punctuation of a poem is amended so as to make that poem more accessible to a modern reader, there is evidently a risk that the syntax of the poem will be amended as well, and that meanings available in the quarto will disappear from the modern text. And this is all the more likely to happen if the editor who sets about repunctuating the sonnets holds certain truths, about their greatness, magic, and complexity, to be self-evident, for he will certainly not believe that all poems are great, magical, and complex – only some poems, only a certain kind of poem can be all those things. And it may then happen that the process of repunctuating a poem will become a process of representing it as just that certain kind of poem.

## II

What kind of poem Booth finds great, magical and complex I will try to consider at the end of this essay. But it seems unlikely that this poem would qualify:

> When in disgrace with Fortune and mens eyes,
> I all alone beweepe my out-cast state,
> And trouble deafe heaven with my bootlesse cries,
> And looke upon my selfe and curse my fate.
> Wishing me like to one more rich in hope,
> Featur'd like him, like him with friends possest,
> Desiring this mans art, and that mans skope,
> With what I most injoy contented least,
> Yet in these thoughts my selfe almost despising,
> Haplye I thinke on thee, and then my state,
> (Like to the Larke at breake of daye arising)
> From sullen earth sings himns at Heavens gate,

For thy sweet love remembred such welth brings,
That then I skorne to change my state with Kings.

This is the version of Shakespeare's 29th sonnet as it appeared in the 1609 quarto, except that I have substituted the short 's' for the long throughout, changed a few 'u's into 'v's, and the second 'i' in 'inioy' to 'j', and have replaced the 'VV' – the 'double u' – of the opening word with 'W'. Now I am probably no less suspicious than Booth of the notion that we can arrive at 'correct' interpretations of poems, though I think for a different reason, for I cannot imagine an interpretation of a poem which would not proceed from a specific reading-position, and would not be mediated by ideology. But I see no reason to believe that we should not therefore attempt to produce readings of poems which, however much we may dislike the word 'interpretation', inevitably do 'interpret' them in the sense that they foreground some meanings and push others into the background. In fact I do not see what use we could make of poems if we did not do this. That said, I want to offer a reading of this poem of a kind that will certainly violate its beauty and complexity, for I want to offer that reading in the form of a paraphrase and a commentary on my paraphrase. The point of the exercise is to show that one way of understanding this poem would involve giving a very specific gloss to numerous of the words and phrases it uses – words and phrases like 'bootless cries', 'rich in hope', 'friends', 'art', 'scope', even 'love'.

These words and phrases, taken by themselves, or in relation to the particular sense-units in which they occur, seem capable of a wide, in some cases a very wide, range of meanings; but that range will be narrowed considerably when we consider them in the context of each other, and perceive that they can be seen to signal in the poem the presence of a specific discourse, in terms of which they cohere and co-operate to define the historical moment of their utterance, and to specify, within that moment, the social position of the narrator who utters them. That discourse is the discourse of patronage, and, more particularly, that discourse as it is represented in complaints about the lack of patronage; this is a discourse we encounter repeatedly in the poetry and non-fictional prose of the late Elizabethan and early Jacobean period. Its general characteristic, like that of all discourses, is to privilege one particular meaning of the various potential meanings of the words it employs, in such a way as to make them, almost, technical terms, but in such a way also as to suggest that those privileged and special meanings are the meanings the words 'normally', they 'naturally' have.

The discourse of patronage, however, is represented in complaints about the lack or the withdrawal of patronage in such a way as seems at once to accept and to challenge that the 'normal' meanings of words are also their 'natural', their right meanings. For among the characteristics of the discourse of patronage, I want to suggest, are that it represents personal relations as economic relations (or it is, at least, unwilling to consider how there might be a distinction between the two); and that it represents personal reputation as something to be measured in terms not of moral worth or worthlessness, but in terms of honour and shame and their equivalents, which it estimates in terms of material success – or at least, once again, it is unwilling to focus on the distinction between moral and material worth and worthlessness. When this discourse comes to be used in utterances which complain of the lack of patronage, its failure to make such distinctions is apparently made an object of censure, as it must be if the complainant is to base a demand for patronage on the fact that he – for it is men we are speaking of – is morally worthy to receive it; but that censure cannot be pressed to the point where it would appear that to be in receipt of patronage is dishonoura-ble, for the complaint is also a request, and one unlikely to succeed if the petitioner represents patrons and patronised alike merely as complicit in an agreement to distort the language of true value.

My paraphrase is long and clumsy, because it attempts to offer a gloss on a number of the words and phrases in the poem – especially those I have already picked out – at the same time as it tries to produce a continuity of meaning. But I will apologise for it at greater length in a moment:

When I am out of favour with the fickle goddess of prosperity, and shamed in the eyes of men, all alone I weep for my condition as a social outcast, and I pester heaven with my complaints, but heaven is deaf, so that my complaints bring me no profit, and I look on myself from outside, as others see me, and I curse my lot in life. Wishing that I was like someone with better expectations of advancement – as good-looking as this man, as well-supplied with rich and influential friends as that man – envying the ingratiating arts of the one, and the other's range of career-opportunities, contented least of all with the advantages I do possess, and still almost despising myself for thinking this way – it may happen that I think of you; and then my condition, like the lark arising at break of day, no longer complains to heaven but sings hymns at heaven's gate, though, unlike the lark, my condition remains on the dull and melancholy earth. For when I am reminded of the deep affectionate regard you have for my interests, I am in possession of such spiritual wealth, that I would think it a disgrace to change my condition with that which kings enjoy.

Let me offer some criticisms of that paraphrase – a random selection of them – before I make an attempt to justify some of the meanings which it sets out to privilege. For all its length, the paraphrase is particularly inept whenever it encounters some very salient moments of ambiguity. Let's look, for example, at the line 'Yet in these thoughts my selfe almost despising'. It's impossible to decide, and only a paraphrase obliges us to decide, whether the narrator's self-contempt is a part of his despair, or whether it is part of what enables him to transcend it, or whether, because we can't decide which it is, we simply have to say that it is both. The problem turns on the ambiguity of the word 'yet', which embodies a similar ambiguity as is nowadays embodied in the word 'still': that is, 'yet' can indicate that at the moment when the thought of 'thee' enters the narrator's mind, he is still in that state of self-contempt described in the first eight lines of the poem; or it can indicate that he despises himself for despising himself, and that to some degree this reversal makes a passage for the thought of 'thee' to enter his mind; in which case 'yet' will have the force of 'but'. I have chosen to privilege the first of these meanings only because Booth's version, which we will look at later, puts a semi-colon at the end of line 8, and so may privilege the second, especially if we read the sonnet with the expectation that the sestet will somehow counter the drift of meaning in the octet.[1]

Or consider the word 'at' in line 12. It is essential to my contention that we can read this poem as at once critical of, and complicit with, the discourse of patronage, that though the poet's state, and the lark, both sing hymns at heaven's gate, the 'state' is primarily to be pictured as still on the earth, while the lark is in the air. As applied to the action of the lark, 'at' indicates where the lark is, where it does its singing; as applied to the action of the state, 'at' indicates the direction, the object at which the state projects its hymns – we hear this second meaning in such a sentence as 'the dog is baying at the moon', or indeed in such a line as Drayton's 'Like to the Dog that barketh at the Moone'.[2] But there is nothing my paraphrase can do to indicate a double function in the word.

Thirdly among this random set of criticisms, I have chosen to give salience to one particular meaning of the word 'love', which emphasises its status as a term in the discourse of patronage, when even within that discourse itself the word is thoroughly ambiguous, and when it is crucial to its status as part of that discourse that it is ambiguous. By substituting for the word 'love' the words 'deep and affectionate regard you have for my interests', I have tried to defamiliarise the word – to specify out of all its possible and various and compound meanings one which most clearly represents it as a part of the discourse of patronage, and most clearly removes it from the meanings we most readily attach to the word today. Thus, among the meanings my paraphrase pushes away is the one by which we indicate the kind of feeling which, we may imagine, can properly be described as love when it is entertained exclusively for one person: I mean the meaning by which I might say 'I love Tom', and you might reply, 'Oh, I thought you loved Harry'. My paraphrase, on the contrary, refers to an emotion, perhaps more a concern, which someone, and a patron in particular, may feel or entertain towards a number of people; and to the degree to which we read Shakespeare's sonnets as love-poems, in the conventional sense, to that degree we will find the meaning offered by my paraphrase a misrepresentation of the narrator's meaning. My rather brutally materialistic phrase makes the narrator's idea of love, we could say, seem *cheap*.

But then again, among the meanings of the word 'love' which do not indicate the kind of attachment which the OED defines as 'based upon difference of sex' and 'the normal basis of marriage' – among those meanings is the love of God; and if the narrator's thoughts of 'thee' lead him to sing hymns to heaven, then to exclude that meaning, as I have done, will certainly be to limit the range of meanings, or the complex of meanings, in the word. These two objections to my paraphrase take on even more weight if we put them together; it is a frequent device of Elizabethan love-poetry deliberately to blur the distinction between the exclusive love for another person, and love for God, a blurring whose effect is to insist not just on the profundity but also on the purity of an exclusive attachment of 'love'; and to insist also on the ideal perfection of the beloved. Taken together, these meanings – this compound meaning – of exclusive and divine love may certainly seem to reveal the inadequacy, even the inappropriateness, of my paraphrase of the word.

Its inadequacy I admit, and I will elaborate upon it; but its inappropriateness is another matter. In defence of my paraphrase of the word 'love', I have said that of all the meanings that I believe to be partially appropriate here, I have chosen to foreground the one least likely to occur to modern readers; and the one which most clearly connects the word with the other terms from the discourse of patronage which the poem deploys, and which I shall look at in a minute. For in the period when this poem was written, the word 'love' is frequently to be found describing the relations of patron and patronised, or the emotion which for example a petitioner for patronage claims to feel for a potential patron. A late Elizabethan poet who professes 'love' for a rich aristocrat, and who gives expression to that 'love' by dedicating a play to him, will not say that his love is cheapened – he will say indeed that his love is properly requited – if in return for that expression of love he is offered a couple of pounds, which was the going rate. A patron whose love for a poet was more abundant, whose pocket was longer, or whose desire or need for praise and honour was greater, might believe it to be an expedient, or even – for I do not intend to be merely cynical – an appropriate acknowledgement of the poet's 'love', to up the rate, even to as much as a fiver. Best of all, he might put himself out to secure to the petitioner some position, some job – whether a sinecure, or one to which substantial duties were attached – which would guarantee him a more steady income, and so guarantee a continuation of the poet's love, which otherwise, though claimed to be undying, would fizzle out if the next dedication went unrewarded, or the poet was lucky enough to find a more generous patron.[3]

Now as I say, I do not want to be merely cynical about this situation, and there is no reason to doubt that there were relations between poet and patron which were relations of such mutual regard as to make it seem appropriate to us that they should be described by the word 'love', in some such sense as we might attribute to the word now. But they remained economic relations – relations of patronage – whatever else they might also have been: relations in which the patron's love was expressed by money, however it was also expressed. So while we can say that the economic dependence of the poet upon his patron was sanitised, and as it were treated as incidental, by the description of the relation as one of love, we must also say that the patron's love was at least in part represented by his gift of money or position. But if this was the situation in what we can think of as the best possible case – where we can imagine a genuine and affectionate regard between poet and patron – then of course it had to be claimed to be the situation in all cases of patronage. For the more the language of love was played down, the more a relation of patronage would be exposed as one in which the patron was exchanging money for reputation. Furthermore, if, one way or another, it was necessary to represent relations of patronage in terms of relations of love – and, on the poet's part, as a relation of exclusive love – and if one function of that representation was to purify and idealise what was always of course an economic transaction, it is not surprising that the distinction between love for another and love for God should be blurred in the discourse of patronage, just as it was in love poems which seem concerned with relationships conceived of as non-economic.

## III

All this may serve to justify my point that the word 'love' had a specific
function within the discourse of patronage, but all this does not, of
course, justify my paraphrase – it does nothing to support my claim that
in this poem the word is being used as part of that discourse. That claim is
based on an argument which, like all such arguments, is necessarily
circular. What I am claiming, in short, is that each of the words and
phrases such as 'disgrace', 'fortune', 'bootless', 'rich in hope', 'with
friends possest', 'art', 'scope', 'injoy' – that each of these can carry the
specific significance ascribed to it by the discourse of patronage, only
because all the others can; that each of them has a meaning defined for it
by all the others, in such a way as to foreground that meaning, to put it in
front of all the other meanings which, individually, each word or phrase
can bear. Let's start by taking the phrase 'more rich in hope', which,
within the context of the line in which it occurs, seems to offer itself,
perhaps, as defining a wish that the narrator were, simply, a more
optimistic sort of chap.

'Hope' is a term frequently used in the discourse of patronage: let me
take an example from what is probably the most famous pamphlet
written by Thomas Nashe, *Pierce Penniless his Supplication to the Devil*, a work in
which disappointment at the absence or withdrawal of patronage seems
to be less a feeling of temporary loss of advantage than a permanent
condition of life; and which, on that basis, assumes a licence to disambiguate, to undress, if I can put it that way, the terms of the discourse which,
for reasons I have already suggested, it was usually necessary to keep
muffled. This is not the case, however, when Pierce comes to a consideration of the virtues of the dead Philip Sidney:

Gentle Sir Philip Sidney, thou knewst what belongd to a Scholler, thou knewst what
paines, what toyle, what travel, conduct to perfection: wel couldst thou give every
Vertue his encouragement, every Art his due, every writer his desert.

This sentence of course leaves it open, leaves it ambiguous what it is that
'belongs' to a scholar; what kind of encouragement Sidney thought
appropriate to virtue, what it was he thought 'due' to art, or what it was
that a writer 'deserved'. If we say, in each case, that it's money that is
being spoken of, we will seem to cheapen, here too, the very special kind
of 'love' that Sidney apparently evinced towards men of parts. But the
next sentence puts it in no doubt: it is money that's being spoken of, but
somehow money as transfigured, money as guaranteeing a regard which
it cannot of course wholly represent. For Pierce continues:

But thou art dead in thy grave, and hast left too few successors of thy glory, too few to cherish the Sons of the Muses, or water those budding hopes with their plenty, which thy bounty erst planted.[4]

It is, then, money that belongs to a scholar; but which belongs to him only by the same natural law as water belongs to, because it is necessary to, a tree or a flowering shrub.

Or here is Spenser, dedicating 'The Ruines of Time' to Sidney's sister the Countess of Pembroke, and lamenting the death of her brother:

... God hath disdeigned the world of that most noble Spirit, which was the hope of all learned men, and the Patron of my young *Muses*; togeather with him both their hope of anie further fruit was cut off: and also the tender delight of those their first blossoms nipped and quite dead.

And here is the Fox in Spenser's 'Mother Hubberds Tale' complaining that the service he has done his country has got him nowhere:

And still I hoped to be up advanced,
For my good parts; but still it hath mischaunced.
Now therefore that no lenger hope I see . . .
I meane to turne the next leafe of the booke.

Or we could take an example from Drayton's revised version of his eclogues, in which, in the voice of the shepherd Rowland, he complains of his inability to attract lucrative patronage while appearing to complain of some more specifically pastoral persecution:

To those fat Pastures, which flocks healthfull keepe,
Malice denyes me entrance with my Sheepe.

Therefore, says Rowland, 'my hopes are fruitlesse'.[5]

These examples seem to summon 'more rich in hope', in Shakespeare's poem, within the orbit of the discourse of patronage. Once there, the phrase summons a word like 'bootless' within the same orbit: it weakens further the weak senses of the word ('useless' or 'unavailing', as Booth has it, 180), and foregrounds the sense 'bringing in no booty', no profit – no 'fruit', as the common euphemism would have it. It suggests that the 'friends' in line 6, represented as they are as a possession of whoever it is the narrator envies, are precisely the kind of rich and influential friends whose love is represented by the disbursement of money or the offer of a salaried position. It focuses the word 'Fortune', not as mere chance but as fortuitous prosperity, or as the deity who now extends and now withholds the prosperity which, to many writers in renaissance Britain, could come only from patronage: as the Fox again complains

Thus manie yeares I now have spent and worne,
In meane regard, and basest fortunes scorne.

Within the discourse of patronage, in 'disgrace with . . . men's eyes'
comes to mean to be shamed by one's poverty, and to be held 'in meane
regard'. 'Art' comes to refer to that kind of skill in social address which,
whatever one's worth as an artist, will secure lucrative patronage; as
Spenser's Colin Clout complains, success at court is to be won by those
who have

A filed toung furnisht with tearmes of art,
No art of schoole, but Courtiers schoolery.
For arts of schoole have there small countenance.

'Scope' comes to mean neither the subject-matter available to a writer
(180), nor imaginative or intellectual range: that second meaning was
probably not firmly attached to the word for another two centuries – at
least, the only example of that meaning offered by the OED prior to 1775
is the instance we are now considering, in this poem, where the word
seems rather to mean, within the discourse we are identifying, the
freedom of opportunity which money and position can offer.[6]

The presence in the poem of that discourse also suggests that the
narrator does not wish to be more good-looking simply so that, in the
general course of life, he will be more attractive to other people, but
because, as Pierce Penniless points out, 'comliness' may persuade a
patron to look favourably upon a petitioner. It suggests that when the
narrator curses his fate, he is doing something akin to what Pierce does
when he 'curses' his 'birth', the meanness of which obliges him to
become a petitioner. And most crucial of all, it suggests that the 'outcast
state' that the narrator beweeps is not his state of mind, his 'downcast
spirits', his subjective sense of himself as an outsider, of such a kind as
may change to a mood of elation in the right circumstances. It suggests
rather that it is his state 'in regard to welfare or prosperity', as the OED puts
it, or his social condition, something akin to his 'estate', with a sense of
social and economic disadvantage combined: the 'estate' which Pierce
also bemoans, and attempts to relieve, and which he imagines must be
relieved by money, if he is to cease to be a social and economic outcast.
This is not something which can be relieved by a decision to think
positive and look on the bright side, and this point will come to be of
importance when we come to examine Booth's version of the poem.[7]

We do not, of course, have to start the process of identifying the
discourse of patronage by starting as I have, with the phrase 'more rich in

hope'; we could start with almost any of the words and phrases I have referred to, and, having identified its meaning within that discourse, we could observe how it attracts the others into the same discourse. My point is that each word and phrase offers to define the others; and it is together, each supporting the other, that they produce the discourse within the poem.

Let us return now to the word 'love', and to the nature of the relation it suggests between the narrator and 'thee'. Now if we came across this poem in isolation from the sonnets that surround it, we might find ourselves believing – and reasonably enough – that 'thee' is God. The poem would then make a single and coherent statement, that when the narrator is depressed about his economic and social disadvantages in the competition for patronage, he thinks of God, whose love brings such spiritual wealth as to pluck him out of the slough of despair and envy, and make him aware that the love of God offers him rewards and consolations far more worth having than anything to be won in that demeaning struggle. But if we read this poem as one of a run of Shakespeare's sonnets, which continually address a 'thee' who is clearly human, and male, we are unlikely to plump for that solution; in which case we are left with a puzzle, which, by the very nature of the discourse of patronage, cannot be solved.

The puzzle is this: is the relationship of love between the narrator and 'thee' to be understood not as a relation of poet to patron, but as an exclusive attachment of deep affection, entirely uninvolved in economic considerations of the kind that appear to infect the friendship spoken of earlier in the poem? If it is, then the love that 'thee' has for the narrator seems to work more or less as the love of God would work, in releasing him from the degrading circle of envy and interest. Or is the love of the kind that a patron may be supposed to have for a petitioner? We cannot tell; because if it is that second kind of love, then its effects will still have to be described in spiritual rather than material terms, so as to represent that economic relation as so sanitised, so purified, so much a marriage of true minds, that the material wealth the relationship may bring to the narrator is not to be mentioned alongside the spiritual refreshment and encouragement it brings him. When I say 'is not to be mentioned', I intend both senses of the phrase: it is not worthy of mention, and it must not be mentioned – it is unmentionable.

I can put the point best this way. The poem may say, and this we could call the best possible case, that the special and exclusive love of 'thee' for 'I' is like the love of God, and makes all the economic worries that the speaker has been prey to entirely beneath consideration. Or, at the other extreme, the poem may be actively concealing a less beautiful and magical meaning, a meaning that runs like this: 'when I'm pushed for money, with all the degradation that poverty involves, I sometimes remember you, and you're always good for a couple of quid'. But whatever is being said or not said here, the discourse of patronage invoked earlier in the poem refuses to allow us to decide, precisely because, as I have argued, it is the nature of that discourse that it represents the economic relations of patron and petitioner in terms that must be indistinguishable from other kinds of purer, more ideal relationships of love.

The fact that we cannot find a solution to this puzzle does not make it a waste of time to attempt to define its terms; for to do so enables us to do something to situate the poem at the historical moment of its production: a moment, for example, at which the commercial market for writing was not so developed as to enable a writer to be a professional writer in the sense that he could hope to be supported by his sales, and be exempt from the need for patronage; but a moment, also, when the growth of literacy and learning, and other more purely economic factors, meant that there were far more petitioners for patronage than the potential patrons were able or willing to patronise. To attempt to define the terms of the puzzle also enables us to locate the identity of the narrator as something produced by that historical moment and spoken within a discourse that moment provides. The best possible case, as I have called it, is the case in which the narrator may be understood as claiming that he is freed, by the transcendent power of love, from the social and economic conditions that the discourse of patronage exists to describe and conceal; that he is freed, therefore, from speaking within the terms of that discourse, and is able either to speak within the terms of another, or to speak a quasi-religious language of love which transcends the limitations that all discourses impose on our utterances. But even that case cannot escape the embrace of the discourse of patronage, precisely because that discourse has its own power, to appropriate for its own purposes the most expansive and the most hyperbolic expressions of authenticity. And even in that case, the claim to an authentic love, which confers on the narrator an authentic, an unconditional identity (or one subject only to the condition that he is truly loved), and which escapes the constraining representation of personal relations as economic relations, can represent that escape only in the terms prescribed for it by the discourse of patronage, which pushes the narrator into behaving as if all

that is required to show that one's authentic feelings and identity transcend the constraints of the social, the economic, the historical, is to
elude the terms of a particular discourse which in any case refuse to be so
eluded.

## IV

But I suspect that my main priority should now be to answer the
objection that no reader of this poem could conceivably doubt the
presence within it of the discourse of patronage, and that I have spent
several pages in the laboured statement of the obvious. And any reader of
this essay who has consulted Booth's commentary on this sonnet may
have found it particularly odd that I should have situated my reading of
the poem in the context of a disagreement with his editorial method. For
almost all the meanings I have pointed out as belonging within the
discourse of patronage are offered by Booth in his glosses on the poem.
He does not, it is true, have anything to say about 'love', which is for me
the word which suffers most from the parasitic action of the discourse in
the later lines of the poem. But for 'more rich in hope' he offers alongside
the generalised meaning 'who has more hope, who is richer with respect
to hope', a second, 'who is prospectively more wealthy, who has better
expectations of wealth', a meaning which certainly attracts attention to
the fact that the hope may be for material advancement, if not for the
specific kind of material advancement that patronage can offer. The word
'art' is glossed by Booth as '(1) skill; (2) learning: and possibly (3) devious-
ness' – again, a gloss which acknowledges, though it also marginalises,
the meaning attributed to the word in the discourse of patronage. 'Scope'
is glossed as 'range of ability', but also as 'range of opportunity', the
meaning I have foregrounded (180).

But to acknowledge these meanings is not the point, if they are not also
recognised as constituting a particular discourse, and thus as inviting us
to understand the poem as an utterance made within the terms of that
discourse. And Booth's edition does not allow the interpretation I have
offered, because though some of the meanings which that discourse
attributes to the words in the poem are available in Booth's commentary,
they are not available as the constituent parts of a connected discourse in
his text of the poem. In that text a different discourse is foregrounded –
one which cannot allow the meanings I have pointed out even to appear
as some of them do in Booth's commentary, as 'suggestions' or
'overtones' (xi). This different discourse is foregrounded by Booth's

repunctuation of the poem, which certainly has the effect of 'moderniz-ing' the poem, though not therefore of enabling a modern reader to 'respond' to it 'very much as a seventeenth-century reader would'.

This is Booth's version:

When in disgrace with fortune and men's eyes,
I all alone beweep my outcast state,
And trouble deaf heav'n with my bootless cries,
And look upon myself and curse my fate,
Wishing me like to one more rich in hope,
Featured like him, like him with friends possessed,
Desiring this man's art, and that man's scope,
With what I most enjoy contented least;
Yet in these thoughts myself almost despising,
Haply I think on thee, and then my state,
Like to the lark at break of day arising
From sullen earth, sings hymns at heaven's gate;
   For thy sweet love rememb'red such wealth brings,
   That then I scorn to change my state with kings.

My decided preference for the quarto version of this poem means that it would be tendentious for me to produce a paraphrase of this version. But fortunately there is another edition of the sonnets which offers a text for this poem virtually identical with Booth's, and which offers its own paraphrase on the opposite page. It goes like this:

When down on my luck and with people set against me, all alone I lament my lot as an outsider: but I reproach heaven in vain with my laments, when I look upon myself and curse my fate. I wish myself like one with more hope, like him in looks and surrounded with friends; I find myself envying this man's art and that man's range, least contented with what I most enjoy. In this mood almost despising myself, I happen to think of you: and then, like a lark rising at dawn from sullen earth, I chant hymns to heaven. For thinking of your love brings such wealth to mind that then I would not change my state with kings.[8]

This paraphrase is by A. L. Rowse; and within the limits of what the exercise can do – it can do little more of course than point one way through a poem, privileging those meanings which the paraphraser thinks it most important to draw attention to – within those limits, this seems to me a just representation of the versions of the poem which Rowse and Booth, in their separate editions, have produced; though Booth, as we shall see, would not agree that it is often desirable or even possible to engage in the exercise at all.

Now evidently Rowse is reading a very different poem, and calling attention to very different meanings, from the poem and the meanings I was concerned with. Most particularly, the discourse of patronage seems entirely to have disappeared from the poem; and with it, of course, all those constraints which complicated and, I argued, frustrated the claim to a transcendent love and a transcendent identity which the narrator makes in the last lines of the poem. For if an interpretation sheds, as I would argue this interpretation has done, those meanings in the poem in which is embodied the specific nature of the economic and social constraints which produce, which condition, the narrator's identity, then it will not be hard to represent the narrator as successfully claiming that his identity is unconditional and autonomous. So what is the difference between the two versions, and what accounts for the fact that each seems to move such different meanings into the foreground? There are two kinds of answers available to that question: the first focuses on how this version differs from the first, so as to produce this new (and, I believe, distinctively post-renaissance) meaning; the second focuses on that idea of the nature and function of poetry, of which, I believe, this second version is an expression. Let's look at the first issue first.

In terms of that issue, then, there is a number of possible answers to the question, but only one seems decisive. We could argue, for example, that simply to modernise the poem's spelling is to invite us to believe that we will find modern meanings in the words, or at least will not be invited to speculate on the possible strangeness of those words. We could argue that the changes in punctuation produce in us a similar expectation that the poem's meanings will be immediately available to us, will be, that is, modern meanings. The decisive answer seems to me to be indeed a matter of punctuation, but of one instance of it only: the decision to place a comma in the twelfth line, after 'sullen earth'. Up to that point it is perfectly possible to identify in this poem the discourse of patronage; after that moment it is extremely difficult to persist in the belief that one has identified it, that there are therefore special and strange meanings which are privileged in the poem, or that the conclusion of the poem and the kind of spiritual success it lays claim to are in any way constrained by those meanings.

To place a comma after 'from sullen earth' is to propose, in the first place, a radically different meaning for the word 'state' from the one I proposed. The argument for inserting the comma turns on the fact that line 12 requires that the poet's 'state' be in two places at once: on 'sullen earth' and also at 'heaven's gate'. This will seem – at least if we don't consider the double meaning for 'at' which I proposed earlier ('baying at the moon') – a perfectly reasonable objection, the more persuasive in that if we remove the end-stop from the previous line and place it after 'earth', all ambiguity is removed, and the 'state', and the lark with which it is compared, become more neatly congruent in their actions: both start from sullen earth, both rise to heaven's gate. Booth's version of this argument is that the punctuation in the quarto:

can mislead a modern reader into assuming that he should understand *lark* as the only riser, *state* as the only singer, and *From sullen earth* as designating only the place from which *state sings*. Actually, the general context (downcast spirits and low status), on the one hand, and both common knowledge of birds and the inevitable unity of the standard phrase 'arising from,' on the other, make any punctuation powerless to deny that *state* and *lark* are both singers and risers. However, both the Q [quarto] punctuation and the line-end pause between *arising* and *From* carry a syntactically blurred image of the speaker('s state) sending hymns aloft from the earth, sending up hymns to heaven: 'then my state from sullen earth sings hymns . . . like to the lark arising at daybreak.(181)

There are arguments against this, of course. There is an argument from euphony, that in terms of rhythm and pitch, the triumphant assertion that is made or attempted in these lines is far more convincing if we read:

> and then my state
> (Like to the Larke at breake of daye arising)
> From sullen earth sings himns at Heavens gate . . .

than if we read

> and then my state,
> Like to the lark at break of day arising
> From sullen earth, sings hymns at heaven's gate.

The second reading obliges us to descend, both in terms of the pitch and of the ideational content of the lines, back to the low level which the narrator (by the argument of the second paraphrase) has successfully left behind him. But euphony may count for little against what seems to be the logic of the emendation. There is another argument, based on my own paraphrase: I have claimed that much of the pathos of the poem derives from the narrator's simultaneous desire and inability to escape from the limiting conditions of earth and perhaps of discourse; and if the narrator's state can do all that the lark can do, that source of meaning and pathos is abolished. But that argument has no status, as we shall see, in relation to a text in which the meanings it presupposes have been at best concealed, at worst erased.

And it is by this change of punctuation that they are concealed. For if both lark and state arise from sullen earth to heaven's gate, we have to find a meaning for 'state' which is compatible with the notion that it can be successfully elevated above the earth – that it can change its position as the narrator's mood, or the content of his mind, changes. And there is of course such a meaning available, by which 'state' would mean not social condition, which must be changed by social action; not economic condition, which must be changed by material means – not in short something akin to 'estate', but 'state of mind'. We can be in a low state, a low state of mind, and then something can happen which puts us in a better state, which moves us from depression to elation. In Booth's notes, which 'attempt to indicate not only what words mean but when they mean it' (x), 'state', in lines 2, 10, and 14, is glossed as '(1) condition (social, economic, mental, emotional, or spiritual); (2) status, rank' (180). The second of these meanings coincides with my reading of 'state' as 'estate', as do some, but not all, of the meanings Booth lists under (1). I entirely agree that in line 2, when the presence of the discourse of patronage is yet to be established in the poem, 'state' can mean 'mental, emotional, or spiritual state' – say, 'state of mind'. But once the discourse is established, then when the word re-occurs in line 10 of the quarto text, those meanings are pushed aside, and the meanings 'social and economic state', 'status or rank', become the primary meanings available to us. In Booth's edition, the reverse happens: all the meanings of 'state' that define the word as part of the discourse of patronage become at most 'suggestions' or 'overtones', and we are left with 'state of mind' as the primary meaning.

Once the meaning 'state of mind' has thus been selected and foregrounded, it has the effect of attracting all those terms, which, I argued, were attracted by each other into the discourse of patronage in the first poem, back out of that discourse again, and towards those meanings which seem most easily compatible with 'state' as 'state of mind'. The 'outcast state' bewept in line 2 seems to become also primarily a state of mind, a *sense* of oneself as an outsider, rather than a condition of social exclusion. 'In disgrace with Fortune' can quite properly be glossed as, simply, 'down on my luck', and whether that luck operates in relation to one's economic success or, say, one's personal relationships, conceived of as purely personal, becomes immaterial. Indeed, the whole vocabulary of the poem becomes immaterial, for the poem becomes a narrative about a state of mind whose position is determined not by material factors but by *itself*. 'Bootless' comes to mean, simply, 'unavailing'. 'More rich in hope' means 'more generally optimistic'. 'Friends' become personal friends, the kind who help you through a bad patch, by listening to your troubles (lots of black coffee), not by securing you a better social and economic status. 'Art' and 'scope' become, primarily, the technical accomplishment and imaginative range of another poet, whom the poet envies for these alone, and not for his better success in attracting patronage. The boast in the last couplet, that the narrator would not change his state with kings, becomes simply a banal declaration that he would not change his cheerful frame of mind with the frame of mind that kings possess – with the covert assumption, of course that money can't buy you love – and not that he would not swap his lowly economic and social status with the highest earthly 'estate' he can imagine.[9] And finally, even love itself is disinfected by that one comma, which purifies the emotion of all those taints of the material and the self-seeking that the narrator of the first poem, I argued, was powerless to wash away.

Now with the probable exceptions of the word 'scope', though I have called the meanings thus attributed to the poem in the second version 'modern meanings', I do not mean to imply that they are not meanings which we can believe were present in the poem for its original readers. Indeed, my account of the first version depends absolutely on the assumption that they were, but that in that version they were present as, if you like, the bright side of each word, of each coin in the purse that is the discourse of patronage, and that their function was to attract our attention to that bright side, to the good meanings, away from the dull reverse side, where friends turned out to be of value for what they did for your pocket, where hope was hope for advancement, and where love was requited according to a fixed scale of charges. By concealing the meanings disclosed by the dull side of the words, however, this text conceals much of the content of the bright side as well, for bright and dull are here relative and binary terms, which require and produce each other. It conceals, in short, all those meanings which have to be recovered by historical enquiry, and announces that all the important meanings of the poem are meanings as available to us in the late twentieth century as they were to those who read the quarto edition of the sonnets when it came out in 1609. It is in this sense that the poem in its second version has developed a 'modern' meaning, and one based on a specifically modern, and a specifically liberal, notion of what it is that poems do and mean.

## V

That brings me to the second answer to the question I proposed, what accounts for the difference between the two versions, or between – for we can reduce it to that – the different punctuations of lines 11 and 12? I can rephrase this question by asking what it is that has persuaded most editors of the sonnets in this century to privilege the kinds of meanings that are produced by this emendation and numerous others in editions of the sonnets? I will offer a very brief answer: that such editors have had a predisposition to believe two things: that great poetry must be universal, must speak the same meanings to all people at all times, to an unchanging human nature; and that the place where we are all the same is in our minds, the site of our individual identities, which are imagined to be primarily self-produced – to be fundamentally uninfluenced by, independent of, transcendent over whatever in the world might seem to press limiting conditions on that individual identity. Insofar as we are individuals, paradoxically it may seem, so far we are all the same; we differ only as there are, laid over our individual and true (true because individual) identities, the accretions of our different social and personal histories and situations. To reveal that common ground of individuality, we must scrape away whatever seems to threaten to condition our identity, and our individuality will be revealed as pristine, shining, unchanged. If Shakespeare can be shown to speak in that identity (which he can be, if we suppress those meanings in his poems which threaten to obscure it), then he can speak immediately to us, if we too, as we turn to read his poems, can persuade ourselves to believe that here, in poetry, is a language which, by privileging the individual, scrapes away the accretions also of our own particular histories. This belief not only homogenises individuality to universality, to a common and so allegedly fuller humanity; it also homogenises the different histories that might seem to condition different subjects and subjects in different periods; for all those histories are reduced to the same abstract notion, 'history' – to 'ideational static' (391), white noise, through which, if we listen attentively, we will be reassured to discover that the same tune is playing, was playing, and so (we may presume) always will be.

Now Stephen Booth would certainly object to my attributing this position to him, and would certainly object also to my associating his text with Rowse's paraphrase: his belief that the greatness of the sonnets is partly a function of their 'dizzying complexity' (xiii) leads him to believe also that few of them 'can be paraphrased without brutality' (387). I want now to try to do justice, though the attempt will have to be brief, to Booth's arguments, as well as to my own suspicions of them and to my claim that, in spite of everything, Rowse's paraphrase describes Booth's version of the poem quite fairly, and that the assumptions that produced both text and paraphrase are as I have described them.

Booth believes that poetry in general, but Shakespeare's especially, works in such a way as continually to produce an ideational surplus, a range of suggested meanings which must be present in the poem if they are triggered off in the mind of the reader. As we encounter a word in a poem, a whole range of possible meanings are available to us, and in that sense must be present in our mind until they are disambiguated by their context, and cannot be assumed to be cancelled even after they are thus disambiguated. But if they are present, however briefly, they cannot be treated as extraneous to the poem's meaning, which is – and this is one reason why poetry cannot be paraphrased – the whole experience of reading the poem, of participating in the 'action' which the poem performs (514–15). Similarly, groups of words may seem to make, as we read them, fragments of sense which turn out to be surplus to the requirements of the whole syntactical structure in which they inhere, and which are therefore disambiguated by that structure; but they are not, therefore, cancelled from our consciousness or from our unconsciousness (391) – they become and remain a part of the experience, the meaning, of the poem. Thus, it has to be assumed that there is some kind of primary meaning in the poem, whose function is to disambiguate, and to define what is the ideational surplus. To offer a paraphrase of that meaning, however, is to threaten to abolish the surplus, to behave as though it contributes nothing of importance to our experience of reading the poem.

With much of this I agree wholeheartedly, and in the next essay I shall be reading some lines of Coleridge to make much the same point. I take issue with Booth, however, over what conclusion we are to draw from the last sentence of my last paragraph. For to me it does not at all seem to follow that because a paraphrase seems to threaten to abolish meanings which are surplus to the primary meaning we should not paraphrase poems. I would argue that whether we should or not, we do effectively paraphrase them when we identify a primary meaning, and it is just as well to try and spell out that meaning, so that we can recognise and test it. I would also argue that we cannot avoid mentally paraphrasing a poem: that it is of the nature of discourses that in any connected utterance they privilege some meanings of words and obscure (though they cannot therefore entirely cancel) others, and that we cannot arrive at any notion of the primary meaning of an utterance except in the terms of discourse. In relation to this particular poem, I am arguing that Jacobean readers could not have constructed a primary meaning for this poem except in terms of the discourse of patronage, whose determining presence in the poem is repeatedly signalled by the poem's vocabulary. To produce a text which conceals that discourse, treats the meanings it privileges as only 'ideational static', is thus the very opposite of enabling the reader to 'respond' to the poem 'very much as a seventeenth-century reader would'. It is, on the contrary, to go a long way towards denying the difference between what a seventeenth-century reader would have identified as the primary meaning of the poem, and the meaning that is attributed to it by the fact that much of its vocabulary is now primarily incorporated within what are now liberal discourses on personal relationships ('friends', 'love'), on the creative artist ('art', 'scope'), and on individual subjectivity ('state' as 'state of mind'), discourses which are no longer in danger of being contaminated by the discourse of patronage.

For Booth, even to suggest what the primary meaning might be, or might once have been, is to do violence to the whole experience, the whole action that the poem is. Though there is, he believes, 'a clear and effectively straightforward sense' (371) in all but a few of the sonnets, it is usually the case that it must not, indeed it *cannot* be stated; and, as we shall see, it is so clear, so straightforward, that to describe it is anyway unnecessary. But Booth also believes that it is a characteristic of the greatness of the sonnets that they give us the sense of 'effortless control of the uncontrollable' (xiii). The effect of this argument is almost to deny that anything in the sonnets can be described as surplus, for almost everything in them is controlled; so that Booth can write 'in the sonnets Shakespeare *uses* [my emphasis] more of the ideational potential in words than the logic of their exposition needs or can admit'. I take it that since it is impossible to demonstrate that Shakespeare or his sonnets (as opposed to the readers of them) 'use', in this active sense, what is surplus to their straightforward meanings, this part of the argument is true by definition, as it were: such control is constitutive of great poetry; since Shakespeare's poems are self-evidently great poems, he and they must be assumed to control, to use, all surplus meanings within infinitely complex but finally coherent and unified statements. He occupies the central position from which all meaning proceeds, and in which the unity of all meanings can – theoretically at least – be reconstituted.

This control, however, is not always Shakespeare's responsibility: sometimes it is indeed the reader who wears the trousers. 'All this complexity and density', writes Booth, 'is not only mastered by a reader but mastered without conscious effort or awareness' (xvii). I should apologise, I suppose, for trying to get some cheap mileage out of Booth's choice of verbs here, and his repeated reference to the reader as 'he'. No doubt he has no intention to exclude women from the circle of readers, and no doubt I have been guilty in my own writings of a similarly casual sexism. But as we shall see in the second and fifth essays in this book, it has been a defining characteristic of liberal discourses on language that they attribute control, 'mastery' of language much more readily, if not exclusively, to men, and it would be a pity to pass up an opportunity to remind myself, as well as others, that these casual choices of verb and pronoun are the signs and instruments of a rather less casual oppression.

The reader's 'mastery', then, enables him to disentangle the surplus from the necessary. But he does not therefore discard the surplus, but produces, at the same time, the 'clear and effectively straightforward sense', and an infinitely ambiguous but still controllable sense whose nature is that it *cannot* be disentangled from the straightforward sense. I had better acknowledge that I am not sure that I follow Booth's argument here, and may be misrepresenting it; for I do not really understand how the assertion of Shakespeare's control, and/or the reader's mastery, is ever going to become more than simply an assertion and a mystery. But I do think I see the purposes of the assertion, which are to assert the unity of the poem by asserting the unity of those, the author and/or reader, who produce its meanings, to claim that Shakespeare's poetry is at once as infinitely complex and as magisterially controlled as great poetry must be, and to insist that it is nevertheless immediately comprehensible to the modern reader, as all great poetry, which is universal in its appeal, must be.

And I can see what follows from these positions, which is that if the reader 'masters' all the infinite complexity of the text; if (as Booth says) the renaissance reader did the same; and if the sonnets have (all but a few of them) a clear and effectively straightforward sense, then whatever meanings the modern reader notices must be co-extensive with all the meanings which a renaissance reader might have noticed. The straightforward sense which the modern reader both does and does not disentangle from the surplus, must be the same sense as seemed straightforward and in that sense primary to the renaissance reader. Both share the same experience of the sonnets, which are universal, therefore, in their meaning, a meaning which in no crucial way depends on any specifically renaissance meanings the poem may contain. For there are, Booth argues, only 'some relatively rare instances in the sonnets where historical changes in idiom invalidate or distort a modern reader's probable response to a line' (xiii). Except in those rare cases – he finds none in this sonnet – the kinds of meanings which I have argued are introduced into this sonnet by the discourse of patronage are relegated to the surplus, are part of what the modern reader supposedly masters, but not part of the straightforward, clear, and universal sense of the poem.

However great the reader's mastery may be, however, he is not omnipotent; for in order to lay bare, Booth believes, that universal sense, it is necessary to re-spell and re-punctuate the text in such a way as will remove – as far as possible – its strangeness, to reveal the clear sense that both renaissance and modern readers experience in reading the poem, a clear sense which is the same to them both. But, as we have seen, that sense can be claimed to be the same to both, only by claiming that the meanings which the modern reader will most readily attach to the poem are universal meanings. Specifically renaissance meanings, few though they allegedly are, must be relegated, by the processes of editing, to what is surplus to the text's straightforward movement towards unity of meaning. And of course if one of the pressures on how the modern reader determines the meaning of a poem is the expectation that great poems speak a universal language, the meanings she or he will seek out will be such as minimise whatever knowledge they happen to have of the discourses of the renaissance and the historically-specific meanings embodied in them: these will be treated as surplus, for they are part of what must be scraped away, though not quite discarded, if the miracle of integration that the poem performs is to be appreciated. An insistence on applying such knowledge, or on allowing it to give more than a casual and provisional shading to the words of a poem, will be a failure to respond to the poem's greatness, its universality.

I do not have the space to represent some of Booth's more subtle qualifications of his positions, but they do not seem to me to qualify his apparent belief that an attempt to understand the sonnets need not involve an attempt to understand the historically specific discourses they employ, and which, I have been arguing, their narrator can never elude. So I want to end this essay by addressing a question to myself. For it could reasonably be objected that if I insist on arguing that the sonnets speak a strange language whose meanings we must work to recover, and which is the production of a historical moment which is strange to us, I can have no means of experiencing the poems as the modern readers that Booth has in mind experience them, as poems which *move* them. So let me assert that I am much moved by this sonnet, in the quarto version, though not in Booth's. I find it moving by virtue of its *attempt*, and I italicise the word, to assert an ideal of transcendent love, and of a transcendent, autonomous identity, and to grasp at these as the means and the result of an escape from the oppression of the system of patronage and the constraints it imposes on the freedom of the narrator. But it is far from true that I find the poem less moving the more I examine the discourse which is the linguistic representation of those constraints, and attempt to understand how it constrains at once the narrator and the language he uses.

I can put it like this. Booth's text locates the affective power of the poem in its alleged power to transcend the conditions in which it was produced. For me, this does not reveal a universal content in the poem: it empties it of content, diminishes its pathos, and represents all the affective power of the poem as a function of the uncomplicated progress from depression to the elation of its final lines. I have argued (and he would no doubt disagree with me) that Booth's text and commentary represent the meanings in the poem by which its historical specificity is defined merely as white noise. To do this is, by implication, to treat the historically specific meanings and discourses of every 'great' poem simply as a metaphor for whatever it is, at any time, that imposes limits to our ability to assert our independence of the histories and discourses that constrain our freedom of action and speech. It makes all poems tell the same dull story, of how an empty individuality easily escapes from an empty history. For me, the pathos of this poem is, I repeat, inextricably a function of how it represents the specificity of the historical moment it produces and which produced it: a pathos which arises from the narrator's attempt to claim a transcendence he cannot achieve. He cannot achieve it, not simply because all such attempts must of their nature fail, but because the historical moment he seeks to transcend is represented by a discourse whose nature and function is to contaminate the very language by which that assertion of transcendence must try to find expression. For me, the pathos of the poem – I can repeat here my earlier point – is that the narrator can find no words to assert the transcendent power of true love, which cannot be interpreted as making a request for a couple of quid.

## Notes

1  In his book *An Essay on Shakespeare's Sonnets* (New Haven and London: Yale University Press, 1969), Booth seems to consider only the meaning 'but' for 'yet' (which he leaves unglossed in his edition), and remarks that 'the division after the octave of 29 is the sharpest in the poem' (48).

2 Poems by Michael Drayton, Esquire (London, 1619), p. 458.

3 See J. W. Saunders, The Profession of English Letters (London and Toronto: Routledge and Kegan Paul, University of Toronto Press, 1964), chapter IV, and Edwin H. Miller, The Professional Writer in Elizabethan England (Cambridge, Mass.: Harvard University Press, 1959). The discourse of patronage, which I identify in sonnet 29, has been identified there also by Arthur F. Marotti, in his essay ' "Love is not love": Elizabethan sonnet sequences and the social order', English Literary History, vol. 49 (1982), pp. 396–428 (see especially pp. 410–11), and, more briefly, by Thomas M. Greene, in 'Pitiful Thrivers: Failed Husbandry in the Sonnets', in Shakespeare and the Question of Theory, eds. Patricia Parker and Geoffrey Hartman (New York and London: Methuen, 1985).

4 The Works of Thomas Nashe, ed. Ronald B. McKerrow, revised by F. P. Wilson (Oxford: Oxford University Press, 1966), vol. 1, p. 159.

5 'The Ruines of Time' (1591), dedication; 'Mother Hubberds Tale' (1591), lines 63–8; Drayton, p. 434.

6 'Mother Hubberds Tale', lines 59–60; 'Colin Clouts Come Home Againe' (1595), lines 701–3.

7 Nashe, 1: 176, 158.

8 A. L. Rowse, ed., Shakespeare's Sonnets, third edition (Basingstoke and London: Macmillan, 1984), p. 61.

9 In two other sonnets (64, 128), the question of a 'change' of 'state' is raised, and in both cases the 'state' is evidently not something that can change by virtue of a change of heart or mood. In sonnet 92, the narrator remarks: 'I see, a better state to me belongs / Then that, which on thy humor doth depend', where the 'pure' language of love poetry seems to be again contaminated by the discourse of patronage. The line may be read innocently, to say that the narrator enjoys or has a right to a better 'state of mind' than the state dictated by the capricious humours of his lover (though even within this reading, a range of other possible meanings of 'state' are possible, as Booth, in an excellent note (300–1) points out). But the conjunction of 'humor' and 'depend' reminds us also of the 'state', the social and economic situation of a petitioner for patronage, 'dependent' upon the 'humour' of the powerful.

# 2

# Masters of suspense: syntax and gender in Milton's sonnets

## I

In 1986, a critical edition of Shakespeare's sonnets was published, edited by John Kerrigan, with a text of sonnet 29 which differs in one important respect from Stephen Booth's:

When, in disgrace with Fortune and men's eyes,
I all alone beweep my outcast state,
And trouble deaf heaven with my bootless cries,
And look upon myself and curse my fate,
Wishing me like to one more rich in hope,
Featured like him, like him with friends possessed,
Desiring this man's art, and that man's scope,
With what I most enjoy contented least;
Yet, in these thoughts myself almost despising,
Haply I think on thee, and then my state,
Like to the lark at break of day arising
From sullen earth, sings hymns at heaven's gate;
   For thy sweet love remembered such wealth brings
   That then I scorn to change my state with kings.

This version seems to do no less to conceal the discourse of patronage than did Booth's. I quote it here, however, not to make that point, but to draw attention to the particular kind of sentence-structure Kerrigan has chosen to attribute to the poem. This is clearer from his commentary on the poem than from his revision of the punctuation of the quarto-text. On line 9, Kerrigan offers the following note: 'Yet. "Still, even then", transformed by "even so" when the recollection of the youth is related. The expected then . . . is delayed, seemingly displaced, until the second half of line 10.'[1] This note makes it clear that Kerrigan has chosen to identify the first main verb in this poem as 'think', in the tenth line, whereas both Booth and the quarto-text seem to offer a main verb in line 2, 'beweep'.

   I can explain what I mean by comparing two different statements. If I write 'When in London, I stay with my aunt', I have written a complete sentence: the question implied by the first clause – 'what do you do in London?' – is answered immediately – 'I stay with my aunt'. The sentence is closed, complete. But if I write 'When, in London, I stay with my aunt', the question remains open, unanswered – 'well, what do you *do*, or what *happens*, when you stay with your aunt in London?' We are left waiting for a main verb which will answer that question, and the suspense involved in that waiting will persist until I offer some such additional statement as 'I catch up on all the family news'. The same is true of the difference between the versions of the poem we looked at in the last essay, and this new version. If we read 'When in disgrace with Fortune and mens eyes / I all alone beweepe my out-cast state', we have already read a complete statement. But if, as in Kerrigan's version, we put commas around 'in disgrace with Fortune and men's eyes', we will come to the end of the second line, and the third, and the fourth, and even the ninth, still waiting for the additional statement which will answer the question, 'what happens?', or 'what do you do?' The answer does not come until line 10, 'Haply I think on thee', and until that line we are in a mounting state of suspense, waiting for the question to be answered and a complete statement to be made. This is the point of Kerrigan's remark about 'the expected *then*'. For the further we get away from the opening 'when', and the question it implies, the more our sense of suspense is likely to become also one of confusion – where on earth is this sentence taking us? In such a sentence-structure, the word 'then' offers a kind of reassurance, for it seems to answer the 'when', and announce that our suspense and confusion are about to be resolved: 'When, in London, I stay with my aunt, and catch up on all the family news, and go with her to the pub, wishing all the time that I didn't drink so much,' and so on, 'then I sometimes remember you'.

To read a sonnet which defers its first main verb until the tenth line is a very different experience from reading one which seeks to create no comparable sense of suspense, and offers its first main verb more or less immediately. This, for example, is the opening of Shakespeare's eighteenth sonnet in the quarto text:

> Shall I compare thee to a Summers day?
> Thou art more lovely and more temperate:
> Rough windes do shake the darling buds of Maie,
> And Sommers lease hath all too short a date:
> Sometime too hot the eye of heaven shines,
> And often is his gold complexion dimm'd,
> And every faire from faire some-time declines, . . .

Every one of these lines contains a main verb – every line is a main clause, which is as much as to say that each of them can be considered as a simple sentence in its own right, except that some are introduced by the conjunction 'and', whose function is to conjoin, to bring into conjunction, these separate clauses. The effect of these simple structures is that we seem invited to read the poem slowly, at a measured pace, never anxiously looking forward, never feeling obliged to read at a run so as to arrive at the resolution of some syntactical complexity. And the composure this syntax allows us to enjoy can be read as representing the narrator's own state of mind as similarly composed. The calm emphatic statements that he makes in the third quatrain –

> But thy eternall Sommer shall not fade,
> Nor loose possession of that faire thou ow'st,
> Nor shall death brag thou wandr'st in his shade,
> When in eternall lines to time thou grow'st,

– derive much of their emphatic effect from the fact that they too are sufficiently prompt and generous with their main verbs to cause in us no anxiety about how they will develop. But their calmness derives also from the fact that the statements that have preceded them have been so syntactically simple. The statements made in the third quatrain of Kerrigan's version of sonnet 29 –

> Haply I think on thee, and then my state,
> Like to the lark at break of day arising
> From sullen earth, sings hymns at heaven's gate;

– may be no less emphatic. But if they seem less calm, more excited, this is because they are at once the expression of the narrator's relief from anxiety, and the means by which our anxiety about how the opening sentence is going to develop, and where it is going to end, is relieved.

What interests me then about Kerrigan's version and others like it, is that they attribute a syntax to the poem which enacts the narrator's change of mood. The narrator's anxiety about his failure to get a share of the pickings patronage has to offer is soothed or temporarily forgotten when he happens to 'think' on thee; and our anxiety about the length and direction of the sentence is similarly removed when we arrive, at last, at the same verb. The semi-colon Kerrigan places at the end of line 8 rather conceals this effect, for he is apparently undecided about whether to call attention more to a possible break between the octet and sestet ('yet' meaning 'but') or to the continuity of the sentence over that break ('yet' meaning 'even then'), and he cannot do both. But in so far as he has tried to represent the poem as one in which the narrator's anxiety is enacted by the suspense created in us by the deferment of the main verb, he has implicitly compared it with a large number of sonnets – the most well known are probably Milton's sonnet on his blindness, and Keats's on his impending death, which alludes to Milton's – in which the main verb is deferred for a long time, and to very similar effect.

The most extreme and apparently self-conscious example of this effect of which I am aware, in a sonnet at least, is to be found in a poem included in a volume of sonnets attributed to Henry Constable, *Diana* (1594), though the poem in question is no longer believed to be by him. Instead of the 'when / then' structure, this poem uses 'As / So', the structure we find in a sentence like 'As trees shed their leaves in autumn, so men lose their hair in middle age'. This is a common structure in Elizabethan sonnets: it is used for example by Samuel Daniel:

> Like as the Lute that joyes or els dislikes,
> As is his arte that playes upon the same:
> So sounds my Muse according as she strikes,
> On my hart strings high tun'd unto her fame.[2]

Here the implied question, 'what is like the lute', is answered in the fourth line, 'my hart strings'. There seems to be no very great anxiety expressed at the level of content, in the narrator's state of mind, and there is equally no impetus to enact or produce anxiety in the syntax. In this version of the structure by Spenser, however, in which the narrator compares himself to a ship that has lost its way, his confusion seems appropriately represented by the deferment of the main verb until line 7:

> Lyke as a ship that through the Ocean wyde,
> by conduct of some star doth make her way.
> whenas a storme hath dimd her trusty guyde.
> out of her course doth wander far astray.
> So I whose star, that wont with her bright ray,
> me to direct, with cloudes is overcast,
> doe wander now in darknesse and dismay,
> through hidden perils round about me plast.[3]

But Spenser is positively hasty compared with the sonnet in Constable's *Diana*:

> As drawes the golden Meteor of the day,
> Exhaled matter from the ground, to heaven,
> and by his secret nature, there doth stay
> the thing fast held, and yet of hold bereaven,

> So by th' attractive excellence, and might,
>     borne to the power of thy transparant eyes,
>     drawne from my selfe, ravisht with thy delight,
>     whose dumbe conceits divinely syranyze:
> Loe; in suspence of feare, and hope, upholden,
>     diversly poyz'd, with passions that paine mee,
>     no resolution dares my thoughts imbolden,
>     since tis not I, but thou that doost sustaine mee.[4]

This extraordinary sentence seems to be as much a comment upon its own development as the representation or production of the narrator's state of mind. The beginnings of the complexity it develops and describes can perhaps be located in line 5, where it becomes apparent that the comparison between the action of the sun, and whatever is going to be the subject of the main clause, 'So . . . ', is not going to be simple, as it was in Spenser's sonnet, but involves some resemblance between the sun which actively 'drawes' moisture from the ground, and something else which is passively attracted, 'drawne'. By line 7, we probably think we know what it will turn out to be that is thus 'drawne from my selfe' – that is to say, it looks as though the subject of this sentence will probably be 'I'. But by the end of line 8 we have still not been offered either the subject or the main verb; and the third quatrain, instead of setting out to resolve this anxiety and suspense, starts off by interrupting the progress of the sentence to point out just how anxious the narrator is becoming; and in doing so it increases our anxiety also, for by taking two lines to do this it defers the introduction of the subject and main verb still further.

When they finally appear, in line 11, the subject is not at all what we expected: it is not 'I', but 'no resolution'; and all the participles in the second quatrain which seemed to be about to describe the subject of the sentence now seem to be best understood as describing its object, 'my thoughts', if they can be understood as describing anything at all. As a result, the comparison we were offered in the first line is never explicitly made: we are offered instead a pseudo-comparison, in the form: 'as the sun drawes moisture from the earth, so no resolution dares imbolden my thoughts', and the question implied by the opening line – 'what is like the sun?' – is itself offered no clear resolution.

When the narrator says that he is 'in suspence of feare, and hope', his immediate meaning, perhaps, is that he is in a state of anxiety and confusion: should he fear the attractive power of his lover, or does the fact that s/he exercises that power upon him give reason to hope that his courtship will be successful? But, crucially, he has chosen to express himself in the technical language of rhetoric. A 'suspense', an uncertainty whether to 'hope' or 'fear', is not only a characteristic of a lover; it is also the effect which a certain kind of oratory seeks to create in its audience, or – in the case of an oratorical soliloquy – the impression it seeks to convey of the speaker's state of mind. Thus when the narrator points to his 'suspence' in line 9 – 'Loe' – he seems to be pointing not only to his anxiety, but to the rhetorical means – the syntactical means – by which that anxiety is being enacted.[5]

# II

What this poem has done is to make explicit a rhetorical effect which is often implicit in sonnets which defer the introduction of the main verb, and which thereby seek to represent the narrator's suspense by creating an analogous suspense in their readers. Spenser's sonnet and Kerrigan's version of Shakespeare's may thus be hardly less self-conscious than this sonnet from *Diana*, in that they may equally be making an appeal, though a silent one, that the reader who is versed in rhetoric should observe their sentence-structure and register what effect it is intended to secure. And to say this is not far from saying that if such a reader was moved by such poems, this was a result not only of their immediate affective power, and of the affective power of their syntax, but of the rhetorical signal they may give, that an appropriate response to them would be a certain kind of emotion, anxiety.

Milton's sonnet on his blindness, probably written in the early 1650s, may give a similar signal:

When I consider how my light is spent,
  Ere half my days, in this dark world and wide,
  And that one Talent which is death to hide,
  Lodg'd with me useless, though my Soul more bent
To serve therewith my Maker, and present
  My true account, least he returning chide,
  Doth God exact day-labour, light deny'd,
  I fondly ask; But patience to prevent
That murmur, soon replies, God doth not need
  Either man's work or his own gifts, who best
  Bear his milde yoak, they serve him best, his State
Is kingly. Thousands at his bidding speed
  And post o're Land and Ocean without rest:
  They also serve who only stand and waite.[6]

By the end of the seventh line of 'Shall I compare thee to a Summers day?', we had encountered seven main verbs; by the end of line 7 of this sonnet, we are still waiting for the first main verb. If the syntax of the first half of the poem is not confused, it is certainly confusing; and seems to oblige us to hurry through it, looking for something that will disambiguate these lines, or will give us the sense, at least, that we have understood what it is that we have been reading. We don't get that sense until line 8, because it is not until then that the implicit question set up by the first line, 'what happens when I consider how my light is spent?', is answered – 'I fondly ask if God exacts day labour', 'I foolishly ask if God demands a full day's work from those to whom the light of day is denied.' Why the question is foolish we can consider in a moment. But the fact that it is described as foolish is not at all irrelevant to the syntax of the sonnet, which contributes to the poem's meaning the notion that the language of someone who chooses to dispute with God, and to challenge his justice and mercy, will necessarily be confusing. This syntax, then, is to be understood as the expression of a mind confused, a mind which is continually deferring the question it wants to ask by an ever more complex account of the conditions the answer must satisfy. At the same time, it invites itself to be understood as an attempt to confuse God, and to entrap him within its complexity.

I shall try to give a brief account of the traps this syntax sets for God and the reader, in its attempt to oblige them to experience a confusion analogous to the narrator's confusion over doctrine. To begin with, it is very possible that we will misread the first two lines, which seem to promise us a different structure from the one they turn out to be offering us. I have asked a number of people to read aloud the opening lines of this sonnet, and most of them started off like this:

> When I consider how my light is *spent*
> Ere half my days, in this dark world and wide . . .

To put the emphasis on 'spent' seems at first sight the sensible thing to do: what seems important about Milton's 'light', his eyesight (but also the light of his faith, as the poem demonstrates), is that it is used up. Indeed, the line alludes to the parable of the wise and foolish virgins in the twenty-fifth chapter of the gospel of St Matthew; a parable which precedes, in that chapter, the parable of the talents, which Milton goes on to allude to in lines 3–6. To emphasise 'spent' is thus to indicate that Milton is comparing himself, unfairly as patience will eventually suggest, to the foolish virgins, who had put too little oil in their lamps, so that, when the hour of the wedding arrived, their lamps had gone out. My light, the poem seems to be saying, is *spent*. But if we read the first line like that, we may have problems at the end of the second: we may read, 'Ere *half* my *days*, in this dark world and *wide*', so that we arrive at the end of the line looking for a new verb of which 'half my days' can be the subject – for example, ere half my days 'are past', or 'are completed'. Our voices register the sense of reaching for a verb that isn't there to be found, for what we do find, at the beginning of line 3, is evidently a new beginning, 'And . . .' So we seem obliged to go back, and to find a new way of reading the lines – this way:

When I consider how my *light* is spent,
    Ere half my *days* . . .

which makes sense, and makes room for that new beginning in line 3. Two things are 'spent': Milton's light, and half his life. The verb 'spent' has two subjects.

The next few lines pose greater problems. There are various ways of understanding the words 'And that one talent . . . Lodg'd with me useless' – that piece of silver, deposited with me and collecting no interest, like the talent lodged with the unprofitable servant in the parable. To go through all the possibilities, however, would take too long, and I will consider only what seems to me the most likely way in which seventeenth-century readers would have understood the words, as composing what they would have called, by analogy with Latin grammar, an 'absolute' construction. Absolute constructions consist, usually, of a noun, here 'talent' or 'that one talent', and a participle, here 'lodg'd'; they are constructions, however, which are 'absolute' in the sense that they are detached from the rest of the sentence, to which they do not declare their precise relation. I can make this clear with a brief example. 'My aunt having died' – that's the absolute construction – 'I went to London'. Now clearly this sentence suggests that there is some relationship between my aunt's death and my going to London. But the sentence doesn't specify what that relationship is. Is it that *because* my aunt died that I went to London? Or *when* she died that I went there? Or if I say it like this –

'My aunt having *died*, I went to London'

then the sentence could even mean, '*Although* my aunt died, I went to London.'

But the difficulty of using absolute constructions in English is not simply that we do not always know, even given the context, how they affect the sense of the sentence. It is also that we sometimes cannot grasp that they are absolute constructions until after we have heard or read them, and so we read expecting them to be completed with a finite verb, not with a participle. In Latin or Greek there is no problem, because these languages signal the use of the absolute construction by using a particular case, a particular form of the noun and of the participle that agrees with it. But English cannot do that. Here, for example, are the opening lines of a poem by Coleridge:

> My pensive Sara! thy soft cheek reclined
> Thus on mine arm, most soothing sweet it is
> To sit beside our Cot . . .[7]

By the time we have read to the end of the second line, we are in no doubt about what is most soothing sweet: it is Sara's cheek reclined on the narrator's arm. But by the time we have read a few more words, we have to change our minds – though that does not mean, of course, that the first meaning we arrived at can be abolished, for that meaning is there, on the page. By the middle of line 3, however, what is most soothing sweet has become 'to sit beside our Cot', because, or when, or even in spite of the fact that Sara is doing what she is doing. In Latin and Greek, the case-endings would prevent all ambiguity, and all the interest as well as the disadvantages of that ambiguity.

In lines 3 and 4 of Milton's sonnet, similarly, we may not realise we are reading an absolute construction until we have read past it; once again, we seem obliged to shuffle the structures before we can make sense of them. We might expect, for example, that the sentence will say, 'When I consider (a) that my light is spent, and (b) that one talent, (which is) lodg'd with me useless . . .' and that a verb would follow, of which 'talent' would be the subject – say, 'is buried'. It may only be when we do not find a verb, or when we do not find the word 'is' before 'lodg'd', to convert the participle into a finite verb, that we can construct what we have read into grammatical sense. And once again, the effect is of confusion and difficulty.

I will not trace out the other problems of construction in these opening lines in anything like the same detail. There is, for the record, another absolute construction, though this time disambiguated by the word 'though', in the lines, 'Though my soul more bent / To serve therewith my maker, and present / My true account' – such a way of determining the force of an absolute phrase would probably have been thought of as borrowed from Greek, but might have seemed unusual even to English readers of Greek in the mid-seventeenth century. The line 'And that one talent which is death to hide' contains the literal sense that the speaker's one talent, his only talent, is to *hide death* – that's what he's good at; we, of course, would put 'it' before the verb 'is', to disambiguate it; we would write, that is, 'which it is death to hide', but so, probably, would most speakers and writers have done in 1650. The clause 'least he returning chide' causes problems too: does it refer backwards, to what has already been said, or forwards, to what is about to be said? Is the narrator saying that he wants to present his true account so that his master, when he comes back, will not chide him? or does he mean that, in case his master, on returning, chides him, he asks his foolish question? The first reading suggests a proper concern not to give God any cause for anger; the second suggests a less innocent concern to pre-empt God's anger by trapping him with a trick question. It may not be that we register these alternatives as we read; but the lack of certainty about what the clause does in the sentence contributes to the confusing quality of the poem's opening.

And all this confusion finally leads up to an attempt to confuse God – by suggesting, with a rhetorical flourish, that it is at the most a contradiction in terms, at the least thoroughly unreasonable, for God to exact day-labour – a full day's work, and one paid by the day – from those who have no sight of the day. If you are blind, the suggestion is, then the concept 'day' is meaningless to you, as a measure of time as well as as an alternation from night; so that the injunction to do a full day's work must be equally meaningless. This attempt to catch God out in a paradox is reinforced by the rhetorical structure Milton gives to the paradox: 'day-labour, light denied'. The two phrases match each other, monosyllable, dissyllable / monosyllable, dissyllable; but at the same time the paradox is underlined by the pattern of assonance, d/l: l/d, in such a way as to try to associate daylight with denial, and labour with light, as if only those who can see the light can labour.

After all this, we come, at last, to the long-deferred main verb, 'I fondly ask'. It may not make sense to us, when it finally appears, of all that has gone before, but it seems to suggest that that hardly matters – all that has gone before is foolish. And the arrival of the main verb does give us at least a *sense* of completion: we have at last *got through* that whole confusing passage of complex syntax and complex argument. The fact that it takes so long for the main verb to arrive, means that we may have felt obliged to read all that has come before at a run; for until that main verb arrives, we cannot easily have a sense that we know where we are in the sentence; we do not know what all the previous clauses are dependent on. This would have been so even if the syntax of the first eight or so lines wasn't so confusing in itself, for, as we saw at the start of this essay, the mere fact of deferring that main verb so long seeks to create a suspense, an anxiety, which seeks to oblige us to read those eight lines at speed, hardly pausing at the punctuation-marks or line-endings in our breathless search for a main verb whose arrival is continually being deferred by the insertion of yet more subordinate and dependent matter. Once the first line has been uttered, the main verb could, grammatically, come anywhere after that first line – we might expect to read, if you like. something like 'When I consider how my light is spent / I fondly ask'; or 'When I consider how my light is spent / Ere half my days, I fondly ask', and so on. As far as the syntax is concerned, the main verb is continually able to make an appearance – the conditions which lead us to expect it are continually established – and yet it keeps not appearing; we keep expecting it; it keeps being deferred. That is the suspense, and that is what builds up, perhaps more than the local difficulties of construction, the sense of the complexity of the poem's opening. We are invited to try to hold idea after idea in our minds, as it were with the promise that when the main verb finally does come, we will then understand how all that we have been reading fits together.

The sentence-structure of the second half of the poem, when patience replies, can be read as an attempt to resolve all this confusion and anxiety by resolving the suspense created in the narrator and in us alike by the deferment of the main verb. If it takes more than seven lines to get through to the first main verb, patience offers us, in the space of six or so lines, no less than seven main verbs. Their effect is to simplify the syntax immensely, and to slow the poem down, to a pace which, instead of inviting us to share the narrator's anxiety, may be taken to represent rather the virtue of those 'who only stand and waite'. The narrator's anxiety, we are invited to believe, is groundless: to do nothing for God is still to be in a state of readiness to do something; to 'waite' for something is also to 'waite' at table, to serve; God exacts day-labour from nobody, whether blind or sighted. We could say that we are invited at the end of the poem to accept the deferment of fulfilment, represented by the deferred syntax of the opening lines, as a condition of living: by acknowledging the need to wait, and by naming the process as 'waiting', the deferment of fulfilment is arrested, is represented no longer as suspense but as a static condition in which we can find repose.[8]

## III

In Milton's 'heroic' sonnets, addressed to some of those whom he regarded as the heroes of the English revolution, he borrows a sixteenth-century Italian sonnet-structure, first addressing a man by name, describing and praising him in relative clauses, and again deferring the first main verb. But the deferment in these sonnets is used to very different effect, as compared with the sonnets we have so far examined. It may still cause confusion and anxiety in the reader, but it does not seem to invite itself to be taken as representing any comparable feelings in the narrator, still less in the heroes addressed. And I want to argue that these poems suggest that the technique may be appropriate to the representation of male subjects, and what are conceived of as masculine virtues, and inappropriate to what is simultaneously conceived of as the feminine. I want to look first at the sonnets addressed to Cromwell, probably in 1652 and to Sir Henry Vane, at about the same date: Vane was a statesman and political philosopher who was executed after the restoration of Charles II.

The sonnets to Cromwell and Vane refer to and comment on a particular phase of the revolution, the attempts in the early 1650s to set up an established church and to restrict the religious toleration which Milton, Cromwell, and Vane all defended. The demand for religious uniformity had led the Presbyterians, in the late 1640s, to break their Covenant with Parliament and to side first with Charles I and, after his execution, with the man who called himself Charles II: they were defeated at Preston, by the river Darwen, in 1648, at Dunbar in 1650, and at Worcester in 1651. It is in opposition to the movement towards an established church that Milton warns Cromwell to reject the 'hireling' priests of an established church, who threaten 'free conscience', and praises Vane for understanding the necessary separation of church and state, and for resisting the incursions of the religious into the secular sphere.

> Cromwell, our cheif of men, who through a cloud
>     Not of warr onely, but detractions rude,
>     Guided by faith and matchless Fortitude
>     To peace and truth thy glorious way hast plough'd,
> And on the neck of crowned Fortune proud
>     Hast reard Gods Trophies and his work pursu'd,
>     While Darwen stream with blood of Scotts imbru'd,
>     And Dunbarr feild resounds thy praises loud,
> And Worsters laureate wreath; yet much remaines
>     To conquer still; peace hath her victories
>     No less renownd than warr, new foes arise

Threatning to bind our soules with secular chaines:
Helpe us to save free Conscience from the paw
Of hireling wolves whose Gospell is their maw.

The character of Cromwell is represented here by what he has done, by his actions; and by actions and successes conceived of as having been performed and achieved against the force of circumstances. Thus his character, also, is something produced in resistance to circumstance: it is his glorious way that he ploughs through; whatever happens does not happen to him – he happens to it, he does it his way, ploughing through a cloud of resistance. The notion of his character as consisting, instead, of qualities and virtues, rather than of actions, is acknowledged only in so far as his qualities and virtues – faith and fortitude – help him produce his character as defined by his actions.

This much seems obvious enough – it is a conventional way of repre-senting the kind of hero whose character is to be understood as active, and as self-produced. If kings are overthrown by 'crowned Fortune', Cromwell overthrows Fortune herself; if the rest of us must struggle to make our own history, in circumstances not of our choosing, it seems that Cromwell can bend all circumstances to his own will, so that his achievements fully match his aspirations. The point I want to make, however, is that this means of representing Cromwell's character pro-duces, and is produced by, a particular kind of syntax. In this sonnet, the first main verb, 'remaines', does not appear until line 9. All that comes before, apart from the name 'Cromwell' itself, consists of dependent clauses – of relative clauses attached to the name 'Cromwell', or of adverbial clauses of time, attached in lines 7 to 9 to those relative clauses. All define the name, the character – and that they do define the name of the man will turn out to be of some importance when we examine the structure of Milton's sonnets addressed to women.

The result of thus deferring the main verb, of continually denying it to us, is once again to attempt to oblige us to experience a suspense, and to read the poem quickly, on the run, in search of the main verb that will link up with the name 'Cromwell', and enable some complete statement to be made. The suspense seems to convert all end-stopped lines, as it were, into enjambed lines, for it seeks to prohibit us from pausing, from attributing to the punctuation any of the arresting power it had, for example, in Shakespeare's eighteenth sonnet. And once again, this syntax invites us to attach a particular importance to the end of the sonnet, and to the account there of what 'remaines / To conquer still'. For though in the first eight and a half lines there are no main verbs, in the last five and a half there are four. As at the end of the sonnet on Milton's blindness, we are invited to read slowly, our attention concentrated relatively more on the statements the poem makes, less on the ostentatiously complex structure of those statements.

Another effect of this syntax is to suggest that Cromwell, whom the poem addresses, is not to be addressed until he has been described: as if in order to reveal Cromwell as the appropriate addressee for the warning 'yet much remaines / To conquer still', it is first necessary to produce a Cromwell who has already conquered much; who having shown himself capable of mastery over circumstances in the past, can be expected to master them in the future. And the speed of reading invited by the deferral of the main verb seeks to make what he has done seem to have been achieved by an inexorable force, enacted by a movement of language which cannot stop until Cromwell does. This is what I meant when I suggested that in these 'heroic' sonnets the deferment of the main verb does not seem to allow itself to be read as representing any anxiety felt by the addressee. The syntax asks to be read instead as enacting the production of a particular kind of character, as enacting the process of a man producing his own identity in resistance to the circumstances that would, in a man less heroic (the implication is), simply produce him. The syntax thus plays a crucial part in the attempt to produce a notion of Cromwell as victorious, not just over his enemies but over the circumstances of history. And this is so, in spite of the fact that Cromwell does not emerge as the eventual, purposive subject of the first main verb when it appears. For throughout all its length, the structure of the first nine lines seeks to ensure that Cromwell's name remains in our minds, at the same time as it seems to allow the words that qualify him to slip out of our attention.

'Cromwell', the name announced at the beginning of the poem, must, for the poem to become grammatical, itself eventually become either the subject of a verb, or the object of an address. The name sets up a syntactical obligation, which sooner or later must be discharged. If the various clauses that qualify the name are allowed to pass out of our minds as soon as we read them, this is because we know to what they belong – they belong to Cromwell. But Cromwell himself must belong with the main clause: the name is waiting, or rather we are waiting, for the name to link up with some substantial statement: either 'Cromwell, who has done all this all this, can do this too', or 'Cromwell, who have done all this, you must do this too'. In this sense, everything that comes between the name and the main clause can be read as functioning, not just as qualification, but as interruption, as preventing the poem from making its main statement. When that interruption is finally brought to an end by the first main verb, Cromwell re-emerges from the sentence, as if his ploughing his way through the circumstantial has been enacted by our ploughing a way through the syntax. And he can emerge as the self-made man, the conqueror, not the victim of history, and so as the hero able to continue to shape history and to do what must still be done. And his name can emerge as a transcendent signifier, which signifies an identity claimed as transcendent over the circumstances of history.

The sonnet to Vane, though he is a civil rather than a military hero, manages to create at least as great a sense of the activity of his mind as the sonnet to Cromwell creates of the activity of his sword. It does this, once again, by deferring the first main verb, 'thou'hast learnt', which this time is held back until the eleventh line:

> Vane, young in years, but in sage counsell old,
>> Then whom a better Senatour nere held
>> The helme of Rome, when gownes not armes repelld
>> The fierce Epeirot and the African bold,
> Whether to settle peace or to unfold
>> The drift of hollow states, hard to be spelld,
>> Then to advise how warr may best, upheld,
>> Move by her two maine nerves, Iron and Gold
> In all her equipage; besides to know
>> Both spirituall powre and civill, what each meanes
>> What severs each thou'hast learnt, which few have don.
> The bounds of either sword to thee we ow.
>> Therfore on thy firme hand religion leanes
>> In peace, and reck'ns thee her eldest son.

Again, we begin with the name; again we are invited to search for the main clause with which that name must, eventually, link up. Before that linkage is made, however, we are first offered one quatrain of what is evidently a compliment to Vane's civic virtue – indeed, perhaps the highest compliment it could be paid, for it announces that his virtue is not outshone by the very models of civic statesmanship, the senators of republican Rome who resisted the invasions of Pyrrhus, king of Epirus, and of Hannibal from Africa. Thereafter, from line 5, the syntax becomes much more confusing, and on a first reading it is very difficult to know what to make of it. In the first four lines, the clauses are easily made sense of, because they all refer back, directly or indirectly, to the name 'Vane'. But from line 5 onwards, the clauses, as it were, look forward: they are dependent upon – they are in fact the objects of – a main verb that is always about to arrive, and yet we cannot predict what that verb will be. It could be about to say, for example, that all these issues are issues Vane must learn about, or that they are new issues – as in the sonnet to Cromwell – that Vane must now turn his attention to; or that they are all issues which it is beyond even Vane's intelligence to grasp, or which – and this is in fact what it does say – he *has* grasped. But the point is that the syntax attempts to oblige us to wade through lines 5 to 10 uncertain of anything except that eventually a main verb will come along and make sense of them; and if we accept that obligation, then as one issue is added to another, our sense of suspense, confusion, of the difficulty of keeping all these issues suspended in our minds, will be increased, until finally the main verb arrives.

Now *any* main verb, almost – even if its meaning was that Vane didn't have the first idea about whether to settle peace, or about the difference between spiritual and civil power – any verb that made sense would have resolved this syntactical confusion. But the particular verb the sonnet offers us – 'thou 'hast learnt' – is of course particularly reassuring; for it indicates that all these difficult issues have been thoroughly sorted out by Vane. The confusion we may experience from the syntax is a measure of the clarity of Vane's understanding. For when the main verb finally appears, and Vane, the name and the man, is finally linked with a substantive statement, the effect is to produce for Vane a powerful and transcendent identity which results from the fact that he, the name, the man, has survived the confusions of the eleven lines that intervene between the name and the verb, in such a way as to suggest that he rises above, transcends, is *on top* of things, is the master of situations which cannot therefore master him.

That noun and verb are perfectly appropriate: it is because he *masters* the complexities of politics that he can appear, in the predictably simple lines – again full of main verbs – that conclude the poem, as the 'son' of the (apparently widowed) religion, the son who is the support and prop of religion. And, more than that, as the eldest son of the widow, the son who has come into his inheritance, and is free to make his life as he chooses. The relation between patriarchy and the notion of a free, unconstrained individual identity is what is being disclosed to us in those last lines. It suggests that if the poem represents the emergence and the achievement of such an identity, by means of a syntax which enacts the process by which the individual essence survives and triumphs over the affairs of the world and the circumstances of history, then that syntax would be entirely inappropriate for the representation of women, whose identity, in a patriarchal society, is conceived as dependent ('leanes') on men, as something created for women, and reflected on them, by the men who master them.

And the notion of mastery may be appropriate also to the notion that the longer the main verb is deferred, and the more qualities and triumphs can therefore be attributed to the man named in the opening words of these two sonnets, the more heroic that man appears to be. The length of the deferment which measures the degree of the hero's transcendence may also measure the length of his manhood. This suggestion may provoke us to decide, as we read these two sonnets, to refuse the invitation the syntax offers us, or the obligation it seeks to impose upon us, to hurry from name to main verb, to experience the need always to be reaching further on for the deferred meaning. We can choose, instead, to linger on each line, to concentrate on each line or clause as itself rather than as a unit in a progressive movement, and so to interrupt and diffuse the urgent and phallocentric energy of the syntax.

## IV

Milton wrote three sonnets to women which begin with an opening vocative, a word of address, as Cromwell and Vane are addressed at the start of the sonnets to them. One of these sonnets to women is in Italian; in an English translation it begins:

Bright lady, whose fair name honours the flowery vale of Reno and the famous ford, truly is he destitute of all worth that is not moved to love by thy gentle spirit.

The sonnet begins not by naming the woman – the conventions of love poetry make naming, except obliquely[9] or by a false name, indiscreet – but by calling her 'lady'. As in the poems to Cromwell and Vane, she is then qualified by a relative clause; but this brief deferment of the main verb can cause none of the suspense it seeks to cause in the other poems we have looked at, for the verb turns up at the very beginning of the third line.

There is also an English sonnet addressed to a 'Lady', perhaps (though there is no way and for our purposes no need to be sure) Milton's intended wife: it begins:

Lady that in the prime of earliest youth,
  Wisely hast shun'd the broad way and the green,
  And with those few art eminently seen
  That labour up the Hill of heav'nly Truth,
The better part with Mary, and with Ruth,
  Chosen thou hast . . .

Here the first main verb, 'chosen thou hast', is deferred only until the sixth line; but what intervenes between the address, 'Lady', and that verb, can again cause no confusion, no great sense of suspense. It consists only of simple relative clauses, referring back to the lady; and all that we are asked to hold in our minds, as we look forward to the main verb to make sense of it, is the object of that verb in line 5, 'The better part with Mary, and with Ruth'.

One way for women in most of the circumstances of patriarchal society to achieve some other identity than that constructed for them by the familial relations with men is to remain unmarried – which meant until recently to remain a virgin, if the identity they were to achieve was to be an honourable one. And we may link this to the fact that the poem does defer its main verb at least until the sixth line; because there is at least something to say about a woman who has made the choice this woman has made; there is something to intervene between the invocation, 'Lady', and the main verb, something to say about what this woman is and has done. But the deferment, I suggest, cannot last long, because she does not, finally, have much manhood to measure: though there is something, there is not, apparently, much to say even about such a woman – only that she avoids the temptations of sex, and devotes herself to religion, and is comparable therefore with Mary and with Ruth. Her identity is constructed by these generic facts, by facts typical of the kind of woman she is, and not, as in the case of Cromwell and Vane, by their specific, individual achievements in and over the circumstances of their time.

It might appear that the third of these sonnets, to Lady Margaret Ley, is an exception to my claim that, in these sonnets of address, syntactical deferment is used to represent the process of achieving a freedom – and a specifically masculine freedom – from circumstantial constraints. The sonnet reads like this:

Daughter to that good Earl, once President
   Of Englands Counsel, and her Treasury,
   Who liv'd in both, unstain'd with gold or fee,
   And left them both, more in himself content,
Till the sad breaking of that Parlament
   Broke him, as that dishonest victory
   At Chaeronéa, fatal to liberty
   Kill'd with report that Old man eloquent,
Though later born, then to have known the dayes
   Wherin your Father flourisht, yet by you
   Madam, me thinks I see him living yet;

So well your words his noble vertues praise,
  That all both judge you to relate them true,
  And to possess them, Honour'd *Margaret*.

Here the main verb is deferred fully as long as it was in the sonnet to
Vane, that is, until the eleventh line. But the process of deferring it, and
eventually linking up the word of address, 'Daughter', to a substantive
statement, is hardly a process by which the identity of Margaret is
produced as transcendent, as unconstrained by whatever intervenes
between the first and the eleventh lines. For the point of this poem is to
represent Margaret as having no identity whatsoever, except insofar as
that identity consists, consists wholly, in her being her father's daughter.
The lines that intervene are devoted entirely to an account of her father;
she can be 'Honour'd Margaret', she can be 'Honour'd', only because so
completely has she shaped and subdued her identity to his, that a sonnet
addressed to her, and apparently about her, can appropriately be written
in the syntax of a heroic sonnet almost entirely about her father. In a
sense, the poem is almost completed at the first comma: all that there is
to say about Margaret is that she is truly the 'daughter to that good Earl';
everything that follows that first line is concerned to show just how truly.

   Margaret is at no point in the poem the subject of a finite verb: just as
she has, of herself, no qualities, she performs, in herself, no actions; and
perhaps, from a masculine point of view, that is just as well, for her
verblessness may help to push back the troublesome reflection that if she
really does possess her father's virtues, perhaps she could also do all that
he could do, given the opportunity. When the main verb finally turns up,
it is the narrator who 'sees' the father living in his daughter. Her *words*, not
she herself, praise his virtues. It is other people who judge her behaviour,
and she is honoured because they recognise her as being nothing but
'daughter to that good Earl', for being as good a man as it is possible for a
woman to be, for having no untidy feminine edges in her character
which might prevent her father's image being superimposed on hers,
and blotting her out. The main verb is deferred only to create space for
the elaboration of the virtues and actions of 'that good Earl', and to
elaborate on Margaret's virtues only to the extent that she has no virtues
except his.

   Only on these terms, I suggest, can a syntax appropriate to the representation of a hero, of an 'eldest son' with all that that implies, be used in
a sonnet of address to one who is no more than a daughter. Though
Margaret is named in this poem, as the women in the two other sonnets

are not, her name does not get into the poem until the very last word. The sonnets to Cromwell and Vane first name their addressees, and then continue to elaborate on the transcendent identity the name signifies. This poem names its addressee only at the point where we can be in no doubt that her name announces not an identity transcendent and self-produced, but one entirely produced by her status as 'daughter'.

## V

I said earlier that it was often a characteristic of representations of heroism – it is often a defining characteristic of heroism – that heroes must be the masters of circumstance, as Cromwell is shown to be. What makes Cromwell in particular a new kind of hero, and the sonnet to him a new kind of poem, can perhaps be described like this. In societies governed by hereditary aristocracies, the hero is frequently understood to master circumstances, but only in deference to conceptions of the familial, social and political duties and functions which must govern his actions. Heroic actions are the constrained products of duty, honour, the fear of shame: to act heroically is not a triumph of the individual will, though the failure to do so may be the result of a failure of the will. Those constraints legitimate the aristocratic hero, and distinguish between virtuous heroism and villainous audacity. Such social and political constraints, however, are not available to legitimate the actions of heroes who rise in opposition to a hereditary aristocratic governing class. Those, therefore, who came to be represented as the heroes of the English revolution, were obliged to stake all on an appeal to their duty to God, to legitimate their actions. But that appeal could be made, was made, no less forcefully by their enemies, and the issue of who had the right to make it was one which, for the revolutionaries, could be decided only by a contest of wills; whoever had the strongest will would prevail, and, in prevailing, would be assured that God was on his side. Cromwell's heroism, therefore, came often to be represented as a function of his will to power. It is represented as inspired by God, but also as self-produced, since Cromwell must act as hero before it can be known for sure that God acts through him – he must fight before he can win. And in Milton's sonnet to Cromwell an appropriately powerful syntax is invented to represent and to reinforce the overmastering power of that individual will. It is the syntax of this poem, and of the sonnets to Vane and Fairfax, which as much as anything else ties them to the moment of their production. It is, just as much, the similar syntax used in the sonnet to Margaret Ley, announcing that she has lost herself in her father, and the pale shadow of that syntax in the poem to the 'Lady', which remind us that the revolutionary claim to transcendence could not have been conceived of as a claim that women could make.

I am not making this point to argue that Milton was a sexist – of course he was. Nor am I arguing that to produce complex sentences, with deferred main verbs, is necessarily to produce a distinctively masculine syntax, a syntax which, by its very nature, can be used only to represent masculine subjects. In the poems with which I introduced this essay, and even in Milton's sonnet on his blindness, the main verb was also deferred, but I felt no compulsion to discuss that deferment in terms of gender-difference. What I am arguing is simply that the variety of sentence-structure used by Milton in his 'heroic' sonnets is used to celebrate a revolutionary energy which claims to subdue circumstance to its own designs. We are invited to acknowledge the reading-speed which the syntax seeks to impose on us as a function of an active power which we cannot find, and cannot imagine, being attributed to women; and so we are invited to understand that syntax as appropriate to the representation of a transcendent subject which cannot be conceived of except as masculine.

I want now to consider some remarks that Coleridge made about Milton, as he attempted to distinguish the nature of Milton's genius from Shakespeare's. For Coleridge seems indeed to have believed that a syntax which defers the main verb was a distinctively masculine syntax, and it will help to broaden the issues raised by this chapter if we examine what Coleridge has to say about them. I can begin by putting together some paragraphs by Woolf on Shakespeare and Coleridge, and a paragraph by Coleridge on Shakespeare and Milton. This, then, is Woolf:

And I went on amateurishly to sketch a plan of the soul so that in each of us two powers preside, one male, one female; and in the man's brain the man predominates over the woman, and in the woman's brain the woman predominates over the man. The normal and comfortable state of being is that when the two live in harmony together, spiritually co-operating. If one is a man, still the woman part of his brain must have effect; and a woman also must have intercourse with the man in her. Coleridge perhaps meant this when he said that a great mind is androgynous. It is when this fusion takes place that the mind is fully fertilised and uses all its faculties. Perhaps a mind that is purely masculine cannot create, any more than a mind that is purely feminine, I thought. But it would be well to test what one meant by man-womanly, and conversely by woman-manly, by pausing and looking at a book or two.

Coleridge certainly did not mean, when he said that a great mind is androgynous, that it is a mind which has any special sympathy with women; a mind that takes up their cause or devotes itself to their interpretation. Perhaps the androgynous mind is less apt to make these distinctions than the single-sexed mind. He meant, perhaps, that the androynous mind is resonant and porous; that it transmits emotion without impediment; that it is naturally creative, incandescent, and undivided. In fact one goes back to Shakespeare's mind as the type of the androgynous, of the man-womanly mind, though it would be impossible to say what Shakespeare thought of women.[10]

And this is Coleridge:

What then shall we say? even this; that Shakspeare, no mere child of nature; no automaton of genius; no passive vehicle of inspiration possessed by the spirit, not possessing it; first studied patiently, meditated deeply, understood minutely, till knowledge become habitual and intuitive wedded itself to his habitual feelings, and at length gave birth to that stupendous power, by which he stands alone, with no equal or second in his own class; to that power, which seated him on one of the two glory-smitten summits of the poetic mountain, with Milton as his compeer not rival. While the former darts himself forth, and passes into all the forms of human character and passion, the one Proteus of the fire and the flood; the other attracts all forms and things to himself, into the unity of his own IDEAL. All things and modes of action shape themselves anew in the being of MILTON; while SHAKSPEARE becomes all things, yet for ever remaining himself. O what great men hast thou not produced, England! my country![11]

We could begin a comparison of these two passages by registering how much less troubled Woolf's prose appears to be by the directions taken by its argument, which is itself much more provisional than is Coleridge's attempt to define and fix the nature of Shakespeare's genius. 'And I went on amateurishly to sketch', writes Woolf; and whatever the pressures that produce this diffident tone, it is a diffidence which makes room for the speculative and the exploratory. 'What then shall we say?' writes Coleridge, but the question pretends to an *aporia*, to a sense of being at a loss, only to announce that the conclusions he is about to draw will not be speculative at all, but the firm pronouncements of a mind resolved: 'even this'. The tentativeness of Woolf's prose enables, or is enabled by, the notion that androgyny is 'a normal and comfortable state'; whereas for Coleridge, I shall suggest, androgyny is far from being that, and is opted for only because to represent Shakespeare in terms of gender-difference is still more uncomfortable, and produces a Shakespeare still more abnormal.

In Woolf's passage, the fusion of masculine and feminine, represented though it is in terms of sexuality and procreation, manages to leave sex and gender unattributed: we do not know, and we do not seem invited to ask, which faculties of the mind are to be imaged as feminine and which masculine. Thus the process of literary creation does not seem to involve the masculine fertilising the feminine – it is the undivided, man-womanly or woman-manly mind that is indifferentiably fertilised by this intellectual congress. This is in marked contrast to the troubled definitions that Coleridge offers, in which anxiety about difference – or, to be more specific, an anxiety about the value of whatever may be classified as feminine – continually disturbs the attempt to describe the greatness of Shakespeare's mind. To develop this point, I shall be claiming that in Coleridge's writing acts of the mind are continually represented as gendered: the justification for that claim will emerge later in this essay.

For Woolf, then, the mind is not the site of an act of fertilisation, performed by the manly on the womanly: it is itself what is fertilised. For Coleridge, it is exactly the *site* of a sexual congress, and yet the gender of the actors participating in that congress seems at once to demand and to elude identification. 'Knowledge', he writes, 'become habitual and intuitive wedded itself to his habitual feelings, and at length gave birth to that stupendous power, by which he stands alone.' The immediate difficulty of this formulation is that it seems to reverse, not only a conventional gendering of the faculties and contents of the mind, but the gendering Coleridge himself usually proposes. Knowledge and feeling are conventionally gendered in the early nineteenth century as masculine and feminine; and by Coleridge, intuition is regularly gendered as a masculine act, which sees into the formless data of experience, or the discrete facts assembled by the understanding, to discover in them an indwelling law. The feminine is usually for Coleridge, and unsurprisingly enough, the formless, or what appears formless until penetrated by the power of intuition. But in this passage, intuitive knowledge, once it is wedded with habitual feeling, is represented as feminine – it 'gives birth' – and in the process feelings seem to become masculine.

Now what knowledge gives birth to, the stupendous power which is the genius of Shakespeare, is evidently and reassuringly a man-child: in the context of the issue of difference which is raised by the images of wedding and giving birth, stupendous power can be conceived of only as masculine. And this formulation, however uncertainly arrived at, appears as the triumphant culmination of a process of definition which began with the masculinity of Shakespeare's genius being put at risk. For those opening negatives – 'no mere child of nature; no automaton of genius; no passive vehicle of inspiration, possessed . . . not possessing' –

were all endeavouring to push away the possibility that Shakespeare's genius may indeed strike us as child-like, as automated and eluding the control of the will, as passive, and as possessed – in short, as a feminine genius. And what follows that series of negatives can be read as an attempt to displace the feminine into the procreative, and to remove it from the creative. The feminine is confusedly identified as participating not in genius itself, but in the production of genius, which is itself unambiguously active, powerful, independent, masculine. The mind may be acknowledged as androgynous, but only if genius is represented as something else, as sundered from mind, as what the mind produces, a man-child.

The comparison with Milton, however, threatens to undo what has been so laboriously achieved, and to return Shakespeare to the realm of the feminine from which he has been so carefully differentiated. It is the process of the comparison that we need to attend to here: the fact that Coleridge takes two bites at it, in two separate sentences, the first requiring to be corrected by the second, and each of them containing its own little drama of correction. In both sentences, Milton is represented as the fixed term in a binary opposition in which Shakespeare is therefore likely to appear as the free, the fluid term. Milton 'attracts all forms and things to himself, into the unity of his own IDEAL'; 'all things and modes of action shape themselves anew in the being of MILTON'. As we shall shortly see, these sentences represent Milton as what Coleridge calls a 'masculine intellect', with the power to give form to flux, a form which is the unity of its own transcendent subjectivity, and which gives its own determination to whatever might threaten to determine it, especially and characteristically feeling and the data of the sense, formless, fluid and feminine.

The evident danger, as I have suggested, of this opposition between Milton and Shakespeare, is that is that it will appear to re-feminise the genius of Shakespeare. In the first sentence, Shakespeare's genius seems to be manifested in a failure of transcendence, in its availability to be occupied by the formlessness of unorganised experience, random, airy, the fire and the flood. What apparently characterises Shakespeare is a lack, an absence of that ideal unity which enables Milton to give his own form to things; things seem to give their own formlessness to Shake-speare. I say 'seems', and 'apparently', because I take it that the word 'one' – the 'one Proteus' – is an attempt to guard against this represen-tation of Shakespeare as simply dispersed among the objects of experience. The word seems to suggest, but too weakly for Coleridge's satisfaction, that the god whose form is continuously changing somehow preserves a continuous identity.

The task therefore of the second sentence is to give that point more emphasis. Shakespeare still 'becomes all things', yet – it is now clearly asserted – he remains 'ever . . . himself'. But what self has Shakespeare to remain? what is it that is always 'himself', if himself is always out there, shapeless and formless, dispersed and disunited in its Protean inhabitation of the other? By ignoring those questions, and by simply reasserting, however much as an afterthought, the unity of Shakespeare's genius, Coleridge can do something to deny the possibility that has been raised once more, that this genius is somehow and uncomfortably feminine. Even by doing this, however, and by apostrophising both poets as 'great men', he cannot now reclaim Shakespeare's genius for the masculine, now that his stupendous power has been so thoroughly dispersed. At best, that genius has now become androgynous, always elsewhere and yet always at home; but its androgynous nature is doomed to be precarious and unstable, because it is required to occupy the position of a term facing the masculinity of Milton in an opposition which has been set up as binary, antithetical, and exhaustive. To put it simply, the comparison of the two poets suggests that they are opposites; that the opposition between them is gendered; that Milton is masculine, so that Shakespeare must be feminine – and so, Coleridge has to add, he is masculine too.

This account of the passage by Coleridge has, as I have already acknowledged, begged a few questions. To begin with, I have been confidently discovering the signs of gender in a passage which may not seem to invite that kind of attention at all, or only occasionally and in the most vague and casual way. Certainly phrases such as 'wedded with', 'give birth', seem to raise the issue, but is there any more persuasive basis to my claim to be identifying a drama of differentiation in such words and phrases as 'power', 'unity', 'passive', 'becomes all things'? – a basis more specific than the general fact, that I imagine no one will now contest, that such words often do appear to be the markers of difference, between a notion of the masculine as powerful and unified, and of the feminine as passive and dispersed. But unless I am claiming that such words are *always* to be read as markers of gender-difference, and I am not, why do I claim that in this passage they are, and that the gender of Milton's and Shakespeare's creativity is an issue raised by the passage? And even if I can make good that claim, so what? Why do I think it matters to Coleridge to attempt to account for the genius of these two poets in gendered terms, or, equally in the case of Shakespeare, to try to avoid doing so? I can begin to address this second set of questions by addressing the first, and by saying something more about the pervasive gendering of acts of the mind in Coleridge's writings; and in the context of our consideration of syntax and gender in Milton's sonnets, it will be helpful to concentrate on how Coleridge thinks of syntax as gendered.

## VI

I can begin by saying that for Coleridge, as for Woolf, there are sentence-structures that can be thought of as characteristically masculine or feminine, but that the form taken by what Woolf thinks of as paradigmatically the 'man's sentence' is significantly different from the form it takes for Coleridge. This is Woolf:

The sentence that was current at the beginning of the nineteenth century ran something like this perhaps: 'The grandeur of their works was an argument with them, not to stop short, but to proceed. They could have no higher excitement or satisfaction than in the exercise of their art and endless generations of truth and beauty. Success prompts to exertion; and habit facilitates success.' This is a man's sentence; behind it one can see Johnson, Gibbon, and the rest.[12]

What is it that for Woolf constitutes the specifically masculine structure of these sentences, so different from the structure that could be represented as masculine, I argued, in Milton's sonnets? It is, I suppose, that they seem to aim at a certain brevity, crispness, and clarity of statement; and they seem to assume that this is to be achieved by the deployment of binary, though not necessarily of antithetical, structures. The whole of the sentence beginning 'success' is a case in point; and so are phrases like 'not to stop short, but to proceed'; 'excitement or satisfaction'; 'the exercise', with its dependent phrase 'of their art', and 'endless generations' with its matching dependent phrase 'of truth and beauty'. These binary structures seem to lay claim at once to a notable care of discrimination, and to a notable completeness of view: 'this but not that', or 'not only that, but this as well'. As Dorothy Richardson put it, 'Clever phrases that make you see things by a deliberate arrangement, leave an impression that is false to life. But men do see life in this way, disposing of things and rushing on with their talk; they think like that, all their thoughts false to life; everything neatly described in single phrases that are not true. Starting with a false statement, they go on piling up their books.'[13] Richardson's notion of the falseness of statements composed of neat descriptions in single phrases is not, I think, shared very

wholeheartedly by Woolf – her sense of the value, for some purposes but
not for all purposes, of the 'man's sentence', may partly account for her
untroubled notion of the great mind as androgynous. But if we substitute
for the notion that such statements are false, the notion that they are
necessarily limited in the uses they can serve, we seem to arrive via
Richardson at something like an account of what for Woolf may have
been characteristically masculine about the structure of the 'man's sentence' she has exemplified.

The structure of the man's sentence for Coleridge is markedly
different. It is a structure he looks to discover in a sequence of prose-
writers that starts from Hooker in the late sixteenth century and runs on
through Bacon to Milton, James Harrington, Algernon Sidney and a few
other writers of the mid-seventeenth century – 'masculine intellects', he
calls them. What characterises the 'manly, unaffected, and pure' elo-
quence of Hooker, Bacon and Milton, for example, is its 'stately march
and difficult evolutions', and an abundance of connectives by which
those evolutions are elaborated and signalled. It is a prose absolutely the
opposite of what he describes as the 'crumbly-friable' style, 'asthmatic',
'short-winded' and 'short-witted', which instils 'the habit of receiving
pleasure without any exertion of thought, by the mere excitement of
curiosity and sensibility'. That habit, he says, 'may be justly ranked
among the worst effects of habitual novel-reading'.[14] We need not speculate on whether the 'excitement of curiosity and sensibility', once it has
been related to the habitual reading of novels, is placed by Coleridge in a
box marked 'feminine', to establish that its opposite, in any case, 'correct
and manly prose', is a product of the masculine intellect. So, by the way –
for the point is worth making in the context of Milton – is the style of the
best epic poets. Thus Dante's style is notable for its 'logical connexion,
strength, and energy', so that 'you cannot read Dante without feeling a
gush of manliness of thought within you'.[15] Readers might like to try to
analyse the imagery in that sentence for themselves.

The clearest example of manly prose is taken by Coleridge not from
Milton but from Hooker, whose style, he remarks, is distinguished by
'the superior number . . . of the thoughts and relations'.[16] This is the
example in question, taken by Coleridge to stand for a prose, he says,
'exclusively addressed to the learned class in society' – as we shall see
later, and again in my final essay, the characteristics of gender-difference
in the acts of the mind often reproduce the characteristics of the distinction between the learned and the ignorant.

Concerning Faith, the principal object whereof is that eternal verity which hath discovered the treasures of hidden wisdom in Christ; concerning Hope, the highest object whereof is that everlasting goodness which in Christ doth quicken the dead; concerning Charity, the final object whereof is that incomprehensible beauty which shineth in the countenance of Christ, the Son of the living God: concerning these virtues, the first of which beginning here with a weak apprehension of things not seen, endeth with the intuitive vision of God in the world to come; the second beginning here with a trembling expectation of things far removed, and as yet only heard of, endeth with real and actual fruition of that which no tongue can express; the third beginning here with a weak inclination of heart towards him unto whom we are not able to approach, endeth with endless union, the mystery whereof is higher than the reach of the thoughts of men; concerning that Faith, Hope, and Charity, without which there can be no salvation, was there ever any mention made saving only in that Law which God himself hath from Heaven revealed?

Of this passage, Coleridge remarks:

The unity in these writers is produced by the unity of the subject, and the perpetual growth and evolution of the thoughts, one generating, and explaining, and justifying, the place of another, not, as it is in Seneca, where the thoughts, striking as they are, are merely strung together like beads, without any causation or progression.[17]

The structure of Hooker's sentence is quite remarkable, not just for its length, but for the way it seeks to oblige us to experience its length, by deferring the main verb, 'was', which eventually appears as the one hundred and seventy-third of 190 words. There is a sense in which the suspense this deferment seeks to create in us is quite appropriate to the content of the sentence, for each segment of each of its tripartite divisions is telling us of a meaning which is itself always deferred. Consider, for example, the second sequence of tripartite divisions, beginning at line 6 with the words 'concerning these virtues'. Each of these three virtues is represented as 'beginning here', and as ending in an intuitive, inexpressible, unthinkable future; each clause speaks of a transcendence, the knowledge of which is deferred, suspended, projected forwards, as we also are to be projected forwards in search of the magic verb that will seem to complete our knowledge by completing this statement of our ignorance, and to unify these three separate virtues by relating them all to the same, to the one main verb.

The eventual unity which the syntax confers on these virtues, by making them effectively if not grammatically all the subjects of the same verb, is related by Coleridge to the unity in the writer, the unity of his grasp of his 'subject', but the unity also of a personal subject. The writer as subject is apparently dispersed among all the proliferating clauses of this sentence, only to be revealed, or at any rate proclaimed, as unified at the end, and as having, by his ability to construct and organise this astonishing proliferation of thoughts and relations, to have been always already in charge, always only pretending to be dispersed and to share our anxiety, in order to demonstrate how thoroughly unified he is, how thoroughly he resists and transcends determination by, and fragmentation among, the clauses which continually threaten to lead the sentence off into one sidetrack or another, into directions which will not lead to a properly unified conclusion. This is, quite evidently, a sentence which seeks to demonstrate the power of the intellect. Of a sentence of his own, and of which he was especially proud – for it ran to 241 words, and the first main verb was the two hundred and sixteenth – Coleridge tells us that it was particularly praised by 'an eminent statesman and orator'.[18] The sentence by Hooker attempts to instantiate a transcendent, we might say a 'stupendous' power of intellect, and its construction is predicated on the power to 'command' attention. It must not be interrupted, for to defer the main verb is to defer meaning, and for the sentence to mean, we must be content to hear it through to the end.

The ability to construct such sentences as these is described by Coleridge as the power of method. The language of a man – and it will be a man – who has this power is characterised, he explains, by 'the habit of foreseeing, in each integral part, or (more plainly) in every sentence, the whole that he intends to communicate'. And there is an evident match between Coleridge's account of the genius of Milton, and his account of the man of method, who 'organizes the hours, and gives them a soul: and that, the very essence of which is to fleet away, and evermore *to have been*, he takes up into his own permanence, and communicates to it the imperishableness of a spiritual nature'. Of such a man, 'it is less truly affirmed, that He lives in time, than that Time lives in him'.[19] And if we look back to Coleridge's comparison of Milton and Shakespeare, we will see that by contrast with the methodical and 'masculine' intellect revealed in this sentence by Hooker, Shakespeare is again in danger of being represented as one who 'lives in time', who gives up the permanence of his own nature to that which is fleeting, fluid, formless.

According to Coleridge, it is possible to display an excess of method, as Hamlet does, though the examples of this fault are rare. It is more common to speak with an absence of method, and to exemplify this fault Coleridge cites three other characters from Shakespeare: Pompey, in *Measure for Measure*, Juliet's nurse, and Mistress Quickly, in *Henry IV Part II*.

He quotes a speech by Mistress Quickly, in which she is replying to Falstaff's question, 'What is the gross sum that I owe thee?':

Marry, if thou wert an honest man, thyself and the money too. Thou didst swear to me upon a parcel-gilt goblet, sitting in my dolphin chamber, at the round table, by a sea-coal fire, on Wednesday in Whitsun week, when the prince broke thy head for likening his father to a singing-man in Windsor – thou didst swear to me then, as I was washing thy wound, to marry me and make me my lady thy wife. Canst thou deny it? Did not goodwife Keech, the butcher's wife, come in then and call me gossip Quickley? – coming into borrow a mess of vinegar: telling us she had a good dish of prawns – whereby thou didst desire to eat some – whereby I told thee they were ill for a green wound, &c. &c. &c.[20]

The absence of method in such utterances as these is 'occasioned', writes Coleridge, 'by an habitual submission of the understanding to mere events and images as such, and independent of any power of the mind to classify or appropriate them'; 'the general accompaniments of time and place are the only relations which persons of this class appear to regard in their statements.'[21] By 'persons of this class', Coleridge refers to the whole class of the immethodical and uneducated, and not specifically to women. But the effect of that inclusiveness, in the context of a gendered notion of syntax which appropriates the 'masculine' to the style of Hooker, is to characterise ignorant men as feminine, and so to suggest that the paradigmatic case of the absence of method is the woman.

In Mistress Quickly's sentences there is no deferment, no suspense, no eventual revelation that, though we might have been lost, she was always present in the sentence, actively foreseeing its development and the final assertion of its unity. In her second sentence, for example, the grammatical subject and main verb are immediately declared, and then what Coleridge has called the 'subject' – the topic of the sentence – is equally promptly dispersed among 'the general accompaniments of time and place'. And so she finds it necessary to try to re-establish the direction and unity of the sentence by repeating the subject and its verb, as if they have been lost, forgotten. By her final sentence, the subject and main verb are still being offered first, but the whole sentence exists for no other purpose that Coleridge can see than to disperse goodwife Keech among the circumstantial, with the effect that the speaking subject is also thus dispersed, and becomes evermore an object determined by a memory which recalls everything except the point of speaking at all. This is certainly a sentence that can be interrupted, and Coleridge does interrupt it, curtailing his quotation with three testy ampersands.

Nowadays, of course, many of us have argued ourselves to a point where we may declare an ethical preference for Mistress Quickly's syntax over Milton's and Hooker's, and precisely because of the way in which it represents subjectivity not as transcendent but as conditional. We may wish to do so particularly if we compare Mistress Quickly's speech with such sentences as these from *To the Lighthouse*, which derive their ability to proliferate and play once again from the fact that the first subject and main verb are offered early, and we are not therefore obliged to be continually looking forward to a meaning continually being deferred:

Standing now, apparently transfixed, by the pear tree, impressions poured in upon her of those two men, and to follow her thought was like following a voice which speaks too quickly to be taken down by one's pencil, and the voice was her own voice saying without prompting undeniable, everlasting, contradictory things, so that even the fissures and humps on the bark of the pear tree were irrevocably fixed there for eternity.

This next sentence is in fact rather closer to Mistress Quickly's word-order, repeating its main verb as did Shakespeare's hostess:

All of this danced up and down, like a company of gnats, each separate, but all marvellously controlled in an invisible elastic net – danced up and down in Lily's mind, in and about the branches of the pear tree, where still hung in effigy the scrubbed kitchen table, symbol of her profound respect for Mr Ramsay's mind, until her thought which had spun quicker and quicker exploded of its own intensity . . .[22]

These sentences, and Mistress Quickly's too, can perhaps be regarded as examples of the 'sentence of the feminine gender' which Woolf des-cribes, in some remarks on Richardson, as 'elastic', as 'capable of enve-loping the vaguest shapes'.[23] It is of course the sentence, not the speaking subject, that does the 'enveloping' – the subject in these 'feminine' sentences seems rather to be enveloped by those shapes. And that point returns us to the danger, as it must have seemed to Coleridge, of repre-senting Shakespeare's genius in stereotypical feminine terms: not power, but its opposite, passivity; not possession but being possessed; not unity but dispersal; not method but the lack, the absence of it. How then could the notion of a feminine Shakespeare ever have arisen? If the conse-quence of feminising Shakespeare is to deprive him of the 'stupendous power' of his genius, where does the impetus come from, the impetus that must be resisted as best it can, to describe his genius as feminine, and thus to perpetrate a grotesque contradiction in terms?

## VII

Of the various possible answers to those questions, I shall concentrate on one that will enable me to find my way back to Milton. Although in this essay I have been considering Milton as the author of heroic sonnets, and as the author of (according to Coleridge) a particular kind of prose, the comparison between Milton and Shakespeare was primarily, for Coleridge, a comparison between the supreme practitioners of two different genres of writing, the epic and the dramatic. And the difference between these two genres was a matter of the kind of imagination and subjectivity each demanded and displayed. 'There is the epic imagination', Coleridge is recorded as having remarked, 'the perfection of which is in Milton'; and 'there is a subjectivity of the [epic] poet, as of Milton, who is himself before himself in everything he writes.' There is also a dramatic imagination, 'of which Shakespeare is the absolute master'; and, accordingly, 'there is the subjectivity of the *persona*, or dramatic character.' It is not simply in Milton and Shakespeare, it is ideally in the epic and in drama, that in the one the poet attracts all things into 'himself', and in the other the poet becomes all things, all characters in all their individuality and variety.[24]

This distinction relates to Coleridge's description of Shakespeare as 'characterless'. Shakespeare, according to the records of Coleridge's table-talk, 'is the Spinozistic deity – an omnipresent creativeness'; his poetry is 'characterless; that is, it does not reflect the individual Shakespeare; but John Milton himself is in every line of *Paradise Lost*'. It is perhaps this remark by Coleridge which, more than any other, threatens to represent Shakespeare as feminine. Speaking of Shakespeare's female characters, he remarked: ' "Most women have no character at all", said Pope, and meant it for satire. Shakespeare, who knew man and woman much better, saw that it, in fact, was the perfection of woman to be characterless'.[25] Now the point of Pope's line is that because women have no firm, determinate character they can adopt all characters, as circumstances and caprice direct. In arguing against Pope, Coleridge does not exactly contradict him: it is because, he makes clear, the proper function of women is to sympathise, to feel with others, to become them, to take as their own the identities that inhabit them, that the perfection of women is to be characterless.

For he goes on: 'every one wishes a Desdemona or Ophelia for a wife – creatures who, though they may not always understand you, do always feel you, and feel with you'.[26] And that is the point: the characterless woman, however laudably undetermined, is unstable, because determinable. But the characterless woman can be stabilised as wife; she then takes on the fixed, permanent, imperishable nature of her husband, whom she may not of course 'understand' – 'my wife doesn't understand me' – but with whom she 'feels', she sympathises. Her characterlessness is thus preserved from a proliferation into character by being determined in relation to one fixed character which is not her own: 'she feels *you*', she feels as if she is you. But if the woman remains, as we say, 'single', like the lady 'in the prime of earliest youth', in Milton's sonnet, she is always in danger of becoming plural; if she does not have a husband to feel, she may end up by feeling you, and you, and him in the flat downstairs, and him over the road. Her determinability is ever liable to become promiscuity, to appropriate or to be appropriated by an infinity of characters not her own, or an infinity of circumstances such as, in Mistress Quickly's speech, determine the subject. She will become characterless in exactly Pope's sense, of being all things to all men, but never herself, for she has no self to be.

The opposition of epic with drama began to be understood, around 1800, as an opposition between two kinds of gendered subjectivity: one kind which was heroically self-determined, like Cromwell's or Vane's, and another which was always sympathetically dispersed into other *personae*. In these terms, the opposition could not but attract 'our myriad-minded Shakspear',[27] as Coleridge called him, into the category of the feminine, the characterless in Pope's pejorative sense, the 'hydra-headed', for it could not help representing him as inherently plural and unstable. What then could rescue him from, and enable him to transcend, that femininity? The answer of course was his *universality*, for there are two ways of valuing myriad-mindedness. Shakespeare, as Coleridge repeatedly tells us, is the 'universal' poet. If we attempt to understand him merely as a dramatic poet, he will be contained within a category, the drama, that was becoming gendered as feminine, as the site of variety, of sensibility, of sympathy, of the fallen and dispersed subject.[28] But if we contemplate him in terms not of his productions, but of his productive *power*, his genius, then his possession of the quality that contains all qualities, his universality, will establish him as the complete exemplar of the poetic imagination, to which are appropriated all the varieties of poetic imagination and creativity. This will explain how he can create a Hamlet, and write the syntax appropriate to excess of method; and how he can also create a Mistress Quickly, and do her syntax too. Milton's genius will no longer be the antitype of

Shakespeare's, but a specific modification of it, a specific aspect of Shakespeare's totality, a totality in which all binary oppositions, all differences, are resolved. Shakespeare will be unity and variety, reason *and* sensibility, the power to methodise but also the disposition to sympathise, the dramatic but also the epic. He will also, alas, have to be androgynous, and we will have to make a virtue of that necessity.

In all this, however, the notion that a syntax in which the main verb, and so meaning, is deferred, remains for Coleridge a syntax which is epic. heroic, and manly. It remains the case for me, however, that we can say no more than that such a syntax has a long history of being used to represent an idea of masculinity which, in Milton's sonnets and in Coleridge's criticism, has itself a history of being used to instantiate a certain conception of the subject, and of the fully human. As such, it testifies to a fear that we – we men – may indeed be the children of nature, automata, passive vehicles of the circumstantial, possessed by experience and not in possession of it; and its function is to represent and dismiss that alternative and threatening conception of identity as other, and so as feminine.

## Notes

1 Shakespeare, *The Sonnets and A Lover's Complaint*, ed. John Kerrigan, (Harmondsworth: Penguin Books, 1986), p. 211.

2 Samuel Daniel, *Delia*, 1592, sonnet XLVII.

3 Spenser, *Amoretti and Epithalamium*, 1595, sonnet XXXIIII.

4 Henry Constable, *Diana*, 1594, seventh decad, sonnet VIII; the reasons for disputing Constable's authorship of many of the poems in this volume are given by Joan Grundy in the introduction to her edition *The Poems of Henry Constable* (Liverpool: Liverpool University Press, 1960).

5 See Heinrich Lausberg, *Handbuch der Literarischen Rhetorik*, 2 vols. (Munich: Max Hueber Verlag, 1960), §229, and the cross-references given in that paragraph.

6 The texts and translations of sonnets by Milton discussed in this essay are taken from *Milton's Sonnets*, ed. E. A. J. Honigmann (London: and New York City: (Macmillan and St Martin's Press, 1966). The notes to this edition may be consulted for explanations of allusions in the poems I discuss.

7 'The Eolian Harp', in *Coleridge: Poetical Works*, ed. E. H. Coleridge (London: Oxford University Press, 1912), p. 100.

8 In the interests of brevity, I have suppressed some of the complications of meaning and syntax in the second half of the sonnet. For an excellent account of them, see Stanley Fish, 'Interpreting the *Variorum*', in *Is There A Text in This Class? The Authority of Interpretive Communities* (Cambridge, Ma., and London: Harvard University Press, 1980) – see especially pp. 154–8.

9 For the suggestion that the name of the 'lady' is alluded to in this sonnet, see Honigmann, p. 90.

10 Woolf, *A Room of One's Own*, (Harmondsworth: Penguin Books, 1967 edition), pp. 96–7.

11 Coleridge, *Biographia Literaria*, eds James Engell and W. Jackson Bate, 2 vols. (London and Princeton: Routledge and Kegan Paul and Princeton University Press, 1983), vol. 2, pp. 26–8.

12　*A Room of One's Own*, p. 77.
13　Dorothy Richardson, *Pilgrimage* (London: Virago Press, 1979), vol. III, p. 14; cited by Stephen Heath in his essay, to which mine is indebted, 'Dorothy Richardson and the Novel', in *Teaching the Text*, eds Susan Kappeler and Norman Bryson (London: Routledge and Kegan Paul, 1983), pp. 126–47.
14　Coleridge, *Lay Sermons*, ed. R. J. White (London and Princeton: Routledge and Kegan Paul and Princeton University Press, 1972), p. 107; Coleridge, *Shakespearian Criticism*, ed. T. M. Raysor, 2 vols, (London: J. M. Dent, second edition, 1960), vol. 2, p. 243; Coleridge, *The Friend*, ed. Barbara Rooke, 2 vols. (London and Princeton: Routledge and Kegan Paul and Princeton University Press, 1969), vol. 1, p. 20. *The Notebooks of Samuel Taylor Coleridge*, ed. Kathleen Coburn (London: (Routledge and Kegan Paul, 1957–　), vol. 3, §3670; *The Friend*, vol. 1, p. 20.
15　Coleridge, *Miscellanies, Aesthetic and Literary*, ed. T. Ashe (London: George Bell and Sons, 1892), p. 143.
16　*Biographia Literaria*, vol. 2, p. 55.
17　*Miscellanies*, pp. 178–9.
18　*The Friend*, vol. 1, pp. 32–3 and 33n.
19　*The Friend*, vol. 1, pp. 449–50.
20　*The Friend*, vol. 1, pp. 450–1.
21　*The Friend*, vol. 1, p. 451.
22　Woolf, *To the Lighthouse* (London: Hogarth Press, new edition, 1930), pp. 42–3.
23　Woolf, in *Contemporary Writers* (London: Hogarth Press, 1965), pp. 124–5, quoted by Heath, see above, note 13.
24　*Table Talk*, 23 June 1834 and 12 May 1830.
25　*Table Talk*, 12 May and 26 September 1830.
26　*Table Talk*, 26 September 1830.
27　*Biographia Literaria*, vol. 2, p. 19.
28　For a discussion of this issue, see John Barrell, *The Political Theory of Painting from Reynolds to Hazlitt: 'The Body of the Public'* (London: Yale University Press, 1986), pp. 283–307.

# 3

# The uses of contradiction: Pope's 'Epistle to Bathurst'

## I

More than any other century, the eighteenth-century was the age of the long poem: it was by writing at length that poetic reputations were made. But those reputations were not easily made, for critics were rarely satisfied that the problem of how to organise a wide range of topics into a coherent whole had been overcome. Edward Young's *Night-Thoughts* (1742–5), according to Johnson, exhibited 'a wilderness of thought . . . in the whole there is a magnificence like that ascribed to Chinese Plantation, the magnificence of vast extent and endless diversity'. 'The great defect' of James Thomson's descriptive poem, *The Seasons* (1726–46), he commented, in a judgment equally famous, 'is want of method; but for this I know not that there was any remedy. Of many appearances subsisting all at once, no rule can be given why one should be mentioned before another; yet the memory wants the help of order.' In his essay on Oliver Goldsmith's *The Deserted Village* (1770), John Scott went rather further: 'Modern poetry has, in general,' he wrote, 'one common defect, viz., the want of proper arrangement. There are many poems, whose component parts resemble a number of fine paintings, which have some connexion with each other, but are not placed in any regular series.'[1] Scott's point, it seems, is directed against modern poetry in general, because modern poetry was, to him, generally concerned to be descriptive, and descriptive poetry must of necessity sacrifice the advantages available to a diachronic medium, in the attempt to annex those of a synchronic.

Like Scott, Johnson in his remarks on Thomson does not go so far as to suggest that poetry should abandon the attempt to represent 'appearances subsisting all at once'; but, like Scott, he sees that attempt as inevitably inimical to method. The *Night-Thoughts*, however, was not a descriptive poem, or at least no one in the eighteenth century seems to have classified it as such. If it seemed to be a 'wilderness', this was the result not of the juxtaposing of word-pictures in random order, but of the fact that, as Young explained, 'the method pursued in it was rather *imposed*, by what spontaneously arose in its Author's mind ... than meditated, or *designed*'. It was perhaps Young's own willingness to point out the absence of an organising principle in his poem that led Johnson to represent its lack of unity as a magnificent 'diversity' and 'copious-ness',[2] but still he registered that absence.

On this showing, then, three of the most popular long poems of the century were remarkable for their 'want of method', and to these we can certainly add a fourth, William Cowper's *The Task* (1785), a poem which moves from topic to topic with greater freedom than any other of the century. But if eighteenth-century critics were quick to point out the 'want of method' exhibited especially by long poems in the newly-inven-ted genres of poetry – the meditative poem, the descriptive poem, the moral essay – they did not often comment upon what has seemed in this century the inevitable consequence of that want, that such poems appear regularly to contradict themselves. In this century, critical discussion of *The Seasons*, for example, or of Pope's *Essay on Man* (1733–4), has been largely preoccupied, either with pointing out contradictions in those poems – say between Thomson's accounts of history as progress and as decline, or between Pope's representation of moral behaviour as natur-ally or providentially determined and as subject to the control of the will – or with arguing that those contradictions are apparent only. Eighteenth-century critics exhibit no similar degree of concern with the consistency of the argument of either poem, and this in spite of the interest in 'method' we have already observed, and in spite of the fact, too, that in common with many other long poems of the eighteenth century, both these poems seems to invite us to inspect that consistency by prefixing to every book a summary of its contents, an 'argument'. Obviously enough, this phenomenon begs a number of questions. Did eighteenth-century critics as a rule concern themselves with whether or not the argument of a poem was consistent? If they did not, what did they mean by 'method', by 'proper arrangement'? If they did, are we to assume that they judged the arguments of most contemporary long poems not to be so inconsistent as to justify adverse comment? Or that for some reason they chose, or were able, to overlook contradic-tions which have seemed only too conspicuous to many recent readers of eighteenth-century poetry?

We can put some of these questions into focus by offering a version of what has become a routine exercise in the criticism of Pope's poetry, the analysis of the famous instance of contradiction, real or apparent, in the account of Old Cotta the miser and his prodigal son, and the paragraphs surrounding it, in the 'Epistle to Bathurst'.[3] The account is introduced by these lines:

> "The ruling Passion, be it what it will,
> "The ruling Passion conquers Reason still."
> Less mad the wildest whimsey we can frame,
> Than ev'n that Passion, if it has no Aim;
> For tho' such motives Folly you may call,
> The Folly's greater to have none at all.                    160
>     Hear then the truth: "'Tis Heav'n each Passion sends,
> "And diff'rent men directs to diff'rent ends.
> "Extremes in Nature equal good produce,
> "Extremes in Man concur to gen'ral use."
> Ask we what makes one keep, and one bestow?
> That POW'R who bids the Ocean ebb and flow,
> Bids seed-time, harvest, equal course maintain,
> Thro' reconcil'd extremes of drought and rain,
> Builds Life on Death, on Change Duration founds,
> And gives th' eternal wheels to know their rounds.          170
>     Riches, like insects, when conceal'd they lie,
> Wait but for wings, and in their season, fly.
> Who sees pale Mammon pine amidst his store,
> Sees but a backward steward for the Poor;
> This year a Reservoir, to keep and spare,
> The next a Fountain, spouting thro' his Heir,
> In lavish streams to quench a Country's thirst,
> And men and dogs shall drink him 'till they burst. (155–78)

The problem posed by the passage these lines introduce has been familiar enough since Courthope published his edition of the poem in 1881. We can take a hint as to how to approach it from the commentary on the poem written by Pope's friend William Warburton. 'In the first part' of the epistle, he explained, 'the *use* and *abuse* of Riches are *satirically* delivered in *precept*. From thence to ver. 177, the causes of the abuse are *philosophically* inquired into: And from thence to the end, the *use* and *abuse* are *historically* illustrated by *examples*.'[4] We can translate this into the suggestion that the poem is characterised by a series of discursive shifts, and that between the lines we have quoted, and those that follow, there is a shift between what Warburton thinks of as the 'philosophical' and the 'historical', or 'exemplary' – though we shall label the discourses rather differently.

The argument of these three paragraphs has been conceived within a hybrid discourse, one we often encounter in the second quarter of the eighteenth century, and one of whose constituents is that form of theodicy whose governing maxim is *concordia discors*. God's providence is evident in the harmonious reconciliation of extremes, of contraries; the harmonious duration of the universe is based on the very changeability of its constituent elements. In the moral universe, no less than the physical, extremes of behaviour are the means by which God produces the general good of the whole of human society. To this end, human behaviour has to be imagined as entirely determined by providence: different modes of behaviour are functions of the different ruling passions that 'Heaven' implants in 'diff'rent men', and over which they have no control – for whatever power to restrain the passions Pope may grant to 'Reason' elsewhere in his poems, in the opening couplet of this passage he categorically denies it any such capability.

According to Warburton, everywhere anxious to acquit Pope of the charge of fatalism, this couplet says that the ruling passion will conquer reason unless we employ 'the greatest circumspection' to ensure that it does not. But of course it says no such thing, and this is no doubt the kind of interpretation Johnson had in mind when he remarked that 'Dr Warburton has endeavoured to find a train of thought' in this and the 'Epistle to Burlington' which 'was never in the writer's head'.[5] That Pope is nevertheless confused in his fatalism is clear enough from lines 159–60, where he seems to declare a rational or an ethical preference for mere 'whimseys', mere caprice, directed to determinate ends, over aimless passions by which no such ends can be secured; the declaration seems to be predicated on the supposition that human beings are autonomous moral agents, a supposition which is painstakingly denied elsewhere in these paragraphs. But this supposition, of course, mentioned here only to be ignored, soon returns to contradict, in a more thoroughgoing fashion, the argument that is being elaborated in these lines.

On this theodicean discourse is grafted the discourse of what we shall call economic amoralism, the scandalous discourse, associated most notably with the economist Mandeville, which said what should never be said, and which produced an account of economic activity too evidently convenient to emergent capitalism to be openly acknowledged. For it proposed that virtue was not just an irrelevant consideration in the conduct of economic life, but that an insistence on the principles of virtuous conduct actually interfered with the maximisation of pleasure and happiness that was the proper end of all economic activity and social life. If luxury was vicious, it was also the great agent in increasing the number of people in employment, in raising standards of living, and in ensuring continued economic progress. Because people are naturally luxurious, naturally vicious, the operations of vice, left to themselves, will guarantee a continuously expanding economy, and the maximum diffusion of happiness. Only moral regulation of economic behaviour, moral intervention in the market-place, can endanger this happy result.

The attempt of the discourse of economic amoralism to challenge conventional condemnations of luxury, avarice and improvidence was scandalous not simply because it represented an attempt to withdraw economic activity entirely out of the sphere of moral regulation, but because it attempted to do this at the same time as it effectively conceded to human agents a free will by which, perversely, they could choose not to indulge their vices. It was thus a discourse at once too useful to be ignored in defences of emergent capitalism, and too direct to be allowed unambiguous utterance in the tradition of high literature, officially committed to moral instruction as well as to pleasure. Thus to those who, writing within that tradition, were anxious to represent emergent capitalism as a morally legitimate form of social and economic organisation, but were concerned equally not to prescribe inconvenient limits to the operation of acquisitive economic activity, the problem presented by the discourse of economic amoralism was to find a way of modifying it, so as to reinsert economic activity within the sphere of the good, while ensuring that not much if any of the economic freedom the discourse offered was sacrificed. The result was a knotting together of economic amoralism and theodicy into a hybrid discourse – what we shall call the discourse of economic theodicy.

As a result of this knotting, the discourse of Mandeville acquired a moral legitimacy, a polish that it had forfeited by blurting out its meanings in so unvarnished a form. By this means, greed could be allowed full scope, and yet be represented not as vice, but as having a sanction which made it more than merely virtuous, by seeing it as a passion implanted by God which no human considerations of vice and virtue could uproot. It is God who makes misers, and God also makes spendthrifts. Both are intended by God, are part of his purpose, are the discords by which a concordant universe is produced. Far from being weakened by its appropriation by theodicy, the discourse of economic amoralism was thus considerably strengthened; for the freedom of the will was by this means abolished, and no one could now choose to restrain their rage either to hoard or spend.

Apparently to convince us of these truths more thoroughly, the poem

now offers to expatiate on the nature of the miser, the 'reservoir', 'pale
Mammon', and his spendthrift heir, the 'fountain'. And so it offers us
these contrasting portraits, as if to show that the behaviour of neither is
reprehensible, since both are the unconscious agents of the providential
plan:

> Old Cotta sham'd his fortune and his birth,
> Yet was not Cotta void of wit or worth:                                    180
> What tho' (the use of barb'rous spits forgot)
> His kitchen vy'd in coolness with his grot?
> His court with nettles, moats with cresses stor'd,
> With soups unbought and sallads blest his board.
> If Cotta liv'd on pulse, it was no more
> Than Bramins, Saints, and Sages did before;
> To cram the Rich was prodigal expence,
> And who would take the Poor from Providence?
> Like some lone Chartreux stands the good old Hall,
> Silence without, and Fasts within the wall;                                190
> No rafter'd roofs with dance and tabor sound,
> No noon-tide bell invites the country round;
> Tenants with sighs the smoakless tow'rs survey,
> And turn th' unwilling steeds another way:
> Benighted wanderers, the forest o'er,
> Curse the sav'd candle, and unop'ning door;
> While the gaunt mastiff growling at the gate,
> Affrights the beggar whom he longs to eat.
> Not so his Son, he mark'd this oversight,
> And then mistook reverse of wrong for right.                               200
> (For what to shun will no great knowledge need,
> But what to follow, is a task indeed.)
> What slaughter'd hecatombs, what floods of wine,
> Fill the capacious Squire, and deep Divine!
> Yet no mean motive this profusion draws,
> His oxen perish in his country's cause;
> 'Tis GEORGE and LIBERTY that crowns the cup,
> And Zeal for that great House which eats him up.
> The woods recede around the naked seat,
> The Sylvans groan – no matter – for the Fleet:                             210
> Next goes his Wool – to clothe our valiant bands,
> Last, for his Country's love, he sells his Lands.
> To town he comes, completes the nation's hope,
> And heads the bold Train-bands, and burns a Pope.
> And shall not Britain now reward his toils,
> Britain, that pays her Patriots with her Spoils?
> In vain at Court the Bankrupt pleads his cause,
> His thankless Country leaves him to her Laws. (179–218)

But though these portraits of Cotta and his son seem to be introduced to reinforce the argument of the preceding paragraphs, they seem to do the very opposite. For the discursive history of these two exemplary types situates them within some other discourse than that of economic theodicy – a satirical discourse, which prescribes an entirely opposite account of economic activity to that proposed in the paragraph that introduced them. The satire of types is a moralizing discourse. It sees each type it identifies as exemplary of some kind of moral deviation; all types, insofar as they are available to satire, are deviants from the central, normative position occupied by whatever individual is adduced as evading typical classification. In this satirical discourse, extremes of behaviour are not necessary to God's providential plan, but rather evidences of humankind's vicious and wilful tendency to frustrate that plan. To attempt to appropriate these characters to the discourse of economic theodicy is, on the evidence of these two paragraphs, extremely difficult. They arrive carrying the discursive baggage of satire, and so tenaciously do they refuse to be parted from it, that instead of being appropriated by the discourse of economic theodicy, they appropriate the poem to their own purposes. The result (though this has, of course, been disputed – see note 4 below) is a complete contradiction between the three paragraphs we first examined, and these two.

This new process of appropriation can be examined in the first couplet about Old Cotta. In terms of what we have read before, this couplet may seem to operate as an unproblematic exemplification of the truth of what has just been announced. That is, it can be read as saying that though, according to some merely human calculus of moral behaviour, Old Cotta's miserliness made him a disgrace to his family and social position, in fact he was not stupid, and certainly not void of worth. Such judgments have nothing to do with the case, for the behaviour of the miser is as much a part of the providential plan as anyone else's. Cotta's worth is not to be measured by merely human notions of virtue, but by the function God intended him to perform, and in those terms he is worth no more nor less than anyone else. But as we read on down the paragraph, this couplet seems to echo in our minds as having said something altogether different, and its second line seems to have been uttered in the voice of some other speaker than the narrator, a voice which is soon further distanced from the narrator when it attempts to make a quite new defence of Cotta: that it was he, not God, who made the decision that he should be a miser, and that he chose miserliness on grounds of principle. This voice considers the evidence of Cotta's meanness, and attempts to reinterpret it as evidence of a scrupulous moral concern, until it is silenced at line 189. And so from the first couplet, which can be read as a vindication, if not of the miser, then of the wisdom of Heaven in implanting within him the passion of avarice, the paragraph becomes, by its end, a moral and satirical attack on miserliness itself. The paternalist moral considerations dismissed by the discourse of economic theodicy as irrelevant, have reasserted their relevance to economic behaviour by means of the discourse of the satire of types.

The triumph of this latter discourse is confirmed in the account of Cotta's son. Once again, the passage is divided between the satirist, and the voice of an advocate for young Cotta, who represents his prodigality as the principled behaviour of a Hanoverian patriot. Once again, the authority and victory of satire is ensured when the counsel for the defence falls silent at line 213; and once again, the voice that is not heard is the voice of the discourse of economic theodicy. And in this paragraph, especially, our desire to find a consistent argument would lead us to expect that voice to be allowed to speak. For the whole point of the lines in which the topic of miserliness and prodigality was first introduced, was that God is vindicated in creating misers by the fact that he also creates spendthrifts. He creates the first, because they naturally, they inevitably lead to the creation of the second. The riotous expenditure of spendthrifts enables money to circulate, to percolate down to the poor, and so ensures the maximum diffusion of money and happiness. The discourse of economic theodicy insists that we should attend to the effects, rather than the motives, of misers and spendthrifts, and that in those terms we will see that their creation by providence is entirely vindicated. But the discourse of satirical types has turned out to be largely uninterested in effects: what is fought out, by the competing voices of these last two paragraphs, is an argument about whether or not the motives of Cotta and his son are selfish, or can be justified in terms of disinterested, unselfish moral principle. The passage so far can thus be seen as an exemplification of that discursive disjunction, by which throughout the first three-quarters of the eighteenth century, writings on the vulgar topic of wealth and trade invite us to understand behaviour in the utilitarian terms of its effects, while writers within the polite tradition of ethical philosophy endeavour, with increasing lack of success, to contain the discussion of behaviour within a discussion of intentions.

Indeed, the next paragraph makes it quite clear that beneficial effects can only be relied upon if they are the result of benevolent human intentions, and cannot be expected from what are now to be understood as the capricious operations of 'Fortune' rather than the providential arrangements of Heaven:

> The Sense to value Riches, with the Art
> T' enjoy them, and the Virtue to impart, 220
> Not meanly, nor ambitiously pursu'd,
> Not sunk by sloth, nor rais'd by servitude;
> To balance Fortune by a just expence,
> Join with Oeconomy, Magnificence;
> With Splendour, Charity; with Plenty, Health;
> Oh teach us, BATHURST! yet unspoil'd by wealth!
> That secret rare, between th' extremes to move
> Of mad Good-nature, and of mean Self-love.(219–28)

Now Bathurst is appealed to as the model by which the rest of us may learn to regulate our economic behaviour by the very moral principle that earlier had been seen as irrelevant to it, and that, in terms of the discourse of economic theodicy, could only have been represented as interference in the natural and beneficial operations of the divine economic plan. The contradiction has now become focused on the word 'extremes', which in the first paragraphs of the passage were so far from being reprehensible that they were the necessary discords out of which God produced harmony. Now, however, such extremes of economic behaviour as are represented by Cotta and his son are entirely reprehensible, and Bathurst must teach a prudent mode of paternalism by his exemplary observance of the golden mean. If he succeeds, of course, then in terms of the first paragraphs the economic system will collapse, for without extremes there can be no balance. But if he fails, then in the terms of this paragraph the economic system must also collapse, for it is the responsibility of moral agents to 'balance Fortune', which God, apparently, does not do.

Or rather, it is suggested in the final paragraph we want to consider, God does mend the faults of Fortune, but it is our duty to help him do so, by attempting to pattern our economic behaviour on his own exemplary economic interventionism:

> To Want or Worth well-weigh'd, be Bounty giv'n,
> And ease, or emulate, the care of Heav'n, 230
> Whose measure full o'erflows on human race;
> Mend Fortune's fault, and justify her grace.
> Wealth in the gross is death, but life diffus'd,
> As Poison heals, in just proportion us'd:
> In heaps, like Ambergrise, a stink it lies,
> But well-dispers'd, is Incense to the Skies. (229–36)

In these lines, God is apparently acquitted of the charge that he is responsible for the maldistribution of wealth that is the prior condition to its equitable redistribution. It is now Fortune who makes misers and prodigals, as clearly as at line 166 it was God. And now God's task, like Bathurst's, is to clear up after the accidents of Fortune. The task of human beings, as moral agents, is to regulate both the intentions and the effects of moral behaviour, their own and that of others. The moralism of the discourse of the satire of types has entirely supplanted that of economic theodicy; and the next passage will be devoted to praising the Man of Ross who, precisely, eased and emulated God's care, and certainly did not wait for him to get round to balancing the extremes of wealth he, or Fortune, had created.

## II

For three paragraphs, then, we seem to have encountered a discourse that functions to insulate economic activity from moral inspection, and to do so rather more firmly than Mandeville, or than other early eighteenth-century writers on wealth had managed. And then for four paragraphs, we have encountered a discourse which, if not positively hostile to the values and beliefs of emergent capitalism, is certainly concerned to propose that economic behaviour should be regulated by a consideration of moral principle that earlier had been shown to have no bearing at all on the matter. But this contradiction need not be seen as an embarrassment to the discourse of economic theodicy with which the passage began. It can be seen, indeed, as immensely convenient to it, a further stage in the knotting together of discourses by which hegemony is confirmed. Both the contradictory statements made in the passage can perfectly well find their place within the ideology of laissez-faire capitalism. The first statement can be taken as an announcement that the free economic activity of individuals should not be constrained by an insistence on judging it by irrelevant moral considerations. God worries about what is good and bad, and leaves us to get on with whatever he has created us to do. The second statement can be taken as announcing that economic activity should be policed – indeed, that it is policed, by such men as Bathurst – by scrupulous standards of morality based upon a careful adherence to the golden mean.

The convenience of saying both these things will be evident if we reflect upon the contradictory arguments by which the financial institutions of the City of London have, at the time of writing, successfully resisted pressure to subject them to external regulation. On the one hand, the nature of the market is such that it cannot function if it is fettered by moral regulation; on the other, it is already regulated by the principles of a scrupulous morality, and could not function if it were not. The second half of this argument is not, of course, quite the same as that elaborated by Pope, but the argument that he offers is no less convenient a justification of acquisitiveness. For while it claims that the equitable distribution of the gifts of fortune is the true end of morality in matters of economics, it represents 'the rich man', as Warburton put it, 'as the substitute of Providence, in this unequal distribution of things'.[6] The inequalities of wealth produce rich men, and rich men must continue to exist, if by their benevolence inequalities of wealth are to continue to be abolished – a moral justification for acquisitiveness quite as convenient as the amoral justification offered by the discourse of economic theodicy, and in some contexts no doubt more so.

It is, then, no embarrassment, but a positive advantage, to the interests of the rich and the reasonably well-off – in short, to almost all the likely readers of this poem, and of poetry in general – that both these contradictory statements should be uttered. And it will therefore also be convenient that there should be forms of literary expression available to the polite culture by which such contradictions could be enunciated. We want now to suggest that the institutions of poetry and criticism in eighteenth-century Britain invented just such forms. These may not have been invented for the *purpose* of giving utterance to contradiction. The power of ideological formations to conceal their function, even and perhaps especially from the class whose hegemony they confirm, is such that we could hardly expect to find evidence of such a purpose; and their power to conceal contradictions, again perhaps especially from those who give them voice, makes it difficult to imagine that new forms could have been invented for a purpose which was not itself open to inspection. But such forms certainly *facilitated* the utterance of contradictions; and we want further to suggest that the institutions of criticism managed to train the readers of poetry in the forms thus invented to read it in such a way as ensured that they would overlook the contradictory nature of the ideologies those forms were able to express.

From the beginning of the eighteenth century, what were perceived as new forms of poetry began to be invented, and we can see their invention as a response to a pervasive sense that some of the older genres, epic and pastoral in particular, were incapable of representing the nature of the modern world, the diversity, as it was understood to be, of modern

European society. The heroes of epic were now unimaginable, for the essential condition of epic heroism was that the hero should somehow represent, within himself, all the members of his society. But the proliferation of interests and occupational identities within a commercial society meant that no individual could now fulfil that representative task. The ideology inscribed within the conventions of pastoral – more or less egalitarian and entirely pre-commercial – disabled that genre too from describing the divided and ramified forms of commercial society. Satire, of course, could do just that, but satire, uncompounded with any genre more hospitable to the values of commercial society, could represent that society only in negative terms. There were, however, classical genres which seemed to have the potential for more positive representations of the modern world: the epistle, for example, which was inhospitable to the high-principled morality of satire, 'suitable to every subject', and could treat 'all the affairs of life and researches into nature';[7] and the didactic poem, which had conventionally been interrupted by frequent digressions, as it were to sweeten the pill of its didacticism. The branch of didactic poetry most committed to the representation of economic activity in a positive light was the georgic, which had also traditionally been ventilated by digressions, and was thus hospitable to a diversity of topics which could be used, as could the ranginess of the epistle, to represent the diversity of modern experience. These were all forms which no critic of authority had methodised, reduced to rule, or separated out; and thus they could even be combined with each other, or with other genres, to produce the characteristic vehicle of eighteenth-century poetry, the poem of mixed genre, variously mingling satire, the epistle, and the didactic poem whether philosophical or georgic.

Such mixed compositions by their very nature evaded classification by genre: thus The Seasons, according to an early critical account, 'notwithstanding some parts of it are didactic', might also 'with propriety' be termed a 'descriptive' poem; the 'epistle' to Bathurst was described at one time as an epistle, later as an essay, and was written according to 'a new Scheme of Ethic Poems'.[8] And at the start of the century it was generally agreed by critics that the suitability of a subject for treatment in this genre was a question less of its dignity or its usefulness to the purposes of society, than of the degree of variety it admitted. The advantage of agriculture as a subject, Addison explained, was that it could offer 'a pleasing variety of scenes and landscapes', and 'surprize and variety' were the essential characteristics of the genre. According to another critic, moral philosophy was 'foreign to a nature that delights in the

Variety of Didactic Poetry'; natural philosophy was 'so far ... from possessing Variety, that it ... concentrates thousands of objects into a single Concept'; and poems which treated of the rules of criticism were bound, if they were to be of any use, to set out those rules with the utmost conscientiousness and the least possible variety. But if none of these subjects can 'charm the mind with Variety', there remains 'the fourth sort of Theme', 'compounded out of them all': 'country scenes' offer so 'joyous' a 'Variety of Imagery' that the greatest effort in this genre, Virgil's *Georgics*, 'will never weary its readers, since its variety is ever-lasting'.[9] If other critics sometimes arrive at different valuations of the suitability of subjects for didactic poetry, their principle is the same. Some believe that natural philosophy is 'agreeable to the Variety' of the genre; all agree that agriculture affords an 'agreeable Variety'.[10]

The preoccupation with variety in didactic poetry seems to invite us to regard the summaries prefixed to different books of poems of mixed genre, and variously termed 'The Argument', 'The Design', 'The Plan', or 'The Contents', in a double light. On the one hand, such summaries are clearly intended to exhibit the coherence, the 'method' of the composition, which according to William Enfield, writing at the end of the century, was 'perfectly consistent with that variety, which characterizes genius',[11] but which, according to John Scott, was seldom found co-existing with it. On the other hand, they could be used also to exhibit the variety of topics the poem had succeeded in treating. Thus the 'argument' of the 'Epistle to Bathurst' summarises the paragraphs we have been examining in four topics:

That the conduct of men, with respect to Riches, can only be accounted for by the ORDER OF PROVIDENCE, which works the general Good out of Extremes, and brings all to its great End by perpetual Revolutions, v. 161 to 178. How a Miser acts upon Principles which appear to him reasonable, v. 179. How a Prodigal does the same, v. 199. The due Medium, and true use of Riches, v. 219.

That the second and third of these topics could exemplify the extremes referred to in the first is clear enough; and that the last could take the form of a conclusion based on the second and third is equally evident. But how we could logically proceed from the first to the fourth is no less mysterious in the argument than it is in the poem. The point of these 'arguments', which seem to invite a critical inspection of the rational development of the poems they introduce, takes on a new light if we see them also as advertising the variety of the topics to be treated. An argument or summary could no doubt be read as representing a poem's

process of development and its variety at the same time. Or different
styles of argument could foreground either connection or variety. In the
first collected edition of The Seasons, published in 1730, Thomson managed to summarize 'Spring', which then ran to 1,205 lines, in an 'Argument' of only seventy-one words, identifying only five or so separate
topics. But this argument was itself a summary of 'The Contents' prefixed
to 'Spring' in the second edition of that poem in 1729, which, consonant
with Thomson's belief that no subject could compete with the the
variety of the 'Works of Nature', ran to little less than four hundred words
and listed forty-five distinct topics.[12]

Our discussion of Pope's epistle has suggested that the various topics
admitted into a properly various poem will each enter encased in its own
discursive history; so that the critical requirement that didactic poems,
and poems of mixed genre, should contain a variety of topics can be read
as, in effect, a demand or a licence for them to exhibit a variety of
discourses. And as the 'Epistle' has also suggested, this in turn is a tacit
licence, if not a demand, for them to contradict themselves. The article of
faith in much twentieth-century criticism, that the value of a poem is a
function of the unity it exhibits, produced a considerable volume of
writing about Pope which argues that such contradictions are only
apparent. We want to suggest that these efforts may be as misconceived
as they have been unsuccessful, insofar as they are predicated upon the
assumption that the concern with unity and consistency, was as important to Pope and Thomson as it has been to modern criticism. We are
arguing that the concern for method and unity in eighteenth-century
poetry was accompanied by a tacit permission for long poems of mixed
genre to contradict themselves.

The permission could remain tacit, partly because the excellence of
such poems was conceived of as residing in their variety. A criticism that
legitimates the employment of a variety of discourses within a poem is
one that legitimates a new notion of what makes a work coherent. It does
not demand that a poem of mixed genre should be, as a whole, consistent;
it demands that each topic, as it is elaborated, should exhibit a discursive
unity, and that the separate topics should cohere, should be glued together
in such a way that we can see the join, but are not offended by its
abruptness. When the introduction of a topic is announced, the introduction of its appropriate discourse should be clearly signalled, as the
evidently fictional name of the miser, and the ironised voice of the
reasonable advocate who speaks on behalf of Old Cotta, announce the
introduction of the discourse of the satire of types. The art of signalling a

change of discourse was the art of 'managing' the 'transitions'. And we repeat that a successful 'transition' was not one which concealed discursive shifts, but which made them appear, at least, to be appropriate and 'natural' – as, in the couplet that introduces Old Cotta, the continuing voice of the discourse of economic theodicy is audible at the same time as the voice of the new, satiric discourse. As Warburton remarked, the 'philosophical' portion of the poem 'naturally introduces' the 'historical'.

In *The Seasons*, descriptions of landscape, which represent the social as well as the natural world as providentially ordered and perfectly harmonious, repeatedly give way, and on occasion within a single paragraph, to exhortations to civic virtue, which represent society as corrupt and in urgent need of reformation. These in turn continually give way to more description of landscape. Nobody in the century seems to comment upon the contradictions these transitions produce. But John Aikin was so intrigued by Thomson's capacity or willingness to switch suddenly from one of these topics to the other, that he directly posed the question of whether, and of how, Thomson got away with it. It all depended, he decided, on 'the manner of their introduction. In some instances this is so easy and natural, that the mind is scarcely sensible of the deviation; in others it is more abrupt and unartful.'[13]

It was by virtue of his excellence in the management of transitions, according to Addison, that Virgil was able to include topics which 'are almost foreign to his subject'. His digressions 'are not brought in by force, but naturally arise out of the principal argument and design of the Poem'. Another critic praises Virgil for digressions 'naturally arising from the main subject', and for 'his happy address in returning again to his subject', when 'he seems to have wandered far from his purpose'. Others expect no more than that transitions should be so managed that they 'seem to arise naturally' out of the main subject, that they should 'seem of a piece with it'. 'Darting about' is essential to the didactic poem, writes yet another, but it must be 'nimble': we should notice, we should admire the transitions, but we should not be embarrassed by them.[14]

## III

By a concentration on the separate topics within a poem, and the art of connecting them 'naturally', or of making the connections between them *seem* natural, the question of whether a poem was consistent disappeared behind the question of whether its separate topical units were pieced together by an art which concealed itself but not its operations. And this habit of regarding poems in terms of their thematically, if not aesthetically, discrete units must have been reinforced by the tradition of practical criticism, deriving in large part from the French critic Bouhours, but in England influenced also by the epistemology of Locke, by which poems could be broken down into, and evaluated in terms of, still smaller ideational units. In the most extreme versions of this style of criticism, the different 'thoughts', 'images' or 'pictures' a poem contained could be classified into sublime, grand, noble, pretty, agreeable, fine, delicate, true, false, beautiful, soft, natural, simple, gay, and so on. Or by the tradition of verbal criticism, poems could be judged in terms of their success in handling the different figures of speech that could be discovered within them, or in terms of their 'expression' in the different styles they could be identified as employing. Such modes of criticism represented the 'beauties' or the 'faults' of a poem as things to be looked for in units of a couple of lines or so, far more than in the unity of its design or argument.[15]

Contradiction is still registered, of course, and punished by criticism, when the rules internal to a particular discourse are infringed. But contradiction among discourses, provided that their introduction is clearly signalled, is not at all reprehensible. So far, then, the evidence suggests that eighteenth-century critics were not concerned by the fact that long poems contradicted themselves, largely because, for them, the coherence of a poem was something distinct from its consistency, and because the procedures by which such poems usually did give rise to contradiction were examined in a rather different light, as the means by which they came to exhibit the variety of the world and of the poet's genius.

But there is another body of evidence which suggests that poems of mixed genre in particular were often not read in such a way as would enable either their coherence or their consistency to be an object of attention. As another French critic, the Abbé Du Bos had remarked, and as a number of English critics repeated, the subject of a didactic poem may be 'so exceedingly curious, as to induce you to read it over once with great pleasure; yet you will never peruse it a second time with the same satisfaction you taste even from an eclogue. The understanding feels no pleasure in being instructed twice in the same thing; but the heart is capable of feeling the same emotion twice, with great pleasure.'[16] If criticism was willing to acknowledge that 'the mind can hardly attend a second time' to 'passages that are merely instructive', this amounts to a permission to skip and dip, to leaf through the volume reading only

those passages that, elsewhere, criticism regarded as ornamental digressions from the principle argument. Thus Fanny Burney records the opin-
ion of Mr Fairly, that Young 'was an author not to read on regularly, but to
dip into, and reflect upon'; and Pope's Essay on Man, according to Johnson, was valued especially for its 'flowers', its 'splendid amplifications
and sparkling sentences', so that 'many read it for a manual of practical
piety',[17] a repository of moral instructions and maxims. Nor was this a
permission accorded to readers of didactic poetry only: it seems to have
been allowed for all non-narrative poems of mixed genre, which were
probably most often read piecemeal by readers searching for the isolated
'beauties' they contained.

Two developments which gathered momentum in the final third of
the century, and which are connected with the expansion of the reading-
public, combined to make 'dipping' easier, or even unnecessary. The
first of these was the proliferation of literary periodicals, in which
reviewers of poetry were expected to identify and quote at length the
'flowers' or 'beauties' of the long poems they discussed. The ideological
convenience of this practice is well-exemplified in contemporary
reviews of The Deserted Village, a poem in which the condemnation of
luxury was not counterbalanced by any contradictory assertion of the
political and economic advantages it secured. Those reviewers who
comment on Goldsmith's attack on luxury do so only to question or
condemn it. But this, they assert, does nothing to destroy the beauty of
the poem, which resides, for them, in its 'beauties' – in a series of
affecting passages which they quote at length. The political argument of
the poem could either be ignored or dismissed, with the implication that
political economy has now taken over the cognitive functions of poetry
with respect to social and economic questions. The poem was thus
boiled down in the reviews to three main passages: the descriptions of
the village schoolmaster, the village clergyman, and the village ale-
house.[18] In the 'dedication' prefixed to the poem, Goldsmith had asked
for the 'unfatigued attention' of the reader, but what he got seems to have
been very different: if the poem was quickly accepted as a classic, it was
largely because these three 'pictures' were accorded classic status.

Copies of periodicals were kept, in this period, far more assiduously
than now: one of their functions was certainly to identify and to reproduce what were reckoned to be the most remarkable passages, not of
poems only, but of any book reviewed at length. But only in the case of
imaginative literature was it not also one of their functions to summarise
and comment upon the argument (where there was one) of the works

under review. So that as the cognitive function of imaginative literature was appropriated elsewhere, so poetry in particular came to be read for the 'ardent images' the 'fine sentiments', it could offer. And that Goldsmith's classic passages may have become more familiar through excerpts, than by being turned to in copies of the poem itself, is suggested by the second development I referred to, the proliferation of anthologies of poetry, aids to the acquisition of good morals, sentiments, or taste, or of the power to recite with appropriate expression.

With the exception of the voluminous *Elegant Extracts*, the anthologies selected and printed only the 'beauties' of long poems, and facilitated the process by which, like Goldsmith's 'Parish Priest', Pope's account of the 'Man of Ross' must have become more familiar than the 'Epistle to Bathurst' in which the account appears, and Young's poem best known for its paragraphs 'On Procrastination', 'On Covetousness', 'On Friendship', and 'On Irresolution'. 'In any well-used Copy of the Seasons,' wrote Wordsworth, 'the Book generally opens of itself with the rhapsody on love, or with one of the stories, (perhaps Damon and Musidora); these also are prominent in our Collections of Extracts; and are the parts of his Works which, after all, were probably most efficient in first recommending the Author to general notice.'[19] The anthologies of passages of verse for reading aloud sometimes contain instructions as to the appropriate tone of voice or gesture to be employed, even the appropriate emotion the reader should experience, in the recitation, but never concern themselves with explanations of the meaning of the passages selected. This concentration on 'sentiment' at the expense of 'meaning' no doubt did much to ensure that among even those readers who were moved to look up the poem, the extracts from which they had particularly enjoyed, not many would be troubled by the issues of the 'method' of the poem, or its consistency.[20]

'If a book has no index to it, or good table of contents', wrote Isaac Watts, 'it is very useful to make one as you are reading it; . . . but it is sufficient in your index to take notice only of those parts of the book which are new to you, or which you think well written, and well worthy of your remembrance or review.'[21] If one function of 'The Contents' of the second edition of 'Spring' was to call attention to the variety of its topics, another must certainly have been to enable the reader to locate the topics and passages that would offer most pleasure on a re-reading. The Contents of *The Seasons*, then, functioned much like the alphabetical index that came to be appended late in the century to the *Night-Thoughts*, the spontaneous lack of design of which could not allow Young to prefix an argument to it. Under 'O' we read:[22]

|                                                                        | Night. | Page. |
| --- | --- | --- |
| Obligations, religious and moral, all rendered void on the plan of infidelity | vii. | 168 |
| Ocean, description of the | viii. | 197 |
| Oeconomy, true, described | vi. | 132 |

The 'arguments' of long poems should perhaps always be understood as indexes or tables of contents, as well as 'designs' and displays of variety: as invitations, that is, to regard the poem in one light as consistent, in another as various, and in a third simply as a repository of detached passages whose coherence with the surrounding passages was as unimportant as their logical connection. If we look at the 'argument' of the 'Epistle to Bathurst' in this third way, it seems to encourage the reader to search for one passage that explains that the use of riches is not an affair of moral judgment, but of God's providential design, and to search for another that argues, on the contrary, that conduct with respect to riches should be regulated by 'the true Medium' of moral behaviour. By this means the contradictory components of capitalist ideology can be enunciated, but can be prevented from coming into contact with each other, by being made available to be sampled separately, as different readers and different occasions demand. Each can appear, almost, as a separate maxim. The poem becomes a repository of economic wisdom, a manual of capitalist piety, which accurately represents the contradictory pieties it contains, but does not invite an inspection of the relations between them. And for those who do read the poem through and attempt to connect up these separate passages, the decencies of the art of transition still conceal the contradictions they conjoin, by the very openness with which they display the variety of its topics and discourses.

The enunciation of the contradictions of ideology may not be the function for which long works of mixed genre, the characteristic production of eighteenth-century poets, were invented. But it is certainly one of the functions which they performed. In this chapter we have attempted to sketch out what should perhaps be regarded as one of the most impressive achievements of eighteenth-century literary culture in England. That achievement is one by which the institutions of criticism displaced inconsistency into coherence – into an aesthetic success – and trained the readers of poetry to admire most the poems which, by their very nature, were most liable to contradict themselves, and so enabled those readers to make use of contradictory meanings in the formation of their beliefs and in the conduct of their lives.

## Notes

1 Johnson, *The Lives of the Poets* (London: Oxford University Press, 1964), vol. 2, pp. 437, 359; Scott, *Critical Essays on Some of the Poems by Several English Poets* (London 1785), p. 251.

2 Young, *Night-Thoughts*, Preface; Johnson, *Lives*, p. 437.

3 *Of the Use of Riches, an Epistle to the Right Honourable Allen Lord Bathurst*, first published 1732/3. Quotation is from the text in Alexander Pope, *Epistles to Several Persons (Moral Essays)*, ed. F. W. Bateson (London and New Haven: Methuen and Yale University Press, 2nd ed., 1961).

4 See *The Works of Alexander Pope*, eds Whitwell Elwin and William J. Courthope (London: John Murray, vol. 3, 1881), pp. 121–2. It has of course been denied that the passage we are about to discuss contradicts itself – most notably, by Earl Wasserman, *Pope's 'Epistle to Bathurst'* (Baltimore: Johns Hopkins University Press, 1960), pp. 29–40. Wasserman's argument is too detailed to be discussed in this essay; it may suffice to say that it seems to us that he does not allow sufficient weight to lines 161–6; and that finally his claim that the passage develops a consistent argument can be reduced to a claim that lines 155–78 are written within a discourse different from that employed in the paragraphs thereafter, and that therefore they should not be regarded as inconsistent; whereas to us it is that very discursive shift which produces the contradiction that Courthope observed. Laura Brown, *Alexander Pope* (Oxford: Basil Blackwell, 1985), pp. 108–17, also sees a contradiction in this passage; we differ from her largely in analysing this in terms of a discursive disjunction. Extracts from Warburton's commentary are quoted from *The Works of Alexander Pope, Esq.*, ed. William Lisle Bowles (London: J. Johnson et al., vol. 3, 1806), p. 297.

5 Bowles, p. 294; Johnson, *Lives*, vol. 2, pp. 324–5.

6 Bowles, p. 302.

7 Anon., *The Art of Poetry on a New Plan* (London: John Newbery, 1762), vol. 1, p. 116.

8 *Art of Poetry*, vol. 1, p. 137; William Bowyer's note to his translation of Joseph Trapp, *Lectures on Poetry* (London, 1742), p. 189 – the Lectures were first published in Latin, 1711–19.

9 'An Essay on Virgil's Georgics', in *The Works of the Right Honourable Joseph Addison, Esq.* (London, 1721), vol. 1, pp. 249–50, 254; Thomas Tickell, 'De Poesi Didactica', a lecture delivered at Oxford in 1711, translated in Richard Tickell, *Thomas Tickell and the Eighteenth-Century Poets* (London: Constable and Co., 1931), pp. 202–3, 206–7.

10 See for example Trapp, *Lectures*, pp. 190, 192, 196, 201, and Joseph Warton, 'Reflections on Didactic Poetry', in *The Works of Virgil*, ed. Warton, 3rd ed. (London, 1778), vol. 1, pp. 156–235.

11 William Enfield, *The Speaker* (London, 1797), p. l.

12 See James Thomson, *The Seasons*, ed. James Sambrook (Oxford: Oxford University Press, 1981), pp. 2–3 and 309.

13 Aikin, 'An Essay on the Plan and Character of Thomson's Seasons', in *The Seasons. By James Thomson* (London: J. Murray, 1794), pp. xl–xlii. For eighteenth-century discussion of the unity of *The Seasons*, see Ralph Cohen, *The Art of Discrimination: Thomson's 'The Seasons' and the Language of Criticism* (London: Routledge and Kegan Paul, 1964), esp. pp. 84–130.

14 Addison, *Works*, vol. 1, pp. 250, 252; Warton, vol 1, pp. 399, 401, 429; *Art of Poetry*, vol. 1: pp. 177, 233, and see Trapp, *Lectures*, p. 196; Tickell, pp. 206, 207–8.

15 See John Oldmixon, *An Essay on Criticism* (London, 1728), pp. 27–40, and Pope, *Peri Bathous*, passim.

16 Warton, vol. 1, p. 401; *Art of Poetry*, vol. 1, p. 233; Du Bos, *Refléxions Critiques sur la Poësie et sur la Peinture* (Paris, edition of 1746), vol 1, p. 64.

17 *Art of Poetry*, vol. 1, p. 233; *The Diary and Letters of Madame D'Arblay*, edited by her Niece Charlotte Barrett, new edition, revised (London, no date), vol. 3, p. 165; Johnson, *Lives*, vol. 2: p. 274.

18 See *Goldsmith: the Critical Heritage*, ed. G. S. Rousseau (London and Boston: Routledge and Kegan Paul, 1974), pp. 76–87.
19 For extracts from Goldsmith, see for example Thomas Janes (ed.), *The Beauties of the Poets*, 6th edn. (London, 1799), p. 73, and Enfield, p. 252; for Pope, see for example Enfield, p. 254; for Young, see for example John Adams (ed.), *The English Parnassus* (London, 1789), pp. 30–2; *The Poetical Works of William Wordsworth*, eds Thomas Hutchinson and Ernest de Selincourt (Oxford: Oxford University Press, edition of 1961), p. 747.
20 We are grateful for the help of Peter De Bolla, who discussed with us the topic of this section of the essay, and made available to us his work in progress, 'The Discourse of the Sublime'.
21 Watts, *The Improvement of the Mind* (London, 1741), ch. 4, § 8.
22 Young, *The Complaint: or, Night Thoughts* (London, 1795), p. 318. Throughout the century, editions of *Paradise Lost* had been published with such an index; *The Seasons* appeared with an index in the edition published by A. Hamilton (London, 1793).

# 4

# Being is perceiving:
# James Thomson and John Clare

## I

The 'knotting' of discourses that we examined in the 'Epistle to Bathurst' is quite as much a feature of James Thomson's *Seasons*. The poem took twenty years, from 1726 to 1746, to arrive at its final form, and there is no reason to suppose that, had Thomson survived (he died in 1748), it would not have continued to change and to grow in length. The poem became less exclusively descriptive, and more openly political, concerned with the question of how the state of Britain was to survive and progress; and it was this development that produced the issue that concerned John Aikin (see above, page 93), how does Thomson manage the transitions between the political discourse, appropriate to the representation of 'courts and cities, camps and senates', and the primarily pastoral discourse concerned with 'sylvan scenery'. I want to begin this essay by examining one such transition, partly to exemplify again the process of knotting, and partly to introduce a new character, George, first Baron Lyttelton, who in the first part of this essay will be performing a double-act with Thomson. Lyttelton, the son of a baronet, was ennobled in 1756; during Thomson's life, he was, in a fairly informal way, Thomson's patron. He was the author of poems and of various prose works; and during the 1730s was a member of the loosely affiliated opposition to Walpole, an opposition which represented itself with considerable success as uniquely in possession of the virtues necessary to preserve the health of the body politic from the corruption of Walpole's ministry.

The transition in question occurs in the later versions of 'Spring', within an extended blank-verse paragraph, and at a point in the poem where, according to 'The Contents' in the second edition, we are invited to learn how it is that spring still 'attunes' the world to 'harmony'[1]. The paragraph immediately follows the claim that spring enables those of 'generous mind' to 'taste / The Joy of GOD to see a happy World!', and it appears to exemplify the truth of that claim by describing a walk taken by

Lyttelton, through his landscaped park at Hagley, his 'British Tempe', where
the harmony of the world is figured by the harmony of the sounds of
nature and of song. The walk, and the movement of Lyttelton's mind, are
represented as a 'straying', a 'wandering', and it is the inconsequential,
digressive randomness that these words suggest which both enables and
conceals the discursive shift:

> There along the Dale,
> ...........................
> You silent steal; or sit beneath the Shade,
> Of solemn Oaks, that tuft the swelling Mounts
> Thrown graceful round by Nature's careless Hand,
> And pensive listen to the various Voice
> Of rural Peace: the Herds, the Flocks, the Birds,
> The hollow-whispering Breeze, the Plaint of Rills,
> That, purling down amidst the twisted Roots
> Which creep around, their dewy Murmurs shake
> On the sooth'd Ear. From these abstracted oft,
> You wander thro' the Philosophic World;
> Where in bright Train continual Wonders rise,
> Or to the curious or the pious Eye.
> And oft, conducted by Historic Truth,
> You tread the long Extent of backward Time:
> Planning, with warm Benevolence of Mind,
> And honest Zeal unwarp'd by Party-Rage,
> BRITANNIA's Weal; how from the venal Gulph
> To raise her Virtue, and her Arts revive.
> Or, turning thence thy View, these graver Thoughts
> The Muses charm: while, with sure Taste refin'd,
> You draw th' inspiring Breath of antient Song;
> Till nobly rises, emulous, thy own.
> Perhaps thy lov'd LUCINDA shares thy Walk,
> With Soul to thine attun'd. ('Spring', lines 911–37)[2]

The transition, from the harmony of rural sounds to natural philosophical speculation, enables a movement from the contemplation of nature
to the interior content of Lyttelton's mind. And when he has thus been
'abstracted' from his immediate surroundings, the process of 'wandering' enables him to be represented as turning to a political discourse,
which seems to imply a comparison of the heroes of the past with the
factious and venal politicians of the present. Within the terms of this
discourse, the world is no longer harmonious; it has fallen into a 'Gulph'
of corruption, from which not God but only human, heroic moral agents
can rescue it. But Lyttelton himself is immediately rescued from such

disruptive considerations by the Muses; he recites some classical poetry, and composes some of his own; and the representation of his poetry as 'song' enables a return to the motif of harmony in and with nature, a motif reinforced by the harmony of Lyttelton's soul with his wife Lucinda's.

The discursive shift, nevertheless, has produced a contradiction which the transition has endeavoured to conceal; and once again it is a contradiction of considerable ideological convenience, for it enables the poem to borrow the authority of Lyttelton to assert, at one and the same time, that the world, as seen from the vantage-point of a benevolent aristocracy, is a harmonious place, providentially ordered, where whatever is, is right – and that its harmony is a fragile thing, dependent upon the vigilance and activity of that same benevolent and public-spirited aristocracy. Thus when such men as Lyttelton assert that the happiness of the world, and especially that of Britain, is secured by God, and that no moral or political intervention is required to set it to rights, they must be right, for they enjoy a breadth of vision denied to the rest of us. When they assert, on the contrary, that only by their own virtues and their own virtuous actions can Britain be rescued from corruption and restored to the happiness it formerly enjoyed, they are right, and for the same reason deployed within a different discourse. And elsewhere in the poem, the same or a similar contradiction, between a fatalistic and optimistic theodicy, and a civic-minded alarm at the progress of corruption, produces the same kinds of contradictory statements about wealth and economic activity as we examined in Pope's 'Epistle'.

There follows a passage of landscape description which was added to The Seasons in the edition of 1744, and which I want to compare with a passage by Lyttelton. The passage by Thomson is an account of what Lyttelton sees – and of how he sees it – as he looks westward beyond the confines of Hagley Park, towards the Welsh Hills. It describes a panoramic prospect, whose function, within the passage in which it occurs, may be to claim for Lyttelton a breadth of vision which gives authority to both the contradictory statements made in the previous verse-paragraph. For the description could be read in two very different ways: on the one hand, as a revelation of the natural, and so providential harmony of the landscape and the social world of which it is a representation; on the other, as a demonstration of how that harmony is produced in the landscape by Lyttelton himself, and is something that he, or the class of which he is a member, is uniquely capable of producing, by virtue of the eminence of his position: the 'height' where

he takes up his viewing-position is a metaphor for the high social position that he enjoys. It could be read in either way, I want to suggest,
according to whether its readers are thought of as attending to the
process or to the result of the description: such a passage as this would, in
the eighteenth century, have been understood as an attempt to raise up a
picture in the mind of its readers; and the meaning of that picture
changes, according to whether it is the picture itself, or the attempt to
raise it up, that is the object of a reader's attention. To attend to the
second, I shall be suggesting, is a matter of attending to the syntax of the
description.

# II

In a number of passages of The Seasons, Thomson invented a means of
using syntax, so as to represent a kind of effect his readers were used to
perceiving in the predominant style of contemporary landscape painting, a style originated, as far as was known in eighteenth-century
England, by the French painter Claude Lorrain, who had worked in
Rome throughout the middle decades of the seventeenth century.
Claude's work was so avidly purchased by British collectors of painting
that, by 1750, fully a sixth of his entire lifetime's output of paintings had
found its way to Britain, and there existed in Britain a fair number of
painters who had learned to reproduce the essentials of his style, and
who helped to satisfy an appetite for Claudian views which was too
hungry to be able to be satisfied by the works of the master himself.
Thomson was not the first poet to attempt to recreate in language the
kind of landscape composition that Claude was believed to have originated: the attempt had been made by Pope, and also, as we shall see, by
Lyttelton. What Thomson originated was, as I say, a particular means of
using the resources of syntax to represent both the means by which a
Claudian landscape was composed, and the experience of observing it;
and what that use of syntax originated – within, I mean, the tradition of
verse-description – was a new representation of the relation of self and
nature, which was of value to the landed classes in eighteenth-century
Britain in more ways than has been so far suggested. To explain what it is
that both Thomson and Lyttelton are trying to do, I want to begin by
offering a brief and general account of the compositional structure of
Claude's landscapes – a structure which, with endless variation, he used
in almost all the landscape-paintings he produced.
    Characteristically, a landscape by Claude places us on a high viewpoint

from which is visible a deep and panoramic view of a considerable tract of land. The foreground is animated with figures. The spaciousness, the distance of the painting, is not however articulated for us in the same way as it would have been in many earlier renaissance paintings. That is to say, Claude does not produce the kind of perspective view, by which we imagine that, invisibly printed upon the view, is a series of straight lines, beginning at or near the corners of the picture and converging at the centre of the canvas; the kind of perspective by which objects of the same size would be evenly diminished the closer they are placed to that point of convergence, the vanishing point. The main means by which Claude articulate the two dimensions of the picture-surface into a three-dimensional space, is by a system of roughly horizontal lines, which divide the picture into a series of bands running directly across the picture. These bands or planes are distinguished from one another by colour and tone: broadly speaking, the system requires that the bands should be alternately dark and light. In the foreground the contrast between them is sharp, and involves a greater range of colour than in the distance, where the same alternation is produced within a far narrower tonal range, so as to suggest how the medium of air, through which that distance is perceived, softens and reduces the contrasts and renders objects progressively more indistinct. This is a technique known as 'aerial perspective'.

There is often no physical, or, if you like, geographical connection between one band, one plane, and another. A sense of connection is negotiated between them by diverting some of the lines which mark the boundaries of the planes from the horizontal, so that, if we wish, we can trace a zig-zag path across the surface of the painting. But this is a system of connection mapped out in two dimensions: nothing in any of the foreground planes, in particular, offers a means of physical access from one plane to another: each plane in the picture seems to have a precipice behind it, and each plane seems flat. Sometimes, however, Claude does attempt to make physical or geographical connections between one plane and another; so that a road, or sometimes a river winds through the distance, its windings at once creating the division between one plane and the next, and appearing to link them within a three-dimensional space.

It is by these means, then, that the recession of the landscape is articulated, and it will usually follow that the more alternating planes of dark and light the painter can stack up, one behind another, the greater the distance the picture will seem to represent. But the painter's task, in this style of representation, does not end here; for the painting is concerned not only to *represent* distance, but to ensure that we are *struck* by that representation, to ensure, that is, that the experience of distance is what immediately strikes us as we look at the painting; and it is here that the vertical elements in the composition play their part. One function of these is to block off, or, in the technical language of landscape painting, to mask, certain areas of the landscape, and to frame others for our inspection, in the far distance and usually at the centre of the picture. At that centre distance is the lightest plane in the picture, which is almost invariably the penultimate plane of the composition, behind which we find only a darker strip, sometimes representing distant mountains, but often indeterminately mountain or cloud. The function of this light plane is to ensure that it is this, the distance, that first attracts our eye; so that, denied access by the masks and flats to other areas of the distance, and funnelled by them into the centre of the picture, our eye is first attracted to, and first rests on, the far and glittering distance, ignoring, in its flight to that distance, the foreground, and the figures which there constitute the formal subject of the painting. Thus the structure of the painting seeks to ensure that our first response to the painting is a response to the depth of the view which it represents.

Only after that first initial movement is our eye released, as it were, from the constraining pressures of the composition, to find its own, self-chosen path around the landscape and the various objects within it. But by that time, the main work of the composition has been done; for, as I hope my account has made clear, the primary function of composition in such paintings is to enable, indeed to oblige us, to experience the depth of the landscape, and thus to experience the three-dimensional space which the two-dimensional painting is attempting to articulate; and all the elements I've pointed to in the composition – the contrasts of colour and tone, the arrangement of horizontals and verticals – co-operate towards the achievement of this primary object.

# III

The vale beneath a pleasing prospect yields
Of verdant meads and cultivated fields;
Through these a river rolls its winding flood,
Adorn'd with various tufts of rising wood;
Here half-conceal'd in trees, a cottage stands,

A castle there the opening plain commands;
Beyond, a town with glitt'ring spires is crown'd,
And distant hills the wide horizon bound.

This passage by George Lyttelton, from The Progress of Love (1732, lines 17–24),[3] can be read as an attempt to reproduce the structure of composition we have just examined. The prospect is imagined as being observed from an elevated prospect – as the word 'beneath' in the first line suggests – and as laid out before us in the form of a series of horizontal planes. But though Lyttelton may immediately suggest that this is how he conceives of the landscape he is describing – by, for example, the opposition of 'verdant' meads and 'cultivated' fields, unlikely to be green but rather golden or brown – his readers are hardly in a position to recognise that this is what he's doing, until the end of the sentence, when his structure and intention become unambiguously apparent, and when he is evidently using each line of verse to represent each separate plane of the landscape.

Thus the final plane is made up of distant hills bounding the horizon; and the penultimate plane, with its 'glitt'ring spires', invites us to visualise it as the brightest part of the composition. This bright penultimate plane is represented as being 'beyond' whatever is being described in the previous couplet; and in that previous couplet, the separate lines again appear to be conceived of as separate planes, one nearer to us – 'here' – and one more remote – 'there'; one inviting us to visualize it as shadowy – 'half-conceal'd in trees' – the other as more open to the light – 'the opening plain' (and the contrast of shadowy cottage and brighter, commanding castle leaves us in no doubt as to which social class enjoys a place in the sun). And if we go on now to the previous, the second couplet, there the winding river will seem to have been conceived as performing the function I described earlier, of dividing yet connecting the planes which are also differentiated by the opposition of colour implicit in 'verdant' and 'cultivated'. Thus if we read the passage backwards – rather as, I was suggesting, we are invited to read a landscape by Claude – it seems unambiguously to represent a landscape composed as Claude composed: a landscape of alternating planes, ending in a penultimate bright plane and a final, bounding plane – 'bound' is a technical term from landscape painting and gardening – which closes the horizon.

Now this is all very well, of course, except that we do not read poems from bottom to top, and we will have to offer rather different account of this passage if we read it from top to bottom. Read like that, the passage discloses an awkward gap between what poetry, what language can do, and what a picture can do – a gap only awkward, of course, for the more doggedly descriptive poets of the eighteenth century, who conceive their task to be to attempt to 'raise up pictures', to make the signs of language function as much as possible like pictorial signs, in such a way as would enable words immediately and instantaneously to reveal the complex pictorial image they are attempting to conjure up in the reader's imagination. Let me put the problem more clearly, for it is a problem which, as we shall see, the Thomson passage can be read almost as setting out to address. Only when we have worked our way down to the last couplet of Lyttelton's landscape are we in a position to be sure that what he has attempted to represent is a landscape structured as a landscape-painting would have been by Claude; only when we have all the pieces in the jig-saw can we grasp the structure as a whole, the structure that makes the *landscape* a whole. Thus, the experience of reading the passage is an experience of discovering, word by word and line by line, a structure which would, in a landscape-painting, have been immediately apparent to us, and immediately responded to, by the fact that so many of the elements in the painting exist to attract our eye immediately to the distance. But there is no such immediacy available to Lyttelton or to his readers: they, we, are obliged, as it were, to store up pieces of information until the moment comes when they can be interpreted as constituting a structure.

The issue of where, for example, the meads and fields are to be imagined in the prospect, or even that they are to be imagined as occupying some determinate position; the fact that the adjective 'cultivated' is primarily to be read as a sign of colour, not of land-use, and so is to be read in contrast to 'verdant' – issues such as these are not resolved, may not even be comprehended as issues at all, until the paragraph and the structure it discloses are complete. Thus the experience of reading the passage is, first, an experience of collecting random, unsorted information; second – by the time we arrive at the 'here'/'there' opposition – an experience of understanding that these bits of information are somehow to be comprehended in terms of the spatial relations between them; and finally – when we have read the final couplet – of discovering that it is in terms of a specifically Claudian structure that those spatial relations are organised. What has not been represented, as I say, is the immediacy by which the structure of landscape is communicated in a Claudian painting. The glittering spires, which would have been carefully positioned by Claude in the penultimate plane of a painting, must necessarily appear in the penultimate line of the description; so that instead of being the first things that attract our eye, and give unity and structure to all the other elements in the composition – elements which, in a painting, exist so as to ensure that our eye is first attracted to that distant glitter – they are the second last image we encounter, and one we arrive at by a slow and even-paced journey through these end-stopped couplets. The attempt of language to aspire to the condition of visual art is frustrated by the very means by which the attempt is made; and the passage becomes, not a recreation of the Claudian structure, but more like an analysis of it. The process which is initiated by our slow discovery of the structure of Lyttelton's prospect is a process of learning, not of immediate response.

## IV

Meantime you gain the Height, from whose fair Brow
The bursting Prospect spreads immense around;
And snatch'd o'er Hill and Dale, and Wood and Lawn,
And verdant Field, and darkening Heath between,
And Villages embosom'd soft in Trees,
And spiry Towns by surging Columns mark'd
Of houshold Smoak, your Eye excursive roams:
Wide-stretching from the *Hall*, in whose kind Haunt
The *Hospitable Genius* lingers still,
To Where the broken Landskip, by Degrees,
Ascending, roughens into rigid Hills;
O'er which the *Cambrian* Mountains, like far Clouds
That skirt the blue Horizon, dusky, rise.

In one way, this passage by James Thomson ('Spring', lines 950–62) can be seen as an attempt to grapple with the problem, so clearly exhibited by Lyttelton, of attempting to represent in the diachronic medium of language what can be represented only in the synchronic medium of visual art; and to this attempt, the fact that Thomson is composing in blank verse, not in heroic couplets, is crucial; for, as we shall see, it enables him to create a pace in his writing, which seeks, as it were, to pass itself off as an experience of immediacy. The pace at which the early part of this passage asks to be read seems intended to persuade us that what we in fact visualize – if we visualize it at all – word by word, object by object, we are visualizing instantaneously, inasmuch as no word in the lines which disclose the structure of the landscape seems available to be dwelt upon. The syntax seems to attempt to oblige us to read through and over the passage, at a run, and allows us no place to rest. In fact, the passage starts almost with a couplet, its structure hinted at but not completed by the false rhyme of 'Brow' and 'around'. That near-couplet seems to perform much of what is performed by the opening line of Lyttelton's passage, announcing to us, once again, that we are in the presence of a prospect visible to us from an elevated viewpoint, a 'Height'. But the contrast between Thomson's opening and Lyttelton's is more striking than their similarity. Lyttelton's prospect is passive, it is 'yielded' up for our inspection and analysis: Thomson's prospect is active, it 'bursts', it is immense, literally, unmeasurable; far from inviting us to discover its structure, it is represented as threatening, as denying our ability to comprehend, to organise, to unify it, and to experience it as structure. An implied opposition is set up between the perceiving subject and the landscape: whereas in Lyttelton's passage the vale seemed to invite us to discover in it a structure which is 'natural', in the sense that it is unproblematically there to be discovered, this prospect, in denying that it is or has a structure, seems to deny any such easy compatibility between mind and nature.

That sense of conflict, and of the refusal of this landscape to be measured, organised, contained within a fixed frame, is reinforced by the fact that the prospect 'snatches' the eye, or rather that the eye is 'snatch'd' by it; it is not the landscape but the eye which is passive, powerless. It is essential, however, to the proposed pace of the passage, and to what is represented as the almost violent power of the prospect, that as we read the third and subsequent lines we do not know what it is that is 'snatch'd': it is a full five lines before we discover it to be 'your Eye'; and the task of this deferral, this division of the participle from its noun, is to oblige us, as I said, to hurry through the intervening lines, to read them as fast as possible, as if impatient to unite the participle with the noun it qualifies. For until we have thus united them, and encountered the main verb, 'roams', of which 'your Eye' is the subject, we experience a state of suspended comprehension, in which we seem obliged to pay as little attention as possible to what those lines say, in order to pay as much as possible to the fact that they say *something*, that together they have a structure, and make *some* complete statement, with a subject, and a verb. But if it does thus hurry over the lines that intervene between 'snatch'd' and 'Eye', our attention is also being hurried through the landscape and into the distance; and as it thus traverses the landscape, so it will register, though it will not dwell upon, the structure of that landscape.

Notice, for example, how singular nouns give way to plural nouns, as we approach nearer to the noun and verb, a movement which stands for a movement of the eye towards the horizon: as the view expands, so the number of objects it contains increases, from, say, a singular field to a plural number of towns. Notice also the sudden reversal in the order of enumeration, in the lines 'and Wood and Lawn / And verdant Field, and darkening Heath between', a reversal whereby we register that the plane represented by the heath is to be located *between* the presumably verdant lawn and the explicitly 'verdant Field'. This enables us to register also that the order of enumeration works in terms of alternating objects of dark and light, as the eye, passing from the 'Hill' into the 'Vale' displayed beneath it, is snatched successively over dark wood, light lawn, dark heath, light field, the dark trees that embosom the cottages, and (we may by this time presume) towns which glitter in the penultimate distance. That they are in the penultimate distance is not revealed, of course, until the end of the passage, and the mention of the hills beyond them; for it is, in this representation, as in a painting by Claude, to the penultimate plane of the landscape that the eye is immediately snatched, and not beyond it. When the eye has arrived there, however, it is represented as free, as I suggested it was in my discussion of Claude; as free to find its own, its own more leisurely path, around and across the landscape, roaming and stretching its view from the hall in the foreground, animated by the allegorical figure of Hospitality as a foreground in Claude is animated with figures, back to the less hospitable, the rough and broken hills and to the mountains which seem to close the view at the horizon.

I say 'seem' to close it, for here Thomson attempts an effect of ambiguity analogous to an effect I referred to in Claude; for it is not clear in this passage that the 'eye' can distinguish the dusky mountains from the clouds which may or may not – and that is the point – indistinctly appear in the distance. The mountains appear 'like far Clouds' – clouds which, the absence of the definite article seems to suggest, are not present in the landscape, and are present in the passage only as objects of comparison. But the mere mention of them, in that simile, has the effect of making them present to our mind; and the fact that a definite article subsequently appears – these clouds 'skirt the blue Horizon' – suggests, but imprecisely, indistinctly, that they are *there*, in the view, in the same way as Claude's distant mountains may often be clouds, or his clouds may often be mountains.

But let me return to the first movement of the eye, which is 'snatch'd' across a bursting and immeasurable prospect which, nevertheless, is represented as being measured, controlled, contained within the limits of the very confining structure that at first it had seemed to spread and burst out of. If we allow the syntax to determine the speed of our reading, then when we finally arrive, breathless if we have been reading aloud, at the phrase 'your Eye excursive roams', we are in a position, as I said, to pause, because we have finally been able to make out a comprehensible order in the sentence and in the landscape. And we may also be struck by how the relation of eye and prospect has changed in the lines we have thus hurried over. The eye at the start is passive, is snatched, is moving at a pace apparently imposed upon it by the energy of the landscape, as that is represented by the energy of the deferred syntax; at the end of the lines, the eye is not only active, and the subject of an active verb, but evidently moving at a very different pace: it 'roams', unconstrained by any power to *make* it move, a power, indeed, which the prospect now seems to have lost. That this is so is an appropriate result of what has gone on in the intervening lines, in which the landscape has been tamed and rendered powerless by the representation of a structure within it; so that the very power it exerts on the eye, to snatch it towards the horizon, is surrendered to, only for it to be converted into the power by which the eye is able to organise and constrain what had earlier been constraining it.

I can put it this way: that when the lines begin, the mind is represented as the object of the constraints of the landscape which condition it, which prescribe its direction and pace of attention; by the end of the ninth line, the mind is represented as liberated from those constraints, independent, unconditional, in a way that is analogous to the attempt made in Shakespeare's twenty-ninth sonnet (see above, pages 41–2), to announce the achievement, at the end of that poem, of an unconditional identity liberated from the social and economic constraints represented by the discourse of patronage. It is this apparent achievement by the eye, or mind, of an identity unconstrained from without, independent of the circumstances of the natural, which enables the second movement of the eye, as it returns to the foreground and makes its active but unhurried exploration of the range of the prospect from immediate foreground to the far and indeterminate distance.

I can focus this achievement on an account of the meanings of the word 'excursive', as these are attributed to it partly by the noun 'excursion' from which it derives. The primary meaning of 'excursion', as offered by the OED, is a 'running out', an '*ex-cursus*', a meaning which the dictionary defines as 'an escape from confinement'. This meaning was still active when Thomson was writing, and is clearly appropriate to the sense in which the eye can be claimed to be 'excursive' in its freedom, not only from the confinement of its viewpoint, but finally also by the constraints imposed upon it by the landscape. And related to this meaning of 'excursion' is a specifically military one, now remembered chiefly in the phrase 'alarms and excursions'; in this sense an excursion is, according to the OED, 'an issuing forth against the enemy; a sally, sortie, raid'. This meaning too has a clear appropriateness to this context, and for two reasons. To begin with, some of the terms in the language of natural description in the eighteenth century are derived from the language of military campaigns and of the science of fortification. One other element of that language appears in the passage from Lyttelton: when he writes that the castle 'commands' the opening plain, the word directs us to the dialect of fortification,, and to the need for artillery to be so positioned as to command as much as possible of the terrain within its range. But this military sense is clearly appropriate, also, to the sense in which what is being dramatised in Thomson's passage is a struggle, a contest for power and supremacy, between the mind and nature.

There are, on the other hand, meanings of 'excursive' which give a more relaxed definition to the eye: which are appropriate to the movements it makes not when it is engaged in that struggle, but when it has won it, and has escaped the constraints imposed on it by the bursting prospect, and 'roams' the landscape. Thus an 'excursion' is also what the OED defines as 'a journey, expedition, or ramble from one's own home, or from any place with the intention of returning to it' – and to this meaning is related another which represents an excursion as a deviation from a definite path or a prescribed course: a digression can be an excursion, as can, apparently, the erratic movement of a planet from its accustomed orbit. These meanings are appropriate, then, not only to the sense in which the eye, having achieved its freedom, is free to roam, but to the sense in which, in roaming, it is free to move at a pace and in directions no longer prescribed for it by the prospect, but of its own determination. The word points, in short, both back to the moment of constraint and of conflict with nature, and forward to the moment when an unconditional freedom and identity are achieved by the mind in its successful attempt to control nature, by surrendering first to the movement the prospect prescribes, and by making that movement the path by which the prospect is subdued.

# V

What then is at stake in this elaborate comparison of how Lyttelton and Thomson differently attempt to represent the compositional structures of the Claudian landscape tradition? It is not simply a matter of the fact that Thomson's choice of blank verse enables him to employ a syntax by which he can attempt to represent the *experience* of looking at a Claudian landscape, while Lyttelton's choice of the heroic couplet limits his description to a representation, as it were, of the analytic process of discovering how such a landscape is organised. Of more importance to the argument I am trying to develop, is a distinction between the two passages in terms of the relation each proposes between the mind or the eye or the perceiving subject, on the one hand, and the landscape, or nature, on the other. But to put it that way is already to propose that Lyttelton *does* propose to represent the landscape in terms of such a relation, of mind and nature considered as in some sense separate, and as requiring that a relation be negotiated between them; and that is, I want to suggest, exactly what he does not propose. For precisely because the vale 'yields' its prospect, without a struggle, the conflict hinted at in that word 'yields' never occurs – any conflict has been already settled, the word may suggest, before the writing begins. The structure which the prospect 'yields' comes across, as I have said, simply as something there, in nature, waiting to be discovered. The perceiving self is aware of no threat or constraint to its identity, and therefore is never obliged to construct its identity as something different from, and in opposition to, a constraining nature.

In Thomson's passage, on the other hand, though the structure of the landscape may still be conceived of as something which is there, is natural, and waiting to be discovered, it is not a structure that the prospect yields, but rather one that it must be *made* to yield. The first problem the perceiving subject encounters in the prospect is the demand that it should yield to the prospect, a prospect which seems to insist that it is the subject, and that the eye must therefore be represented as an object passively suffering the actions of the prospect. If Lyttelton represents the relation of mind and nature as one of indifferentiation, or at least of unproblematic accord, Thomson represents that indifferentiation as something which nature imposes on the mind, by subsuming the identity of the mind to its own identity, by imposing its own identity on the mind. And this initiates in the mind a struggle to differentiate itself from the prospect, to become itself the subject of the landscape – a struggle which it can win only if it can announce itself as having entirely escaped the definition which the prospect attempts to impose upon it, and so as being entirely free, unconditional, the grammatical subject of its own verbs, its own self-chosen actions.

The passage by Lyttelton is from an eclogue, a poem which announces itself as Pastoral – this is the prospect seen by the shepherd Damon, from a viewpoint to which he has ascended to bewail the inconstancy of the shepherdess Delia; while Thomson's passage is from a poem of no clearly definable genre, but which owes most to the tradition of georgic poetry. It is a reasonable generalisation, at least as far as the eighteenth century is concerned, to claim that the discourse of Pastoral proposes a relationship between the earth and its human inhabitants which appears to be one of unproblematic harmony, from which all hint of the exploitation of nature by its inhabitants is made absent, by an idea of nature so fruitful, so abundant, that it yields up the necessities and accommodations of life without resistance, and therefore without demanding in exchange that we should labour to obtain the fruits of nature. Because we are not required to engage in a struggle for existence, a conflict with nature, we do not therefore need to differentiate ourselves from nature, and to define our identity as something which requires to emancipate itself from constraints, and which recognises that emancipation as complete when nature has somehow been bested, by effort, by industry, by labour.

The Georgic, on the other hand, is a discourse which conceives of nature as niggardly, as reluctant to yield its fruits, as always threatening to run wild, as hostile to us, and so as needing to be subdued by work. Though georgic poetry is full of smiling prospects, those prospects have been *made* to smile, and beyond them are always the rough and rigid mountains which, in Pastoral, protect the shepherd community from attack, but which, in Georgic, resist the action of the plough and spade. In Georgic, the processes of civilization are precisely those processes by which we struggle to achieve a sense of our identity as something which is differentiated from the constraints of nature, and that is achieved only when we are in a position to make nature submit to our own identity, our own will; to *make* it yield, to make it improve its yield, and to make it smile in acknowledgement that it is happy to be thus subdued. The Georgic thus imposes on us a moral imperative to labour; the Pastoral proposes the ideal life as a life of idleness.

Two things in particular happened to the Pastoral around the start of the eighteenth century. It had become established, especially since the

Restoration, as a discourse most appropriate for the compositions of the amateur writer, such as Lyttelton was, and specifically of the aristocratic amateur writer, such as Lyttelton was. It appeared to be especially appropriate for the expression of that aspect of aristocratic life in which it could be experienced as an idle life, a life unproblematically supported by the abundance of nature – if only because, from the elevated viewpoint of the aristocracy, the work required to make nature abundant was so far beneath consideration as to be invisible. It was not agricultural workers who produced that abundance, it was, simply, nature; and the abundance of nature was sufficiently proved by the abundance which, several times a day, was placed upon the tables of the aristocracy, and by the rents which, several times a year, were paid to them by their tenant farmers. But the second thing that was happening to Pastoral, in the opening decades of the eighteenth century, was that it was ceasing to be written, except insofar as it could be brought into various kinds of relation with Georgic. And that fact, that it was ceasing to be written, tells us of another aspect in which the aristocracy viewed themselves, that is, as an economic class determined to extract as much wealth as possible from its estates, by rack-renting, which it was believed obliged tenants to farm more efficiently, and by exploiting the natural resources of the estate for example by mining and by manufacturing industry.

These two aspects of the aristocratic life, as idle and as energetically exploitative, as careless and as careful, may appear to be in contradiction, but of course they require and support each other. The idea of life as idle requires to be supported by a view of life as, properly, to be supported by labour, by someone else's, if not one's own; but equally, an aristocracy can distinguish itself from the most successful members of the middle classes, partly by making a display of its idleness and consumption. Neither of these two aspects of the aristocratic can easily exist without the other; but in the self-image of an aristocracy, one or the other may be given prominence at different times; and it is fair to say that, in the decades after the Restoration, the first, the careless, the pastoral, predominated over the georgic, and that in the early decades of the eighteenth century the second, careful image came to predominate. We cannot say that Pastoral then ceased to be taken seriously as a vehicle of poetry – for as the expression of an ideal of idleness, it had earlier been essential to its nature that it was not preoccupied with moral seriousness, that it was not in earnest. But the arts of literature themselves came then to be treated as a means of giving expression to the more serious view of the aristocratic life, and the Georgic came to predominate over the Pastoral as the discourse in which rural life, and the relations of nature and civilization, could most usefully be described. The reasons for this tilting of the balance in the self-image of the English aristocracy cannot be easily summarised and perhaps cannot easily be explained; but we are unlikely to be wrong if we say that it was partly the result of the recent achievement of landed or titled status by a relatively large number of men whose fortunes had been made in commerce; partly the result of increasing intermarriage between the landed and the commercial classes, a transaction in which status was exchanged for wealth; and partly the result of whatever more general causes we might turn to to explain the development, not simply of commercial capitalism in the period, but of the discourses in which it could be more positively, more approvingly described.

Two aspects, in particular, of that development may be particularly important to the passage from Thomson that I have been discussing. The first of these is what we call the 'agricultural revolution' – that complex of processes by which, among other things, the productivity of English agriculture was so dramatically increased during the course of the eighteenth century. One thing which *The Seasons* does is to direct attention to the progress of agriculture as something requiring to be supported and admired, and for that reason in particular the poem came to be much read by the spokesmen for agricultural experiment and development, and to be much quoted in their writings. To such people the poem was important, no doubt, partly in the way that it proposed, by its advocacy of the interests of agriculture, that the relation of nature and civilization should not always be regarded as a relation of harmony, but also as one of opposition, of struggle, in just such a way as the passage we have been considering proposes. That this conflict is presented in the passage as a struggle to impose a merely *visual* order on the landscape does nothing to weaken the point, for most obviously in the instance of enclosure of open fields and wastes, the imposition of a more productive order on the landscape produced, indeed, a new landscape, and one admired because it was believed to be more orderly – more rectlinear, more rationally divided, more the product of art than nature.

The second aspect of the development of commercial capitalism that I want to direct attention to, in relation to this passage, is the development of what we loosely call economic individualism, of that notion of social life which argues for the right of the individual to free and independent action in the conduct of economic life, unconstrained by an ethic of co-operation or of mutualism or paternalism, whether expressed in the

form of positive legal or institutional constraints, or by the discourses
which attempt to define the social virtues. Such a notion is not easily
distinguishable from what we might think of as 'individualism' in general, in many of its various senses. In one of its relevant uses, for example,
the term refers to a notion that individual identity is naturally, or is
properly, self-produced, undetermined as far as possible by conditions
imposed upon it from outside – that real men are 'self-made' men. In
another sense, the word proposes that individual identity is achieved
and guaranteed by its persistence, unchanged except from within,
through whatever external circumstances threaten to determine or set
limits to it. And no less relevant is the sense in which 'individualism'
refers to a primary conern for one's own interests, economic or otherwise, at the necessary expense of the interests of the community as a
whole, which is perceived, of course, as threatening to constrain one's
interests and identity alike. Such notions of individualism in general, and
of economic individualism in particular, combine to represent it as an
imperative that one conceive of one's identity, then, as self-produced,
self-made, as undetermined, and as continuous, not least so as to enable
one to construct one's economic actions prudently, as a continuing
narrative, as a continuum stretching from past to future, initiated by one's
self at one time in order to benefit one's self at some future time. A
necessary condition of one's independence of others comes to be one's
independence of the circumstantial in all its forms, of whatever threatens
to determine, and so to destabilise or de-centre, one's identity.

Such a notion of identity makes the idealist language in which I have
described the passage from Thomson – as a conflict between an abstract
'mind' and an abstract 'nature' – of only provisional use. For what is
finally at stake is the freedom from determination of particular social and
economic interest-groups in the eighteenth century, committed to an
idea of individualism essential to the progress of commercial capitalism
in general, and of the agricultural revolution in particular. It could be
used – as we shall see, it *was* used – to deny, to those in England or in the
empire who did not see their interests as being consulted or advanced by
commercial capitalism, the same subject-position and so the same free-
doms as were enjoyed by those whose interests it evidently did advance.
It enabled them to be constructed as at a 'primitive' stage of 'self-reali-
sation', as *still* merged in their class or tribe, and still merged in nature.
The metaphor by which the progress of civilization could be represented
as a process of 'cultivation' helped in that construction, for it could
represented the normal and proper process of 'human development' as

a matter of differentiation from, and control of nature. And the same notion of subjectivity could be used to impose upon the 'primitive', when it was more convenient to do so, a definition of freedom in individual rather than in collective terms, in such a way as to divide them, as individuals, from the classes and communities to which they belonged. And so it could be used to persuade them that, in working for the interests of their masters they were working for themselves, and that therefore their interests were identical with the interests of those who exploited them.

## VI

The early nineteenth-century poet John Clare was an agricultural worker, the son of an agricultural worker, and began writing poetry at the same time as the parish in which he lived, Helpston in what is now north Cambridgeshire, was undergoing the process of parliamentary enclosure: a process by which the landscape of the parish was restructured on a large scale. Old divisions of property, old roads, old landmarks, were disregarded by the enclosers, as a new landscape of straight lines – rectangular fields, straight roads, hedges and ditches – was imposed upon the parish. The process of enclosure was completed in 1820, when Clare was 27. It is hard for us to imagine the kind of disruption that such a complete reorganisation of the landscape might have had on the least privileged and most poor of the parish, because our relations to the places in which we live is so entirely different. What we have to imagine is a group of people who very rarely had the means or opportunity to travel more than a few miles from home – so that Clare, for example, describes a village only three miles from his own as a 'distant' village;[4] a group of people, therefore, whose knowledge of the world was, to an extent we can hardly reconstruct, an extrapolation from their knowledge of the place in which they lived.

We can approach an understanding of the situation if we look at a couple of phrases by which Clare represents his relations with the landscape of the parish. He describes, for example, the places he knows well, the places he has reason to travel to, invariably on foot, and lying within or just outside the confines of his parish, as his 'knowledge' – to stray beyond them is to go 'out of his knowledge'. *What* he knows, is thus, in a sense, *where* he knows: within that space, he explains, he knows the names of the flowers; he knows the sun rises in the east; but he has no basis for assuming that flowers have the same names elsewhere, or that the sun rises in the same quarter elsewhere.[5] How literally we are to take such statements as these, it is not easy to judge. But they are, at the least, attempts to figure forth a relation of the self and nature which involves the notion that to re-make, by the process of enclosure, the place that he and his neighbours know, is to re-make their knowledge, and even to re-make their identity. For in another passage of his prose-writings, Clare says of a heath which lay to the south of the parish, and which, at the enclosure, was in part converted, from unfenced, unowned, unculti-vated common land, into agricultural land divided into rectangular fields, rectangular properties – he says of this heath that it 'made up my being';[6] that his identity was constructed by, undifferentiated from the heath as it had been before the enclosure. To re-make the landscape of the heath, this suggests, is to re-make his being, to impose upon him an alien identity; or rather, perhaps, to destroy the place that had constituted his identity, and to force a gap, a differentiation, between the two. And what is imposed upon him, in this process, is something analogous to that differentiated identity that Thomson was so *eager* to achieve.

Now these attempts to express a sense of indifferentiation between self and place before the enclosure have to be interpreted with some caution, because they are notions which can only find expression at a point in Clare's career where the sense of what he had been in the past is a matter at once of profound regret, and of a self-patronising amusement – an amusement deriving from a sense of relief that though his body is still largely confined within the boundaries of the parish, his mind no longer is, so that his knowledge is no longer limited by what he knows is true of Helpston alone. On the one hand, he expresses a sense of the violence that has been done to him and to his parish by an enclosure that has forced him entirely to re-conceive his relations with the place in which he lives, the relations between his self and the nature from which it has now been forcibly differentiated. On the other hand, that process of reconceiving has been the result, also, of his brief but considerable success as a poet, which has led to his travelling to London and being introduced to many of the literary personalities there, and has produced in him the sense that he is contributing to a national, or at least a metropolitan literary culture. He regrets a loss of security forced upon him by the enclosure; he welcomes the sense of liberation offered by his success, a liberation which has enabled him to extend the frontiers of his knowledge, and to consider his 'being', his identity, as something self-constructed, or as constituted by his innate genius as a poet, not by the circumstances of his confinement within what now seems a tiny patch of land.

When his brief period of success came to an end, in the middle to late 1820s, and he began to find it increasingly difficult to publish his poetry and to sustain the literary friendships which gave him access to the world beyond the parish, his sense of what he has lost and gained by the permanent effects of the enclosure, and by his now evidently temporary liberation from confinement, changes again; and I can best indicates how it does, by offering a reading of a poem, 'The Lane', which attempts to confront, as I believe, that changed sense of his relations with his local landscape. I shall reproduce the poem, which was never published in Clare's lifetime, as it appears in his manuscript, unpunctuated. When his poems were printed, they were punctuated by his publishers, and the effect of punctuating them is something I shall discuss later. For the moment, the points to bear in mind are that Clare could punctuate in some fashion – he had a kind of grasp of the normative principles of punctuation as these had been formulated in the eighteenth century – but that he did not choose to employ this knowledge, and that he regarded punctuation as a kind of tyranny, an imprisonment of the words of the poem, an imposition on them of a sort of *military* discipline – the image is his, not mine.[7]

> The cartway leading over every green
> A russet strip then winding half unseen
> Up narrow lanes & smothered oer in shade
> By oak & ash in meeting branches made                                    4
> That touch & twine & shut out all the sky
> & teams will snatch to crop them driving bye
> Then over fields deep printed freely strays
> Yet crooked & rambling half uncertain ways                               8
> While far away fields stretch on either side
> & skys above head spread a circle wide
> Letting low hedges trees snug close & fields of grain
> An unknown world to shepherds when descried                             12
> & then the timid road retreats again
> A leaf hid luxury in a narrow lane[8]

The sentence-structure of this sonnet is evidently very different from that of the passage we looked at from *The Seasons*, but equally evidently this difference is not a matter of the length of the sentences each text employs, or even of how long each defers the introduction of the main verb. The whole sonnet, or at least the first twelve lines, consists of only a single sentence, and the first main verb (I will need to qualify this remark in a while) does not appear until line 7 – we have to wait that long to find out what the subject of this sentence, the 'cartway', in all its 'leading' and 'winding', actually *does* – it 'strays'. We can get a sense of the effect of this deferment by comparing the poem, as we compared Milton's sonnet on his blindness, with Shakespeare's eighteenth sonnet, 'Shall I compare thee to a Summers day?' (see above, page 45). In that poem we were offered not one but seven main verbs in the first seven lines; every line was a complete unit of meaning, and we were invited to read the poem at a relaxed pace, with no urgent sense of looking forward to complete a complex and suspended statement. If we read Clare's poem aloud, on the other hand, we may feel ourselves being obliged to hurry over the line-breaks, from phrase to phrase and clause to clause, in our search for a complete statement; and the first time we will be invited to relax will be at the end of line 7, where the subject is united with its main verb, and when we seem to have come to the end of the first complete unit of sense.

Thus the syntax offers us a very urgent sense of the lane's progress through the landscape – the accelerated reading-speed proposed by the syntax invites us to experience the wandering of the lane as restless, as it winds from the open countryside, through the dark tree-tunnel, and out into the open again, and the freedom ('freely') of the fields. And the sense of relaxation the syntax offers, as the lane emerges from the smothering woodland and arrives in the open fields, and as the noun finally links up with its verb, is momentary only, and is immediately attenuated by the word 'yet', and by the five more lines that are made syntactically dependent on that main verb. It is only somewhere in the thirteenth line that we are invited to relax again – when we realise that the first sentence, or the first part of it, organised around the clause 'the cartway . . . strays', has finally come to an end, and that we are now reading a simpler and far shorter unit of sense, with none of the suspense we experience when a subject and its verb are kept far apart. 'The timid road' immediately 'retreats', and the simplicity of that structure con-spires with the rhyme-scheme – for the poem now reverts to the couplets of its opening lines – to bring the poem to a quiet closure.

This sentence-structure produces an intriguingly ambiguous account of the lane's progress, and of the different parts of the landscape it wanders through. To begin with, as we have noticed, the contrast between the open landscape and the closeness of the wood seems to work all in favour of the freedom of openness: the amplitude of the first line, as the lane leads over 'every green', is made to give way to the constriction ('narrow'), the darkness ('shut out all the sky'), and the claustrophobia ('smothered') of the woodland shade; and this part of the poem seems to move as urgently as it does to push the lane through the woodland and back out into the pleasurable freedom of the fields, where the imagery becomes no longer tactile but visual again, indicating that nature has become more distant, and allows more room to breathe. But, as we have also seen, the sentence will not end there; it wanders on, itself now rather 'crooked' and 'rambling', 'half uncertain' of its direction; and the very openness of its structure, the seemingly unlimited possibilities for its continuation, as well as the limitless landscape the lane now finds itself in, seem to become as disturbing as earlier the constriction of the woodland had been. The wide circle spread by the sky, soaring infinitely up and around, and leaving behind (this seems to be the primary meaning of 'letting' here) the reassuringly small-scale landscape of 'low hedges' and 'snug close' or field, present an unknown and threatening world to the shepherds on the ground. It is, then, as if with a sense of relief that the 'timid' lane withdraws into another patch of woodland or another tree-tunnel, a retreat whose narrowness is not now threatening at all, but a comforting luxury, where the lane is 'hid', and so no longer exposed to the insecurity of the limitless. The world is small-scale, manageable again, and we register the change not simply in semantic terms ('retreats', with its connotations of retirement as well as of flight), but in terms of the syntax also, itself now manageable and small-scale.

The sense of discomfort, of being ill-at-ease whether in the smothering woodland or in the stretching fields, is worth examining further. Let us look, for example, at the sixth line, '& teams will snatch to crop them driving bye'. I acknowledged earlier that it was rather less than the truth to say that the first main verb in the poem was 'strays', for 'will snatch' is one as well. But its appearance in the poem a line earlier than 'strays' does nothing to relieve the suspense involved in waiting for the 'cartway' to do something, to find a main verb. On the contrary, it increases that suspense, for the line is an aside, a parenthesis, and will not fit into the analysable structure of the clauses – as the tense, 'will snatch', indicates, it is a sort of intrusion into the narrative present tense of the rest of the poem. The verb refers to a habitual or characteristic activity of teams, presumably of horses. It tells us something about the overhanging branches of the oak and the ash, which is not happening 'at the moment', but it often *does* happen that teams, as they are driven through this tree-tunnel, snatch at the foliage of the lower branches. By the conspicuous lack of syntactical relation between this clause and the rest of the sentence, the suspense is increased, as the true main verb is further deferred, and the cartway is held a line longer in the smothering woodland. The different anxiety experienced in the open fields is communicated by other details of language: most obviously, perhaps, by the intrusion of a hexameter line – 'Letting low hedges trees snug close & fields of grain' – into the pentameter of the rest of the poem, as if the speaker were anxiously trying to name, and so to hold on to, as many as possible of the familiar objects on the ground, in the face of the infinite emptiness of the sky.

The ambiguity of this poem gives expression to what I called the changed sense that Clare came to develop, here specifically of the relative value and meaning to him of the notions of openness and closure. Openness could mean for him the freedom of the open fields before the enclosure of Helpston, and so a landscape in which he was free to wander out in any direction, more or less, from the village, across the fallows, or along the balks and headlands of the fields under active cultivation. The division of the parish into small hedged fields, individually owned and cropped, and the stopping-up of old footpaths, curtailed that freedom, and Clare as well as the landscape was enclosed. But the paradigm, openness and closure, had other meanings for him as well: on the one hand, the closedness, the restriction of a life lived almost entirely in one place, when his success as a poet might have opened to him the prospect of a far freer life in the literary world of London; and, on the other, his fear of a life less constricted, of a loss of identity threatened by a movement out of a landscape which 'made up' his 'being' – a fear which became increasingly oppressive as his literary success declined, and so as his identity as a poet increasingly failed to compensate him for the loss of that identity which the parish, as place, had constructed for him. How then to balance the gains and losses offered by the alternatives of an identity, on the one hand, reassuringly undifferentiated from his home ground, but also smothered by it; and, on the other, an identity released from the determination of circumstance, apparently self-produced, but unable to sustain the pleasures of its freedom except in the context of the success .which had produced it? The problem could not easily be resolved: and 'The Lane' seems to be a means of giving expression to the conflict between the desire for and fear of freedom, and the anxieties and compensations of restriction; a conflict which the poem, by its simple narrative structure, evades the pressure to resolve.

## VII

'The Lane' gives an idea of Clare's sense of the complexity of the situation he finds himself in, vis-à-vis the relations of an idea of identity as autonomous, unconditional, and of identity as undifferentiated from the circumstances which produce and determine it. I hope my account of that poem has made clear, among other things, that a sense of identity experienced as *free* can also be experienced as *constrained* by circumstances, as determined by them; for though freedom is constructed in such arguments as freedom from limitation, it can be experienced as that only from the viewpoint of, or with the desire of finding oneself in, some other specific circumstances which can equally well be experienced as determination. There is no identity which can be experienced as autonomous, self-produced, unless we mean by that only the sense, and the fragile sense, of freedom from some specific form of determination. But I want now to look at a couple of poems which seem to me to express, far less ambiguously than 'The Lane', that aspect of Clare's work in which he conceives of the landscape he describes as what 'makes up his being'. These poems, however, are not the simple utterances of a writer who believes that his identity is, unproblematically, the product of his landscape and of certain all-determining circumstances in which he finds himself. On the contrary, I want to suggest that the poems we are about to look at will seem, in the context of 'The Lane', to construct a mode of expression by which an identity *could* be represented in those terms, however else it could also be represented; so that the poems will seem to be attempts to construct one aspect of a situation which is understood to be complex and to be irresoluble in its complexity. These poems may be regarded, if you like, as attempts to exemplify how we *might* conceive of our relation with a landscape, if it *were* straightforwardly the case that we could conceive as ourselves as entirely 'made up' by that landscape, as perceiving subjects entirely constituted by what it is that we perceive. The poems in question, 'Emmonsails Heath in Winter' and 'The Beans in Blossom', form part of a collection of poems which explore very different aspects and versions of the relations of self and nature.

This is 'Emmonsails Heath in Winter':

I love to see the old heaths withered brake
Mingle its crimpled leaves with furze & ling
While the old Heron from the lonely lake
Starts slow & flaps his melancholly wing                                    4
& oddling crow in idle motions swing
On the half rotten ash trees topmost twig

Beside whose trunk the gipsey makes his bed
Up flies the bouncing woodcock from the brig                          8
Where a black quagmire quakes beneath the tread
The fieldfare chatters in the whistling thorn
& for the awe round fields & closen rove
& coy bumbarrels twenty in a drove                                   12
Flit down the hedge rows in the frozen plain
& hang on little twigs & start again*⁹

Once again, I want to suggest that the best way into this poem, at least if
we are to focus on the difference between what it does and what the
passage from The Seasons was doing, is through its sentence-structure. The
first complete sentence the poem offers takes up the first seven lines – it
ends with the remark about the gipsy. The kinds of connections it makes,
however, do not seem to be quite of the kind that we expect literary
syntax to make. Let us look, in particular, at the first four lines. Now if we
were to persuade ourselves to take these connections at their face value,
there would be two alternative ways of understanding the connection
made here, between the main verb and its objects, in the first two lines,
and the subordinate, adverbial clause in the second two lines: either the
'while' clause would modify 'I love to see', or it would modify what the
'brake' does, 'mingle'. I'll try and indicate the differences by paraphrase.
Either the lines would say 'while the heron does this, I love to see the
brake do that', or they would say 'I love to see the bracken, while the
heron does that, do this'. But either way we would be left with the rather
strange statement, that the pleasure the speaker takes in seeing the
'crimpled leaves' of the brake mingling with the furze and ling, is somehow dependent, and conditional, upon the fact that at the same time the
heron should be starting his slow and melancholy flight – as if, if the
heron was not doing its stuff, there would be no pleasure to be had in the
sight of the bracken. From my experience of teaching this poem,
however, it seems that the oddness of this meaning probably leads most
readers to eliminate it from their minds almost before they become
conscious of it; and they produce, though rather uneasily, some rather
less complicated meaning for the lines, closer to a statement that the
speaker loves to see the bracken do one thing, and he also loves to see

* 'brake': bracken or fern; 'brig': bridge; 'awe': the fruit of the hawthorn tree; 'closen': small
enclosures, or fields; a retention of the old Saxon plural; 'bumbarrels': long-tailed tits (John
Clare, The Midsummer Cushion, eds Anne Tibble and R. K. R. Thornton (Ashington and
Manchester: Mid Northumberland Arts Group and Carcanet Press, 1978), 'Glossary', pp.
493–500. 'Crimpled' seems to suggest that the leaves are crumpled, but frozen into their
crumpled shapes, as if stiffened by a crimping-iron.

the heron do another; and, reading on, that he loves to see the crow do what it does, too; as if the words at the beginning of the sentence, 'I love to see', are mainly used as a peg on which to hang a continuum of images and events, united primarily in that they are all things that the speaker claims he loves to see.

That uneasiness I referred to derives, it seems to me, from the sense that the nature of the connection made by 'while' cannot be so entirely dismissed. It is one thing to read these lines in such a way as to suggest that 'while' does not really *mean* 'while', but the word remains, and with it a sense of the inadequacy of a reading which does not take it into account. For a 'continuum' of impressions suggests that they are experienced one after another, and the word 'while' suggests that they are experienced simultaneously. Now obviously we *do* experience the words that name these impressions successively, and it is of the nature of language that we must do so: we cannot read 'heath' and 'heron' at the same time, as we can see them at the same time. The word 'while' seems to direct attention, however, to the notion that the speaker is experiencing them simultaneously, and not as the separate parts of the kind of composition Thomson offered us, which are discovered successively by the eye as it moves across the landscape from foreground to background. The effect of attending to the word is the sense that the experience of seeing the bracken is connected with the experience of seeing the heron not just because both experiences are pleasurable, but because both are represented as somehow inseparable – they are both parts of the same complex, simultaneous impression, not just this *and* that but this *while* that. And in the same way the experience of seeing the crow is inseparable from these first two experiences, and inseparable also, for the speaker, from the knowledge that, beside the ash-tree on which the crow is perched, a gipsy sometimes sleeps.

This syntax, in short, cannot remove the fact that we experience the words in the poem as a succession; but it can suggest that for the speaker the experience of seeing one thing is simultaneous with, and so cannot be disentangled from, the experience of seeing another. The whole sentence, in short, can be read as representing a complex manifold of simultaneous impressions, which together form a single moment in the complex experience of being on 'Emmonsails Heath in Winter'. And the first word of the next sentence, 'Up', can then serve to indicate a rupture, and so a bringing to an end, of that first moment, by the sudden awareness of what was not there before. The woodcock is first registered as a movement 'up'-wards, and its suddenness and movement inaugurates a new moment of being in this place.

What does all this tell us about the identity of the speaker who is also the subject who perceives these successive moments of simultaneity? If, as I have suggested, the primary ground of unity among the impressions that together compose a moment of experience is less that the speaker finds them pleasurable than that they all happen at the same time, then the identity of this subject seems evidently very different from that of the subject constituted in the passage from Thomson. In that passage, the subject was represented as conceiving of its identity as something to be struggled for, something which needed to announce itself as autonomous, as freeing itself from the determination of the objects it perceived, and so as enduring through successive impressions. In this poem, it seems, the subject's identity is represented as something that is constituted by its perceptions; or, to put it another way, the subject is represented as being constituted as a subject by the complex manifold of impressions that is the experience of being on the heath at one moment in time. The heath, if you like, 'makes up the being' of the speaker, who is represented as having no other being, no other identity, than what is produced by that moment of perception. The subject is not differentiated from the heath, for, at each moment of experience, there is nothing to indicate that the subject is anything other than the place where these simultaneous impressions are registered.

It is true that as, with the word 'Up', one moment gives way to another, we may develop a sense of the continuity of the subject – a sense of it as being something which endures from moment to moment, which can be the place where first one, then another complex of impressions is registered; and to that degree we have a sense of the subject as more than the sum of its impressions at any moment. But if we do have such a sense, it is one we may arrive at, as it were, on the basis of some normative expectation, over and above what the syntax of the poem describes. For all the poem recounts is a series of moments, and it represents the subject not as continuous, but as continually reconstituted by changing moments of experience. The subject never emerges as transcendent subject, like the 'eye' in Thomson's passage; it is at most, at the beginning of the poem, a grammatical subject; in the second half of the poem it is no longer even what it registers, but only what is registered.

We can say much the same about 'The Beans in Blossom':

The southwest wind how pleasant in the face
It breaths while sauntering in a musing pace
I roam these new ploughd fields & by the side

Of this old wood where happy birds abide                                          4
& the rich blackbird through his golden bill
Utters wild music when the rest are still
Now luscious comes the scent of blossomed beans
That oer the path in rich disorder leans                                          8
Mid which the bees in busy songs & toils
Load home luxuriantly their yellow spoils
The herd cows toss the mole hills in their play
& often stand the strangers steps at bay                                         ·12
Mid clover blossoms red & tawney white
Strong scented with the summers warm delight[10]

The structure of the first sentence of this sonnet – down to the word 'still'
at the end of the sixth line – works in much the same way as did the
structure of the first sentence of 'Emmonsails Heath in Winter'; and, in
particular, the word 'while' performs much the same function. Once
again, if we try to take the syntax at its face-value, the poem seems to offer
us some extraordinarily precise conditions in which the speaker finds
the south-west wind, breathing in his face, pleasant: it is pleasant, it
appears, when he is sauntering, strolling idly along, and roaming some
new ploughed fields, by the side of a wood where the birds seem happy
and where they live, and where one of them, in particular, the blackbird,
continues to sing when the other birds fall silent – that's when it's
pleasant. But, once again, it seems likely that we take from the first six
lines of this poem the impression of a complex moment of pleasure,
produced by the simultaneous coming-together of a manifold of impressions in the speaker.

And once again, we can make a clear contrast between this poem and
the passage from Thomson, on the basis of how the subject of these
impressions is constituted. We can focus that contrast on the word
'roam', which is used in both, and which, in the passage by Thomson,
was the verb attributed to the perceiving subject, the 'eye', at the point
when it had disentangled its identity from a controlling nature, and was
celebrating its autonomous freedom to 'roam' the landscape, and not to
be 'snatch'd' over it. But here, the action of 'roaming' seems to imply no
prior struggle against nature, no victory, therefore, and so no proclama-
tion of freedom. It is rather one of a range of experiences – along with the
breathing of the wind, the sense of relaxation signified by 'sauntering',
the places roamed through, and the bird-song – which come together to
compose a moment which is, while it lasts, what constitutes, what
determines the subject, a subject which has no other content than what,
in that moment, it perceives. There is no sense, then, that the freedom to

roam is something achieved by the subject when it has freed itself from the circumstances of the moment, for the impressions it perceives are not conceived of as constraints on its freedom, as events and circumstances which 'snatch' its freedom away. The subject of this opening sentence becomes, by the third line, a grammatical subject, but not therefore a transcendent one.

And once again, the first sentence ends when the moment it represents is intruded upon by another complex manifold of impressions; and just as in 'Emmonsails Heath in Winter' that intrusion was represented as the sudden awareness of a new movement, preceding the registering of what it was that moved, so here it is represented as the awareness of a new experience of pleasure, which is registered before its source is identified. 'Now luscious comes', we read, 'the scent of blossomed beans'. This new moment too is represented by the sentence as a manifold of simultaneous impressions, as far as the successive nature of language will allow; at least, that I take it is the effect of 'Mid which', which seems to represent what the bees do, not as something noticed after the disorder of the beans, but as something registered as part of that disorder, and coinstantaneously with it.

## VIII

I said earlier that such a relation of self and nature as this poem proposes was conceived of, by those who had no interest in sharing it, as a primitive relation. I also suggested that it could be in the interest of such people to impose, from above, a different understanding of that relation, in terms of conflict, differentiation, and eventual autonomy; an understanding of freedom, not only as a freedom from determination by nature, but as a freedom to determine, control, cultivate it. Since the beginning of the eighteenth century, the notion that the lowest members of rural society exhibited a kind of primitive state of mind by virtue of their failure to differentiate themselves as subjects from the raw data of experience had been an important element in accounts of pastoral poetry in particular, and of language in general. Thus it was argued, on the one hand, that pastoral poets ought, for the sake of verisimilitude, to attempt to make their shepherds speak as if incapable of this act of differentiation; and it was argued, on the contrary, that the spectacle of minds thus incapable was so unedifying to the polite as to make pastoral either a worthless genre, or one which would have a claim on the attention of the polite, only if it ceased to imitate the thought-processes of the vulgar, and concerned itself instead with the more polished members of rural society.

This, for example, is the poet Thomas Tickell, writing in 1713:

Men who, by long study and experience, have reduced their ideas to certain classes, and consider the general nature of things abstracted from particulars, express their thoughts after a more concise, lively, surprising manner. Those who have little experience, or cannot abstract, deliver their sentiments in plain descriptions, by circumstances, and those observations which either strike upon the senses, or are the first motions of the mind.

Shepherds, according to Tickell, fall into the second category: they have not 'reduced' their ideas – Tickell means here, primarily, their sense-impressions – to an abstract order, so as to be in control of them; therefore they must not be allowed, in pastoral poetry, to make 'deep reflections'. They must be represented, instead, as expressing, not thoughts, but sentiments, and sentiments which they cannot disentangle from the concomitant circumstances which attended the experience of them, whether or not those 'circumstances' are relevant to what it is they have to say. Their language is constituted by what 'strikes upon the senses', or by what are 'the first motions of the mind' – phrases which picture the mind and senses as passive before the striking power of nature, so that the first motions of the mind will be like the first motions of Thomson's 'eye', which was snatched before it was free to roam. The mid-eighteenth-century philosopher James Harris similarly remarked that the 'vulgar' are so thoroughly undifferentiated from nature, so 'merged in sense from their earliest infancy' that they 'imagine nothing to be real, but what may be touched or tasted'. Their life is so 'merged in a multitude of particulars', that they have no need of a language capable of expressing abstract ideas.[11]

Throughout the eighteenth century, there is a general agreement among writers on pastoral that if pastoral is to represent the speech of the vulgar, it must speak a language full of concrete nouns (whether used literally or figuratively) and spare in its syntax. The only points of disagreement are whether it is worth imitating, or whether, indeed, as Wordsworth argues, the language of those whose passions are thus, he says, 'incorporated' with the forms of nature, is not a more accurate, and so a more philosophical language, than that of more sophisticated speakers, who have, he says, 'separated themselves' from the sympathies of those whose passions are thus incorporated. But Wordsworth of course did not simply offer to *reproduce* the language of such speakers: their language could be the basis of a language of poetry, but only when it had been 'purified', he says, 'from what appear to be its real defects, from lasting and rational causes of dislike or disgust'. Nor was he quite as wholehearted in his admiration for the language of the small farmer and rural worker as even this guarded position may suggest, as we shall see in the next essay.[12]

Had it been possible for Clare's poems to be published as he wrote them, unpunctuated, they would no doubt have produced a complex reaction of pleasure and disgust. Pleasure, because they would have seemed to vindicate theories of what primitive language should be like – a language of the first involuntary motions of the passive mind, unable to differentiate itself from the circumstantial and contingent, from nature and the impressions of the senses. There was (as we shall also see in the next chapter) an easy assurance of one's own cultivation to be derived from contemplating the uncultivated language of the vulgar. Disgust, because they might have seemed too primitive to be edifying. Before Clare's poems could be published, therefore, it was necessary not only to punctuate them, but to correct their grammar – that is, to make the grammar of Clare's dialect conform with the grammar of standard English. By this means something could be done to create a space between the speaker and the things spoken of, to differentiate the perceiving subject from the circumstantial moments of experience with which it seemed entirely 'incorporated'.

The poems could thus be 'purified', to some extent, from 'causes of dislike', at the same time as the repeated failure of the poems to display the autonomy of the subject, by offering conclusions abstracted from experience, general statements about nature of the kind that exhibit the power to 'reduce' particular impressions to abstract classes, would still guarantee the authenticity of the pastoral language, and provide reassurance as to the intellectual superiority of the 'polite' over the 'vulgar' mind. For the majority of Clare's sonnets, in particular, do not end up by offering what Tickell had called 'deep reflections': they do not end up by saying anything abstract or general about the moments of experience they have represented. They just end when the fourteen lines are up. Therefore they could seem the products of a mind incapable of reflecting, and could be taken to exemplify the difference between the educated, differentiated intelligence over the primitive, undifferentiated mind.

We can get an idea of the effect of punctuating Clare's poems, and a clearer idea, therefore, of why they had to be punctuated, by looking again at 'The Beans in Blossom', this time in the form in which it was published in Clare's fourth and final published collection of poems, *The Rural Muse* of 1835: for 'rural', we can understand 'primitive'.

> The south-west wind! how pleasant in the face
> It breathes! while, sauntering in a musing pace,
> I roam these new-ploughed fields; or by the side
> Of this old wood, where happy birds abide                                4
> And the rich blackbird, through his golden bill,
> Utters wild music when the rest are still.
> Luscious the scent comes of the blossomed bean,
> As o'er the path in rich disorder lean                                          8
> Its stalks; whence bees, in busy rows and toils,
> Load home luxuriantly their yellow spoils.
> The herd-cows toss the mole-hills in their play;
> And often stand the stranger's steps at bay,                            12
> Mid clover-blossoms, red, and tawny-white,
> Strong-scented with the summer's warm delight.

Let us look, to begin with, at the effect of punctuation on what was, at least in the manuscript version, the first sentence of this poem. The most obvious effect is the production of a syntax which divides what was before represented as an indivisible moment of simultaneous experience, a 'rich disorder', into a sequence of experiences, and a sequence which presupposes a separation of the subject from what it perceives. The effect of the exclamation-marks, for example, is to confer on the first line and a half the status of exclamatory reflections by the speaker on what it is that he is experiencing: the exclamation-marks convert the lines from statements of the experience into statements *about* it. This invites us to understand the lines that follow as if they were dependent on such a verb as 'I think' or 'I reflect' or 'I exclaim'; as if the poem were saying: 'I feel the south-west wind, and I notice how pleasantly it blows in my face! I think this while sauntering . . . ' and so on. By this means the subject is constituted not simply as the grammatical, but as the transcendent subject of its experiences, and 'while' comes to mark, not the simultaneity of one impression and another, but the simultaneity of reflection and impression.

And by other instances of punctuation the complex moment represented in the first sentence is divided into a sequence of separate moments, through which a differentiated subject is represented as organising its experiences sequentially, so that its own continuity, as it separates one impression from another, is guaranteed. The commas in the fourth line have the effect of separating the phrase, 'where happy birds abide', from 'this old wood', in such a way as makes the one phrase a reflection on the other, something which the speaker offers as an additional piece of information about the wood – 'birds live there' – rather than as something constitutive of the idea 'old wood' and of the complex impression 'wood/birds/song'. A similar act of separation is achieved by the semi-colon in the third line, reinforced by the change of 'and' to 'or'. The effect, yet again, is to divide the moment, to make the exclamations of the first lines into exclamations the speaker makes *either* in this place, the fields, *or* in that place, the wood-side, since he cannot be imagined as making them in both places, and the field and wood cannot apparently be imagined as adjacent.

Or look at the reorganisation of the second sentence – a reorganisation which must have seemed absolutely necessary, to eliminate the traces of a provincial grammar from the poem. Clare frequently uses – and it is a regular dialect use in the eastern counties of England – what is for most of us the third person singular form as the third person plural form. There is an example in 'Emmonsails Heath in Winter', where the fieldfare that 'chatters' in line 10 are revealed to be plural when they 'rove' in line 11. Accordingly, Clare's editor has decided (reasonably enough) that in the eighth line it is the 'beans' that 'leans', and not their scent; and to make that clear, he was obliged to undertake a large-scale reorganisation of Clare's grammar and rhyming. He has to make 'blossomed beans' into 'the blossomed bean', which involves not just a change from plural to singular, but a change from a phrase that refers to particular plants, to one which signifies an abstract, botanical category, the plants 'reduced' into a 'class'. Next he has to find a subject for the verb 'lean': he offers, not very happily, 'Its stalks', but this cramps his style in line 9, so that 'the bees' become just 'bees', and the phrase about them again can be read as a piece of general information about bean-fields, not a specific impression of this bean-field. What is more, 'mid which' is replaced by 'whence', so that we are invited to experience the /bees not as inextricably a part of the complex impression 'beans/path/disorder/bees', but as a new and separate impression. In the moments and spaces defined by the syntax of the manuscript version, there are no internal divisions – there are just, as I said, complex manifolds of what are represented as simultaneous impressions, as far as the successive nature of language can allow them to be thus represented. For the editor, these spaces and moments are divided into, and consist of, separate images, which, as they are produced by his syntax, regulate and give structure to the time and place the poem describes.

In the process, a new kind of perceiving subject is produced: one which, by its ability to divide, organise and reflect upon its experiences, differentiates itself from those experiences, and survives and transcends them. The poem that results is still an appropriately pastoral, in the sense of an appropriately primitive poem, for though the 'first motions of the mind' have lost some of their primal, impetuous flush, still the lack of paraphrasable content evinces an inability to make what Tickell called 'deep reflections'. But it has ceased to be a poem which repesents to a polite readership the notion that there might be another way of apprehending the relations of mind and nature, subject and object, than that by which they claim to apprehend them. The edited version thus confirms the polite in their notions of how such relations are to be conceived: nature is something to be reduced by the processes of abstraction, processes by which we too are abstracted from nature, and by which we become ideal subjects, emancipated from the material world. There is thus an analogy to be drawn between the effect of editing on this poem, and its effect on Shakespeare's twenty-ninth sonnet, whereby the constraints of material life, represented by the discourse of patronage, were concealed or abolished.

It is worth insisting, however, that these poems by Clare are not at all 'primitive', in anything like the simple sense that they were imagined to be by his contemporary readers. They are the products of a self-conscious attempt to invent a language to represent a mode of consciousness that is, as he put it, distinctively 'local'.[13] They are written as a deliberate and considered alternative to the style of landscape description he had encountered in Thomson and other eighteenth-century descriptive poets. In his earliest books of poetry, Clare had made a number of more or less successful attempts to write in the mode of Thomson, but had turned away from those attempts, because he decided that Thomson's descriptive procedures could not be used to represent his own sense of place, his own consciousness, and the mutually constitutive relations of the two. Thomson's procedures were not, for Clare, sufficiently 'local': they could be applied to any landscape whatsoever, and they acknowledged no distinctions between those landscapes with which we are familiar, and those we see for the first time. In that sense they were the appropriate products of a class which, because it could afford to travel, to move from place to place, had developed a means of constructing its relations with places in a way that represented, exactly, the degree of its abstraction, emancipation, from particular localities and their power to determine our 'knowledge' and our 'being'. The language of the poems we have been reading was developed, then, to represent an alternative mode of relation; and the danger they would have represented, in their unpublished form, was that they would have suggested that the ways in which the polite constructed their relations with nature were not the only, the natural, the inevitable ways; and therefore that 'mind' and 'nature', as these concepts were constructed by the polite, might have been constructed for purposes which the 'vulgar' did not share.

In the essay on Milton, we saw Coleridge describe the language of Shakespeare's uneducated women, Juliet's nurse and Mistress Quickly, in terms which are evidently comparable to the terms in which I have suggested Clare's language would have been understood by his polite contemporaries. The women, it appeared, could not tell a story without telling all the circumstances that happened to accompany the incident they were attempting to describe. Clare could not apparently name an object without naming as many objects as happened to be contingent with it. And some twenty years before Tickell announced that shepherds cannot make deep reflections, the feminist Mary Astell had observed that the minds of women in particular, by their exclusion from education, are 'prepossess'd ... with those pleasing Perceptions which external Objects occasion'. Such a mind, she argues, 'forms all its Notions by such Ideas only as it derives from sensation, being unacquainted with those more excellent ones which arise from its own operations and a serious reflection on them.'[14] The next essay will explore the similar terms in which the language of 'children, women, and the vulgar of both sexes'[15] could be described, even at the end of the eighteenth century, and at how their language resembled that of educated men, as well as how it differed from it.[16]

## Notes

1 See above, p. 98, n. 12.
2 All quotations from The Seasons are from James Sambrook's edition of the poem, see above, p. 98, n. 12.
3 Quoted from The Poetical Works of George Lord Lyttelton (London: Cadell and Davies et al.) 1801), p. 18.
4 John Clare, Autobiographical Writings, ed. Eric Robinson (Oxford: Oxford University Press, 1983), p. 60.
5 Autobiographical Writings, pp. 34, 63. The phrase 'out of one's knowledge' was common enough in the late eighteenth and early nineteenth centuries, and was probably regarded by the polite as a vulgarism. My interest is not so much in the fact that Clare uses the phrase, as that he reinforces its meaning by such remarks as those quoted in this paragraph.
6 Quoted in J. W. and Anne Tibble, John Clare, His Life and Poetry (London: Heinemann, 1956), p. 1.
7 The Letters of John Clare, ed. Mark Storey (Oxford: Oxford University Press, 1985), p. 231.

8  John Clare, *The Midsummer Cushion*, ed. Anne Tibble with R. K. R.Thornton (Ashington and Manchester; Mid-Northumberland Arts Group nd Carcanet Press, 1979), p. 474.

9  *The Midsummer Cushion*, p. 445.

10  *The Midsummer Cushion*, p. 401.

11  Thomas Tickell (or possibly Richard Steele), *The Guardian*, no. 23, 7 April 1713; *The Works of James Harris* (Oxford: Thomas Tegg, 1841), pp. 218, 216.

12  Wordsworth and Coleridge, *Lyrical Ballads*, eds R. L. Brett and A. R. Jones (London: Methuen, edition of 1965), pp. 245–6.

13  John Clare, *His Life and Poetry*, p. 84.

14  Mary Astell, *A Serious Proposal to the Ladies*, Part I (1696), in *The First English Feminist: 'Reflections upon Marriage' and other Writings by Mary Astell*, ed. Bridget Hill (Aldershot: Gower Publishing Company, 1986), p. 159.

15  See below, p. 161.

16  This essay is an attempt to re-think the argument of my book *The Idea of Landscape and the Sense of Place, 1730–1840: an Approach to the Poetry of John Clare* (Cambridge: Cambridge University Press, 1972).

# 5

# The uses of Dorothy:
# 'The Language of the Sense'
# in 'Tintern Abbey'

I

*Lines*
*written a few miles above* Tintern *Abbey,*
ON REVISITING THE BANKS OF THE WYE
DURING A TOUR,
July 13, 1798

Five years have passed; five summers, with the length
Of five long winters! and again I hear
These waters, rolling from their mountain-springs
With a sweet inland murmur.* – Once again
Do I behold these steep and lofty cliffs,
Which on a wild secluded scene impress
Thoughts of more deep seclusion; and connect
The landscape with the quiet of the sky.
The day is come when I again repose
Here, under this dark sycamore, and view                    10
These plots of cottage-ground, these orchard-tufts,
Which, at this season, with their unripe fruits,
Among the woods and copses lose themselves,
Nor, with their green and simple hue, disturb
The wild green landscape. Once again I see
These hedge-rows, hardly hedge-rows, little lines
Of sportive wood run wild; these pastoral farms
Green to the very door; and wreathes of smoke
Sent up, in silence, from among the trees,
With some uncertain notice, as might seem,                  20
Of vagrant dwellers in the houseless woods,
Or of some hermit's cave, where by his fire
The hermit sits alone.

* The river is not affected by the tides a few miles above Tintern.

                                    Though absent long,
These forms of beauty have not been to me,
As is a landscape to a blind man's eye:
But oft, in lonely rooms, and mid the din
Of towns and cities, I have owed to them,
In hours of weariness, sensations sweet,
Felt in the blood, and felt along the heart,
And passing even into my purer mind                                    30
With tranquil restoration: – feelings too
Of unremembered pleasure; such, perhaps,
As may have had no trivial influence
On that best portion of a good man's life;
His little, nameless, unremembered acts
Of kindness and of love. Nor less, I trust,
To them I may have owed another gift,
Of aspect more sublime; that blessed mood,
In which the burthen of the mystery,
In which the heavy and the weary weight                                40
Of all this untintelligible world
Is lighten'd: – that serene and blessed mood,
In which the affections gently lead us on,
Until, the breath or this corporeal frame,
And even the motion of our human blood
Almost suspended, we are laid asleep
In body, and become a living soul:
While with an eye made quiet by the power
Of harmony, and the deep power of joy,
We see into the life of things.
                                    If this                              50
Be but a vain belief, yet, oh! how oft,
In darkness, and amid the many shapes
Of joyless day-light; when the fretful stir
Unprofitable, and the fever of the world,
Have hung upon the beatings of my heart,
How oft, in spirit, have I turned to thee
O sylvan Wye! Thou wanderer through the woods,
How often has my spirit turned to thee!
And now, with gleams of half-extinguish'd thought,
With many recognitions dim and faint,                                  60
And somewhat of a sad perplexity,
The picture of the mind revives again:
While here I stand, not only with the sense
Of present pleasure, but with pleasing thoughts
That in this moment there is life and food
For future years. And so I dare to hope
Though changed, no doubt, from what I was, when first

I came among these hills; when like a roe
I bounded o'er the mountains, by the sides
Of the deep rivers, and the lonely streams,                          70
Wherever nature led; more like a man
Flying from something that he dreads, than one
Who sought the thing he loved. For nature then
(The coarser pleasures of my boyish days,
And their glad animal movements all gone by,)
To me was all in all. – I cannot paint
What then I was. The sounding cataract
Haunted me like a passion: the tall rock,
The mountain, and the deep and gloomy wood,
Their colours and their forms, were then to me                       80
An appetite: a feeling and a love,
That had no need of a remoter charm,
By thought supplied, or any interest
Unborrowed from the eye. – That time is past,
And all its aching joys are now no more,
And all its dizzy raptures. Not for this
Faint I, nor mourn nor murmur: other gifts
Have followed, for such gifts, I would believe,
Abundant recompense. For I have learned
To look on nature, not as in the hour                                90
Of thoughtless youth, but hearing oftentimes
The still, sad music of humanity,
Not harsh nor grating, but of ample power
To chasten and subdue. And I have felt
A presence that disturbs me with the joy
Of elevated thoughts; a sense sublime
Of something far more deeply interfused,
Whose dwelling is the light of setting suns,
And the round ocean, and the living air,
And the blue sky, and in the mind of man,                            100
A motion and a spirit, that impels
All thinking things, all objects of all thought,
And rolls through all things. Therefore am I still
A lover of the meadows and the woods,
And mountains; and of all that we behold
From this green earth; of all the mighty world
Of eye and ear, both what they half-create,*
And what perceive; well pleased to recognize
In nature and the language of the sense,
The anchor of my purest thoughts, the nurse,                         110

---

* This line has a close resemblance to an admirable line of Young, the exact expression of
which I cannot recollect.

The guide, the guardian of my heart, and soul
Of all my moral being.
                    Nor, perchance,
If I were not thus taught, should I the more
Suffer my genial spirits to decay:
For thou art with me, here, upon the banks
Of this fair river; thou, my dearest Friend,
My dear, dear Friend, and in thy voice I catch
The language of my former heart, and read
My former pleasures in the shooting lights
Of thy wild eyes. Oh! yet a little while                                        120
May I behold in thee what I was once,
My dear, dear Sister! And this prayer I make,
Knowing that Nature never did betray
The heart that loved her; 'tis her privilege,
Through all the years of this our life, to lead
From joy to joy: for she can so inform
The mind that is within us, so impress
With quietness and beauty, and so feed
With lofty thoughts, that neither evil tongues,
Rash judgments, nor the sneers of selfish men,                                  130
Nor greetings where no kindness is, nor all
The dreary intercourse of daily life,
Shall e'er prevail against us, or disturb
Our chearful faith that all which we behold
Is full of blessings. Therefore let the moon
Shine on thee in thy solitary walk;
And let the misty mountain winds be free
To blow against thee: and in after years,
When these wild ecstasies shall be matured
Into a sober pleasure, when thy mind                                            140
Shall be a mansion for all lovely forms,
Thy memory be as a dwelling-place
For all sweet sounds and harmonies; Oh! then,
If solitude, or fear, or pain, or grief
Should be thy portion, with what healing thoughts
Of tender joy wilt thou remember me,
And these my exhortations! Nor, perchance,
If I should be, where I no more can hear
Thy voice, nor catch from thy wild eyes these gleams
Of past existence, wilt thou then forget                                        150
That on the banks of this delightful stream
We stood together; and that I, so long
A worshipper of Nature, hither came,
Unwearied in that service: rather say
With warmer love, oh! with far deeper zeal

Of holier love. Nor wilt thou then forget,
That after many wanderings, many years
Of absence, these steep woods and lofty cliffs,
And this green pastoral landscape, were to me
More dear, both for themselves, and for thy sake.[1]       160

This essay is about the language of Wordsworth's 'Tintern Abbey'; more specifically, about its two languages, the language of natural description, and the language of the meditations which seem to be produced by the contemplation of nature, of landscape; and I will be saying something about the theory of language which seems to define the distinction between them. As in my discussions of James Thomson and John Clare, I will be working towards an attempt to re-present that distinction, as one between the language produced by a subject who remains (it is imagined) undifferentiated from nature, and the language spoken by a subject who is imagined to have achieved an identity fully differentiated from it. What was at stake in those earlier discussions, and in the distinction between those two kinds of subjects in terms of nature and culture, was a class distinction, defined in its simplest terms, of the different relation of different subjects to the means of production. But 'Tintern Abbey' offers us an opportunity of conceiving that distinction in terms of gender also, so that this essay can be read as taking off from my remarks, at the end of the essay on Milton, on Coleridge's notions of syntax as gendered. Constructions of gender-difference very often supply or repeat the terms in which class-difference is constructed: women are frequently represented as different from men on the same terms as ignorant men are assumed to differ from educated men, or as, indeed, children are assumed to differ from mature male adults. I shall be asking, then, about the nature of the comparison the poem makes between the masculine subject who speaks the poem, and the feminine subject to whom a part of it, at least, is spoken. On this topic, my remarks will turn on the question of whether a woman can .be assumed capable either of uttering or of understanding the language of meditation in the poem, and so on whether Dorothy Wordsworth can be assumed to be capable of understanding the lines addressed to her at its end.

In a chapter of his book *Articulate Energy*, Donald Davie attempts to describe what he feels to be the risks taken by the language of *The Prelude*. He begins by pointing out that 'Wordsworth's world is not pre-eminently a world of "things" ', and that his language is not remarkable for its ' "weight and mass" '. Because, he argues, Wordsworth had castigated some earlier poets, in the 'Preface' to the *Lyrical Ballads*, for 'giving no proof that they had ever truly *looked* at natural phenomena, it is often supposed that his own verse is full of such phenomena rendered in all their quiddity and concreteness'. This, argues Davie, is 'a sort of optical illusion. What Wordsworth renders is not the natural world but . . . the effect that world has upon him'; and in those passages of *The Prelude* where Wordsworth is trying to convey those effects, his words – such words as 'ties', 'bonds', 'influences', and 'powers' – will carry his readers, only for so long as they do not 'loiter', only for so long as those words are taken as 'fiduciary symbols', as 'values of monetary exchange'. In short, 'Wordsworth's words have meaning so long as we trust them. They have just such meaning, and just as much meaning', as the term 'fiduciary symbols' suggests.[2]

I find this argument persuasive, not only for the language of *The Prelude*, but for its 'satellite-poem',[3] 'Tintern Abbey'. If we attempt to understand 'Tintern Abbey' by attempting to define clear conceptual meanings for the words in its abstract vocabulary – 'restoration', for example, or 'mystery', or 'affections', or 'recognitions', or 'something far more deeply interfused' – I believe we will fail; certainly we will not easily convince ourselves that there are any other words into which those ones can adequately be translated. But the problem goes further than that, as we will see if we consider a word which, in its singular and plural forms, occurs no less than nine times in the 160 lines of the poem, the word 'thought'. Now clearly one point the poem is concerned to claim is that 'lofty' cliffs somehow give rise to 'lofty' thoughts, and that with the passage of time these lofty thoughts become more present to us than lofty cliffs can now be; and it is concerned to ask how these things happen. We might be more persuaded of the truth of that notion, perhaps, if we could arrive at a clear idea of what it is that Wordsworth thinks of as 'thoughts'. Is thinking one of a range of various activities of the mind, such as hoping, believing, imagining, feeling, or is it a term which includes some or all of those other activities? It is seldom if ever clear, and we may feel it matters that it *should* be clear, in view of the importance given to thinking as an activity characteristic of a certain kind of maturity, and of distance from immediate experience.

It is seldom if ever clear, also, what these thoughts are of, which are engendered by lofty cliffs, and how it is, therefore, that they can be described as 'lofty'. For though we get *some* idea, of course, of their content, the poem seems far more concerned to impress upon us the notion that these thoughts have such-and-such a character, than that they have such-and-such a content. Look, for example, as well as at the phrase 'lofty thoughts' in line 129, at 'elevated thoughts' in line 96; at 'my purest thoughts', in line 110; at the glowing, but still ungraspable, 'half-extinguished thought', in line 59; or at the 'thought' which endows, in time, the objects in the landscape with 'a remoter charm', in line 83. On two other occasions, the 'thoughts' are qualified by prepositional phrases, but it is by no means clear that it is their content, and not again their character, that is being represented. The 'healing thoughts / Of tender joy' in lines 145–6 may indicate that the content of Dorothy's thoughts will be joy, but as we probably think of joy as a feeling rather than as a thought, the phrase seems at least as likely to communicate that Dorothy will have thoughts of a tender, joyful character, or thoughts, of unspecified content, prompted by her tender joy. The 'thoughts of more deep seclusion', similarly, in line 7, may suggest thoughts *about* more deep seclusion, but the phrase hovers between suggesting that meaning, and suggesting that the 'steep and lofty cliffs' impress on the landscape thoughts proper to a seclusion yet more deep than the seclusion of the landscape itself – telling us, that is, something again about the kind of thoughts, not the content of them; but I will have more to say about this phrase later.

Perhaps the only time in the poem that the word 'thought' or 'thoughts' is used together with a clear suggestion of their content, is in lines 64–6, 'with pleasing thoughts, That in this moment there is life and food / For future years' – but even here, the parallelism around the caesura, 'present pleasure'/'pleasing thoughts', suggests that a sense-unit has already, in some sense, been completed at the end of line 64, by which time Wordsworth has told us, once again, of the character but not the content of the thoughts; and even when that content is revealed, the contrast, between the plural thoughts and the singular statement that defines them, seems to suggest that there is still a surplus on the side of the thoughts, that their entire content has by no means been manifested in the singular statement that follows.

We will find meaning in such words, Davie argues, only as long as we trust them; and it is a point made by the poem as well - which, for all its rationcinative appearance, its deployment, repeatedly, of all those con-junctions by which we seek to display the connections in a rational process of thought, is still continually concerned to suggest that it pro-ceeds not so much by the logical accretion of propositions, but by leaps of faith and trust. 'Perhaps', the poem suggests at line 32, the feelings of *unremembered* pleasure - and we must take it on trust that pleasures which cannot be remembered were indeed once experienced - have had some influence on acts of kindness which have also disappeared from the memory, and so can only be trusted to have occurred. He 'trusts' in line 36 that he may have owed to these feelings 'another gift'. That gift is a 'blessed mood', the visionary power of which at line 50 the poem appeals directly to us to confirm - we 'see into the life of things'.

But do we? - not only the fact that we do, but what we see, is to be taken on trust. The existence of that visionary power is acknowledged, in line 51, to be no more perhaps than a '*vain* belief', or a 'vain *belief*'; but the threat to the meditative direction of the poem offered by that concession is immediately pushed away, by the exclamatory assertion that, in any case, Wordsworth's spirit has, in oppressive circumstances, often turned to the River Wye. In line 66, the thought, 'That in this moment there is life and food For future years', is redescribed as a hope, rather, and a remote one, which Wordsworth must 'dare' to entertain. His character as a youth in the Wye Valley we must, the poem makes clear, take on trust, for he cannot now 'paint' what then he was. In line 89, the notion that the gifts of maturity are an abundant recompense for the loss of youth is what Wordsworth 'would' believe, what he would like, or chooses, to believe. And so on: the poem sometimes declares, and sometimes concedes, that the doctrine that it offers to teach, that lofty cliffs are replaced by lofty thoughts, is the fruit of faith and hope, not of reason and demonstration, and that the content of this meditation, and the state of mind it attempts to represent, can only be the objects of our trust: they are open neither to be proved or disproved.

To explain his approval of, his enthusiasm for, a language whose meanings we must take on trust, Davie refers us to Coleridge's consideration of the 'Preface' to the Lyrical Ballads in Biographia Literaria.

The best part of human language, properly so called, is derived from reflection on the acts of the mind itself. It is formed by the voluntary appropriation of fixed symbols to internal acts, to processes and results of imagination, the greater part of which have no place in the consciousness of uneducated man; though in civilized society, by imitation and passive remembrance of what they hear from their religious instructors and other superiors, the most uneducated share in the harvest which they neither sowed nor reaped.

Davie reminds us that 'this statement is made when Coleridge is objecting to Wordsworth's recommendation of rustic language', on the grounds, says Davie, that 'such language can provide only poor and meagre syntax'. For 'the rustic', continues Coleridge,

from the more imperfect development of his faculties, and from the lower state of his cultivation, aims almost solely to convey insulated facts, either those of his scanty experience or his traditional belief; while the educated man chiefly seeks to discover those connections of things, or those relative bearings of fact to fact, from which some more or less general law is deducible.[4]

I have quoted the passage at rather greater length than is necessary to my immediate purpose, because some of what Coleridge says – which is, for the most part, the conventional wisdom of eighteenth-century theories of pastoral poetry – will be of relevance, if not now, then later on in this essay. For the moment, let us concentrate on what Davie concludes from these quotations, that Coleridge's point is that if a language is deficient in 'fixed symbols' for 'internal acts' of the mind, 'it will also be deficient in syntax'. Thus when Wordsworth in The Prelude or 'Tintern Abbey' 'abandoned rustic diction and took to rendering "internal acts", "processes and results of imagination" ', he used for this purpose 'an elaborate syntax', and 'an important part of his vocabulary' came to be 'made up of fixed fiduciary symbols'.[5]

Davie has clouded things a little, I believe, by writing as though Coleridge's term 'fixed symbols', means the same thing as his own term, or rather the term he has borrowed from St-John Perse, 'fiduciary symbols'; and it may help us grasp the point of Davie's argument better if we distinguish between the two terms. For it may not be true that a language which is rich in fixed symbols, voluntarily appropriated to internal acts, will throw the burden of the meaning of an utterance on to its syntax. By 'fixed symbols', 'voluntarily appropriated', Coleridge has in mind the idea of words as arbitrary signs, their meanings fixed by the meanings they have taken on in earlier instances of their use, as opposed to the idea of words as natural signs, their meanings fixed by some notionally natural connection between word and thing – if such signs, Coleridge seems to suggest, form any part of language, it is the most primitive part. The validation of the meaning of such arbitrary signs will not be within any particular context in which they are used, but elsewhere, in an agreement as to their meaning formed prior to any particular instance of their utterance; and such a compact could fix the meanings of words that denote the relation of acts of the mind and the objects of those acts, as well as the meanings of words denoting the separate acts and objects.

The point that Davie is trying to make is better indicated by the term 'fiduciary symbols', and by holding on to the notion that, in Wordsworth's poetry, the meaning of such symbols depends not on any agreement as to the meaning of words prior to their utterance in any particular instance, but on the willingness to trust that they do have some meaning, that they are promissory notes which, one day, the bank will honour. This is a willingness that the poet creates in us by, and during, his utterance; and it is such a notion of symbols, of words whose meanings are not fixed, but whose relations with other words the poet attempts to suggest as he utters them, that will throw the weight of meaning in a poem on to its syntax, on to the relations it proposes among the abstract nouns he is attempting to appropriate to 'internal acts', to the 'processes', as well as the 'results', of imagination.

It is this notion of words as 'fiduciary symbols', as 'promissory notes' which we trust the poet to honour in the future, that Davie is concerned with as his discussion of The Prelude continues; and it continues by attempting to establish the terms on which the readers of the poem may be persuaded to take these symbols on trust during their experience of reading it. The structure and texture of Wordsworth's blank verse, he argues, invites us to take that verse 'at a run, not pausing on the nouns for fear they congeal . . . but attending rather to the syntactical weave . . . What Wordsworth asks for . . . is for all his words to be considered only in their context.' 'These moods, exaltations, senses, sublimities, and faculties', he argues, will in themselves be no more clearly defined at the end of The Prelude than they are at any stage of our progress through the poem – and his choice here of the abstract nouns that for him typify The Prelude suggests that what he says of that poem may be applied to 'Tintern Abbey' as well, in which moods, senses, and the sublime, are quite as much a feature of the language. But though at the end of The Prelude we will arrive at no clear understanding, no clear definition of those terms, 'the poem will not be a botch'; for what will be clear at the end of the poem is the relation between them, the articulation. In short, argues Davie, 'this is poetry where the syntax counts . . . for nearly everything.'[6]

In no sense, then, will the meanings of the fiduciary symbols be fixed by Wordsworth's utterance; only, Davie suggests, the relations among them. What we learn to trust, as we read, is not that the poet will deliver, eventually, a clear conclusion or doctrine or statement of belief, one that we could abstract from the poem, translate into other terms, agree or disagree with. This is not a rhetorical poetry, in the sense that the poem is seen as a means to an end beyond itself, which, once the poem has arrived at it, will be separable from the process of its development. What we learn to trust is less the words themselves, perhaps, than the voice which speaks them: we learn to trust that the poet, even if he cannot explain them, is somehow in possession of the meanings of his abstract nouns, the proof of which is that he can propose a structure of relations among them, which is the structure of his syntax.

And the implication of Davie's argument is that we will agree to trust the poet's understanding only under certain conditions. One of these conditions is that the poem will continually *attempt* to adopt a ratiocinative mode, as if attempting to produce a conclusion which, when it is arrived at, would indeed be separable from the structure of the argument by which it was produced. It must adopt that mode as an earnest of its concern to satisfy our desire to attach fixed meanings to the nouns it employs, and thus to acknowledge our sense that only when the attempt, made in good earnest, has failed, will we be disposed to accept that the meaning of those nouns is beyond clear definition. And the second condition that this argument appears to propose is that there should be evident in the poem, alongside that ratiocinative mode and sometimes in apparent conflict with it, another mode of reflection, not concerned to provide explanations, but calling attention to itself as meditative, as ruminative, calling attention to the poem as a representation of the poet's mental experience, of what Wordsworth describes in the 'Preface' as 'the fluxes and refluxes', the ebb and flow, 'of the mind when agitated by the great and simple affections of our nature'.[7] The sincerity of the attempt at ratiocination will establish its failure as an honourable one, so that we will accept, along with Wordsworth, that all that is left to us thereafter is a ruminative mode, in which the mind proposes to itself, as its proper object of attention, not so much the meanings it seeks to generate, but its own movements in search of meaning.

## II

Thus far Davie, and as will be clear from the attention I have bestowed upon his argument, I find it, with the reservation I have indicated, as suggestive in relation to 'Tintern Abbey' as I do in relation to *The Prelude*. What I want to do for the rest of this essay is to add two further conditions to those so far suggested as necessarily accompanying the demand that we take on trust the fiduciary symbols that are Wordsworth's abstract nouns. And the conditions I want to propose are such as will, I hope, help to situate the language of 'Tintern Abbey' in a specific historical context, in the context of late eighteenth-century beliefs about, and attitudes to, language, and to gender: beliefs and attitudes to which Wordsworth appeals, in his implicit demand that we take his words on trust, but to which he also refers explicitly, as we shall see. One of these conditions is that the poem's success – and a number of reviewers were enthusiastic about the poem, and used it as a stick to beat the 'lyrical ballads' proper – is achieved not in spite of its failure to define the meaning of its abstract nouns, but absolutely because of its refusal or failure to define them. That failure or refusal is welcomed not, perhaps, out of a belief that the meaning of the fiduciary symbols is too private, too much inherent in the experience of one individual to take on public meanings, but because the power of the poem, the power it communicates to us, is somehow dependent upon the refusal of the poem to communicate fixed meanings. That power, I shall suggest, was conceived of as a masculine power, communicated specifically to male subjects of language. It can be communicated to women only as a promise, only as something they are always about to enjoy.

This first condition I shall consider towards the end of this essay. The second is that we should believe that there is a relationship, however irrecoverable, between the abstract and highly-articulated language of the poem and another kind of language which is also present in 'Tintern Abbey', as it is in The Prelude – the language of natural description, or the language that names the objects in nature. This language is conceived of as entirely unambiguous, but also as lexically and syntactically impoverished. The first language, of course, can be spoken only by a fully autonomous and individuated subject, a subject who is male, educated, fully differentiated from sense and nature; the second can be spoken also by subjects who are not male or not educated or not either, and who are imperfectly differentiated from nature. There seems to be no question of the nouns in this second kind of language describing simply the 'effect' of the natural world, or depending for their meaning on their context, or on any complex of relations among them that requires to be articulated by a complex syntax; so that, although they may crop up in complex structures of rationcinative or ruminative syntax, their appearance always involves a temporary respite from that complexity.

Let us take, for example, lines 78–9, 'the tall rock, The mountain, and the deep and gloomy wood'; or lines 98–100. 'the light of setting suns, And the round ocean, and the living air, And the blue sky'; or lines 104–5, 'the meadows and the woods, And mountains'; or lines 159–60, 'these steep woods and lofty cliffs, And this green pastoral landscape'. These brief lists of natural objects appear as islands of fixity and clarity in the troubled currents of Wordsworth's syntax, and among the objects in these lists, the simplest of all relationships is proposed – that made by the innocent conjunction 'and'. The simplicity of this connection is repeatedly emphasised by continuing the lists of concrete nouns and

noun-phrases over the line-ending, so that the word 'And' can appear in
the emphatic position at the beginning of the line: 'And the round ocean';
'And mountains'; 'And this green pastoral landscape'. This simple,
repeated structure seems to be related to the structure we examined in
Thomson, whereby the eye, before it was revealed as the subject of its
sentence and of the landscape, was

> snatch'd o'er hill, and dale, and wood, and lawn,
> And verdant field, and darkening heath between,
> And villages embosom'd soft in trees,
> And spiry towns . . .

I am not trying to suggest, of course, that for as long as they appear,
these lists of nouns are insulated from the operations of the intellect. But
the kind of operation it seems appropriate to perform on them is well
suggested in lines 15–17 –

> Once again I see
> These hedge-rows, hardly hedge-rows, little lines
> Of sportive wood run wild

– where the qualification, 'hardly hedge-rows', calls attention to the act of
the mind involved in finding the right word or phrase for the objects of
nature, in making the words of the poem more satisfactorily referential.
We are dealing here with signs which, however liable to misrepresent
the objects to which they refer, are treated, it seems, as if they can be *made*
to represent them with some degree of exactness; and the pause in the
momentum of the description, and then the act of redescription, serves
to indicate how different this language is, whose proper objects are stable
enough to be named with precision, from the language of moods,
sublimities, presences.

It is to this language of natural description that Wordsworth refers,
when he speaks at line 109 of 'the language of the sense' – a phrase which
has caused considerable difficulty to a number of readers of the poem,
no doubt because the function which Wordsworth ascribes to that
language – which, together with nature, is claimed to be

> The anchor of my purest thoughts, the nurse,
> The guide, and guardian of my heart, and soul
> Of all my moral being

– seems a function altogether too grand, too awesome, to be performed
by the language of natural description – if not by nature, which for
Wordsworth can do almost anything. What then does Wordsworth

mean by 'the language of the sense'? The first phrase we need to tackle
here is 'the sense', a phrase which the OED does very little to illuminate.
The only definition it offers is 'that one of the senses which is indicated
by the context' – that is to say, the phrase occurs only when the context
has already made clear which of the five senses it refers to, as in this
example quoted from Goldsmith: 'Salts, metals, plants, ordures of every
kind . . . make one mass of corruption, equally displeasing to the sense,
as injurious to the health' – where the context clearly specifies 'the sense'
as 'the sense of smell'. For the singular 'sense' without the definite article,
however, the OED offers 'the senses viewed as forming a single faculty in
contradistinction to intellect, will, etc.', a meaning which corresponds to
one meaning of le sens in French, and which amounts to the same
definition as that which the OED offers for the plural form, 'the senses':
'the faculties of physical perception or sensation as opposed to the
higher faculties of intellect, spirit, etc.'

It is clearly to this meaning of 'the senses' that Coleridge appeals, when
he translates the Aristotelian maxim, 'nihil in intellectu quod non prius
in sensu', as 'there is nothing in the Understanding not derived from the
Senses'. But elsewhere, Coleridge translates the adage thus: 'there is
nothing in the understanding which was not previously in the sense';
and elsewhere again, he writes that 'the REASON without being either
the SENSE, the UNDERSTANDING or the IMAGINATION contains all
three within itself' – where 'the sense' appears to have exactly the
meaning of 'sense' or 'the senses' offered by the OED, as depending on a
contradistinction of the sense from the intellect (Coleridge's 'understanding') and the other faculties.[8]

What then is 'the language' of the sense?[9] Once again, Coleridge
offers us some help. He writes at one point of material nature as 'the so
called elements, water, earth, air, and all their compounds', and notes
that in writing thus he is using 'the ever-enduring language of the senses,
to which nothing can be revealed, but as compact, or fluid, or aerial'. If
the meaning of the phrase here remains opaque, it will seem less so
when Coleridge writes that an 'infallible intelligence' (the Holy Spirit)
'may convey the truth in any one of three possible languages - that of
sense, as objects appear to the beholder on this earth; or that of science,
which supposes the beholder placed in the centre; or that of philosophy,
which resolves both into a supersensual reality'. He is clearly rehearsing
the same notion when he writes of the scriptures that they 'speak in the
language of the Affections which they excite in us; on sensible objects,
neither metaphysically, as they are known by superior intelligences; nor

theoretically, as they would be seen by us were we placed in the Sun; but as they are represented by our human senses in our present relative position'.[10] The languages of science and metaphysics need not yet detain us, though the second can certainly be regarded as akin to the abstract language we have already located in 'Tintern Abbey'. The 'language of the senses' seems by this account to be either the literal language by which we name the objects we behold on earth; or the metaphorical 'language' of images, by which the senses, or the understanding operating on the data of sense, represent terrestrial objects to us.

It may indeed be the second of these, but only as a figurative extension of 'the language of the sense' as that by which we *name* the things we perceive. The 'understanding', according to one of Coleridge's many definitions (and we could use any one of them here) is 'the power of generalizing the motives of the Sense [i.e.: sense-data] and of judging of the objective *reality* of all Appearances by their reducibility to a genus or class'. The understanding, it seems, produces things – let us say a red leather armchair – from the impressions of redness, shininess, comfort, curvilinearity – presented to it by the senses; from these it distinguishes the impressions of heat, brightness, and flickering motion which the senses receive at the same time, and composes these into the thing called the fire in front of which the chair is placed. But it can do this – it can produce objects out of sensations – only because it can *name* them ('let us *say* a red leather armchair', 'the thing *called* the fire'). 'In no instance do we understand a thing in itself; but only the name to which it is referred'; and so, 'in all instances, it is words, names, or, if images, yet images used as words or names, that are the only exclusive subjects of Understanding.'[11] The 'language of the sense' is then a phrase which can be used figuratively, to apply to the 'language' of images, only because it has already been used literally: for images, in this context, are 'used as words or names', to fix a bundle of impressions into an object. The 'language of the sense' is, first and foremost, the language by which we name the things, the material objects we perceive; though, to speak more accurately, we perceive only sensations, and only 'half-perceive' objects, for we also 'half-*create*' them, by the operations of the understanding on impressions or sensations.

There is of course a danger in interpreting a phrase in a poem written by Wordsworth in 1798 by an appeal to the writings of Coleridge some twenty years later. But in this instance the danger seems minimal, in that there is not much in Coleridge's account of the language of the sense which he could not have learned from the mid eighteenth-century philosopher David Hartley, by whom he was much influenced in the 1790s; and so there is nothing in the account which Coleridge could not have communicated orally to Wordsworth, if Wordsworth himself had never looked at Hartley. In a famous passage of *The Prelude*, written in 1799, Wordsworth describes how a baby may be presumed to produce a unified image of an object, its nurse, by combining the various sensations it perceives; by combining, that is,

> In one appearance all the elements
> And parts of the same object, else detached
> And loth to coalesce

Thus the baby is at once the 'receiver' of the impressions of sense, and the 'creator' of the objects those impressions constitute.[12] The passage appears to derive, directly or indirectly, from a section in Hartley's *Observations on Man* (1749), in which Hartley attempts to show how 'the Names of visible Objects' are associated with 'the Impressions which these Objects make upon the Eye'. He argues that the association between names and things is produced by the fact that 'the Name of the visible Object, the Nurse, for Instance, is pronounced and repeated by the Attendants to the Child, more frequently when his Eye is fixed upon the Nurse, than when upon other Objects'. But, more interestingly, he argues that the ability to produce the complex, unified image of an object *depends* upon the baby's learning its name. It is by learning the word 'nurse' that the child learns to distinguish the nurse from the clothes she wears, for however often she changes her dress, the same word seems to name her; it is by learning that the word 'fire' names the fire in different places, and surrounded by different visible objects, that the child learns to separate the bundle of sensations that compose the object, the fire, from those which compose other objects. Much the same is true of how we learn what is common to a range of different objects: it is by the association of the word 'white' with the visible appearances of milk, linen, paper, and so on, that we learn to separate the quality common to those various objects from the qualities that distinguish them from each other. The language by which we learn to name objects is the means by which we learn to distinguish them; it is the first language we learn, and is 'confined to sensible things' – it is 'the language of the sense'.[13]

How is it, then, that Wordsworth can claim to ascribe so aweseome a moral function to 'nature and the language of the sense'? This may appear to be fundamentally the same question as the one I posed earlier: how do 'lofty cliffs' produce 'lofty thoughts', thoughts that are elevated, 'pure', in that they are both somehow *above* nature, supernatural, and are also *morally* elevated. But that question has now been changed, by being associated with a question about language; and we could now rephrase it: how does the phrase 'lofty cliffs', or the ability to use such phrases, produce, or guide us towards, the phrase 'lofty thoughts', or the ability to deploy a phrase like that? How does the language of the sense not only produce, but foster in us, and guide us towards, the language of the intellect and of morality? And how does the language of the sense remain the anchor and guardian, not only of our purest thoughts and our moral being, but of the language by which we describe these spiritual objects of thought?

This question is posed also by Hartley, whose book is dedicated to arguing that the pleasures of sense and of the imagination – including those that we experience from the contemplation of natural beauty – must give way to, and be regulated by, 'the Precepts of Benevolence, Piety, and the Moral Sense'. The pleasure we take in 'a beautiful Scene', for example – say, the prospect of the Wye Valley near Tintern – 'ought to decline', 'by yielding, in due time, to more exalted and pure Pleasures' – say, 'the still, sad music of humanity', neither 'harsh nor grating'. The similarity of this scheme to that of 'Tintern Abbey' is obvious enough; but the important question for us is a question less of morality than of the 'natural history' of the individual: how does Hartley understand the process by which we learn the language of the intellect and of morality?

In the first place, Hartley argues, we learn the meanings of 'the names of intellectual and moral Qualities and Operations' in much the same way as we learn to find the unknown quality in an algebraic equation. That is to say, such names occur in connection with the names in the language of the sense; and by considering the relations of the words we do understand – those which describe 'sensible Impressions only' – with those we do not, we are enabled to arrive at our 'first imperfect Notions' of the names of such qualities and operations.[14] This is much the same as Davie's suggestion, that we understand Wordsworth's abstract nouns by trusting that they do have meaning, as we trust that $x$ in an equation has value; by taking them 'at a run', and by considering them 'only in their context'. Our understanding of these names, Hartley continues, is further refined by encountering them in books, and in attempting to use them ourselves. But in the first place, we are led to understand the language of intellect and morality by its relation to the language of the sense, and in this light the language of the sense can be conceived of as the 'anchor' of the more 'elevated' language, the 'nurse' which fosters our understanding of it, and the 'guide' which leads us to that understanding.

But there is another light in which nature and the language of the sense can be seen to be all those things, to perform all the functions of anchor, nurse, guide and guardian, in relation to the language of intellect and morality. Like Locke, Hartley believed that complex ideas, such as the ideas of objects, are composed of bundles of simple ideas, separate sensations; and he believed further, that what he called 'decomplex' ideas, 'Ideas of Reflection, and intellectual Ideas', are produced by the association of complex ideas. But 'decomplex' ideas are unlike complex ones, in that they have no sensible images associated with them: we cannot refer the word 'intellect' to a visible image, as we can refer the word 'table' to the image of a table. As a result, the names attached to decomplex ideas are far more open to ambiguity, to being misunderstood, than are the names attached either to simple sensible qualities, like 'white' or 'sweet', or to complex ideas, like 'nurse' or 'table'. But in theory, the meaning of the names of decomplex ideas should be able to be fixed, by analysing those ideas themselves down to the simple ideas of sensation, of which ultimately they consist; and if we could do this, we would be able to arrive at 'the proper Use of those Words, which have no Ideas', to the great benefit of philosophy.[15] The ideas of nature, and the language of sensible impressions, are thus to be the fixed anchor by which floating 'Ideas of Reflection', of intellect and morality, and the language which describes them, are tethered to the solid ocean floor. They are the guardians of meaning, the guides by which meaning is to be comprehended; the tangible gold by which the value of the promissory notes of an abstract, intellectual, and moral vocabulary are, or should or might be, guaranteed.

It must of course be the unambiguous way in which the names in the language of the sense refer to their referents that makes nature and the language of the sense, as Wordsworth argues, anchor, nurse, guide, and guardian of his heart, and the soul of his moral being. Of his 'moral' being, because, within the meditative and contemplative language of this poem, in which morality is taken to be the exclusive property of whoever can be claimed to be the subject of nature, not the object of its determination, the capacity to feel for others is something 'learned', and is a function of the capacity to reflect, to have thoughts. 'Our thoughts', Wordsworth argues in the 'Preface', are 'the representatives of all our past feelings'; and in the same sentence it appears that feelings are 'influxes' from outside ourselves, are the sense-data named by the language of the sense.[16] So that however incommunicable and indefinable our thoughts may be – their character, as I tried to show earlier, can be communicated much more readily than their content – this empiricist belief that the basis of abstract ideas is in concrete experience is crucial to the poem's attempt to convince its readers that the language of thought has meaning because it is ultimately derived from objects of sense which admit of being rendered with precision and clarity. This assumed relation, in short, between the languages proper to intellection and to simple naming and description, is not only one of the conditions by which we may take 'fiduciary symbols' on trust – it is represented by Wordsworth as the essential condition for his own trusting of his thoughts.

## III

Now that the problem – how do lofty cliffs produce lofty thoughts – has been represented at least partly as a problem of language, it admits of another solution, which was advanced not only by Hartley but by almost every empiricist philosopher of language in the eighteenth century who considered the relation between the language of sensible impressions and the language of intellection. For the question can now be put another way: how was the language of intellection produced out of the language of the sense? what is the natural history of the development of an abstract out of a concrete language? Hartley's version of the solution is to argue that 'if a Language be narrow, and much confined to sensible Things,' as it will be in the infancy of a language, 'it will have great Occasion for Figures'[17] – in particular for figures of speech based on analogies between those ideas to which words are already attached, and those for which words are desired. The original, literal meaning of a word in the language of the sense can be extended, not only to other objects of sense, but to objects of intellection; and the fact that the same word can be applied to objects of both kinds may act to persuade us that perhaps the capacity of a word to be transferred from things to thoughts may impress upon us a sense of the reality of the relations between them, in such a way as to enable us to trust that abstract expressions do indeed have meaning. In this light, it seems important to the problem the poem is considering, that one of the most striking features of the language of the poem is *repetition*, by which the same word is used here literally, there figuratively, here as part of the language of the sense, and there as part of the language of 'intellectual and moral Qualities and Operations'. The word 'lofty' itself is an obvious example of such a transference; a more interesting one is 'deep', which, together with its derivatives, occurs six times in the poem.

Two of the instances of 'deep' seem to belong more to what we may regard as the language of the sense than to the language of reflection, though neither entirely escapes the more figurative meanings of the word evident in other instances of its use. 'The deep and gloomy wood' in line 79, and the 'deep rivers' of line 70, both occur in passages which I have suggested are moments of spatial arrest in the temporal movement of the ratiocinative and ruminative syntax. The literal, the topographical, the sensational meaning of the word in both cases is underlined by the fact that it occurs both times in the context of accounts of Wordsworth's primitive, appetitive enjoyment of nature, in the period of 'thoughtless youth', when the objects of the landscape had no need of 'a remoter charm By thought supplied'. For, as we shall see, when the word 'deep' is used in a more thoroughly figurative sense, it is used to apply to a later, more mature phase of his development, when the kind of childish, thoughtless enjoyment he had once taken in nature, however much its loss is regretted, is represented as a superficial enjoyment, as compared with the more reflective, more melancholy enjoyment he now experiences.

This maturer enjoyment is characterised at once by his penetrating below the surface of nature, and by his own mind being penetrated far more deeply by what he sees or by what he once saw. To this opposition of the superficial and the youthful, on the one hand, and, on the other, the deep and mature, such a use of 'deep' as that in line 49 appeals – it is when our wild and greedy eyes are made quiet by the 'deep' power of joy that we see into the life of things. The most extreme use of 'deep' in this sense occurs in line 97: Wordsworth has felt, he claims, 'a sense sublime / Of something far more deeply interfused'. The whole phrase is the most extreme example in the poem of a notion that we have no alternative but to reject or to take on trust; and it calls attention to this by the word 'something', a frank admission of a failure to define, or of the impossibility of defining, the nature of that sense sublime. 'Deeply' here refers to an interiority so profound that the mere light of reason will certainly fail to illuminate its depths.

The first use of the word, in line 7, offers itself, by means of its ambiguity, almost as a kind of bridge between the extremes of literal and of figurative use. In the first place, the 'thoughts of more deep seclusion' may be thoughts about, or thoughts appropriate to, a scene which is yet more sequestered, yet more remote from the centres of civilization, than Tintern Abbey is. They may be thoughts, that is, of a more deep seclusion than Wordsworth is now experiencing; and in this sense the word retains a literal notion of spatial separation, even if it operates in terms of a geography as much subjective as objective, a geography as much of thoughts as of maps, a 'landscape of the mind'. But this reading is complicated by the fact that the relation of 'deep seclusion' with 'a wild secluded scene' (line 6) invites itself to be read in terms of the opposition of wildness and depth that runs through the whole poem. Thus, to look on a 'wild' landscape, as Dorothy looks on it, with 'wild eyes' (line 120), and so to experience 'wild ecstasies' (line 139), is evidently to experience it at a superficial level which is entirely innocent of depth. The point is made clear by the insistence, in the second paragraph, that wild eyes must be made quiet, by the 'deep power of joy' (line 49), if they are to perceive things in their depth; it is made clear again by the prospect, announced in the last paragraph, of Dorothy's 'wild ecstasies' in nature maturing one day into a 'far deeper zeal Of holier love' for nature (lines 155–6).

This opposition, then, of wildness and depth is an opposition between an immediate, superficial response to nature, and a response which, mediated by time and reflection, seems to occupy a deep interior space within the mature and reflective adult. In these terms, the 'thoughts of more deep seclusion' may be thoughts of a deeper seclusion than a merely 'wild seclusion', a merely geographical isolation in a natural landscape, can be: a regrettable but still salutary (or so Wordsworth would like to believe) seclusion of the subject from the immediate objects of experience. That suggestion is reinforced by the fact that the steep and lofty cliffs do not simply impress thoughts of more deep seclusion, they also 'connect / The landscape with the quiet of the sky'. The assertion at line 100, that the sense sublime dwells 'in the blue sky, and in the mind of man', so that sky and mind are associated, contributes to an attempt to develop out of the language of the sense another, figurative language, which will be able to describe ideas of reflection and morality. It is this extension which the ambiguous use of 'deep' at line 7 strives to achieve.

But these strategies of repetition and figuration can do no more than begin to provide names for intellectual operations and moral qualities. What they most obviously cannot do is to provide a syntax, a mode of connecting words in well-formed sentences, which both Davie and Hartley took as another essential condition for our trusting that abstract nouns had meanings, and by which Hartley believed we could arrive at an understanding, however imperfect, of those nouns. Can the poem do anything to account for the co-existence within it of a highly-articulated syntax which is descriptive, even mimetic of the operations of reflection and meditation, and the simple syntax of the language of the sense? And does it have anything to say about the historical process by which the first has developed out of the second?

The empiricist theory of language which Hartley and Wordsworth are heirs to derived the most substantial part of its intellectual legacy from the third book of Locke's *Essay Concerning Human Understanding* (1690). In particular, Hartley's concern to produce a philosophical language by rivetting each idea to its one appropriate name had been Locke's concern also, and the primary motive which led him to investigate the nature of language. And as a result, Locke's theory put far more stress on the naming function of language than on any other. He concentrated his attention on nouns and adjectives, and treated most other parts of speech, perhaps including verbs, as 'particles'. About these, he had almost nothing to say: they are, he says, 'marks of some action or intimation of the mind',[18] but he says no more than this, and nothing about syntax. 'It seems fair to conclude', remarks Stephen Land, that 'the only kind of word unmistakeably referred to by Locke in his thesis that words signify ideas is the "name". The formal properties of language have no significant place in Lockean semantics: by excluding from integral consideration all but the naming function Locke inevitably suggests that language is an aggregate of signs rather than a formal system.'[19] And there is every reason to associate with this suggestion the 'language of the sense' as it is referred to in 'Tintern Abbey': a language of names, with minimal formal connections between them, but of names which are nevertheless the 'anchor of our *purest* thoughts' – the word implies most abstract, most removed from sense, as well as most chaste, the thoughts of the 'purer mind', not of the heart, blood, or appetite, but thoughts which must finally be reducible to the language of the sense.

The history of empiricist British linguistics in the 150 or so years after Locke, Land argues, is a process of moving from a theory which conceived of language as an aggregate of signs, 'a collection of words', to one which conceived of it as a formal 'sign system':[20] a movement from an understanding of language in terms of signs to an understanding of it in terms of propositions; and Hartley's algebraic notion of syntax is a part of this development. And we can see the notion of trust, and of taking words at a run, that so engaged Davie, as essential to this new conception of language. We make utterances, or we listen to them, trusting that the formal relations the utterances produce will link together into meaning words which, separated from the contexts of discourse, can hardly be said to mean at all.

Now Locke's theory, and the development from that theory, with its concentration on the sign, to a theory which concentrated on the proposition, both lent themselves to being historicised, in the terms of that characteristically late eighteenth and early nineteenth-century notion of historical process which we sum up in the rule that ontogeny recapitulates phylogeny, that the development of the individual subject recapitulates the development of the race, or of mankind in general. Locke's theory itself could be historicised, by representing the naming of the objects of sense as the first stage of language; the ability to employ a vocabulary of abstract nouns, affixed to 'ideas of reflection', was an ability more likely to be discoverable in developed civilizations. Or the relation of signs to propositions could be historicised by the argument that the theory of language as an aggregate of signs does well enough as an account of the language of primitive peoples, who can express their fears and needs and appetites simply by naming the objects of desire or need, and so have small use for syntax – traces of that notion are evident in the passage I quoted earlier from *Biographia Literaria*, as well as in the 'Preface' to the *Lyrical Ballads*. As civilization advances, primarily through the division of labour and the emergence of cultivated élites, the need to articulate the relations among signs increases, and an increasingly sophisticated system of syntax evolves. The language of John Clare, by this argument, will appear once again as a primitive language, its destiny to evolve into the more abstract and articulate language of Thomson, as the destiny of its speaker is to become a civilized and so a differentiated subject, in control of, and able to organise, the words he uses, rather than being spoken by them.

Or the language of the sense or of Clare could be conceived of as a childish language, destined to mature into abstraction and sophistication as it developed towards the complexities of a propositional syntax able to express thoughts, reflections, rather than simply to name the objects of sense, need and desire. And it is this recapitulation of the history of civilization in the history of the individual, I want to suggest, and the authority which such a notion of history commanded around 1800, that enables the transition in 'Tintern Abbey' from the deep shadowy ruminative tone of its central passages to the assured tone of certainty, of having achieved, having resolved something, at the end. The appeal to this history is made – or rather the linguistic and historical notions are summoned into the poem – by the description of 'the language of the sense' as, in particular, the 'nurse', the 'guardian' of Wordsworth's heart, and by the suddenly unproblematic account of Dorothy's future development, from wildness to depth, in the last paragraph of the poem – from the realm of the wild, the savage, the primitive, the undifferentiated, to the realm of the cultivated, the autonomous, the transcendent.

There is no problem foreseen in the process of Dorothy's development, which can now be seen as an entirely natural process: it is sense and Nature that lead from joy to joy, from the joy of wildness to the joy of depth; Dorothy's wild ecstasies will simply mature, like fruit or cheese, into a sober pleasure. It's all just a matter of growing up: nature and the language of the sense operate, in this process, not as what prevents but as what fosters that process; they are together the nurse and guardian who oversee the the process, the guide who leads us from the experience appropriate to childhood to the experience appropriate to maturity. And yet the language of the sense remains present all the time, as the guarantor of meaning; of the meanings which, by the movement from signs to propositions, from 'animal' and 'thoughtless' youth to thinking loftily and deeply, to fully autonomous and differentiated subjectivity, we produce as adults, for these meanings are only *really* to be trusted because they are analysable into the language of the sense. Wordsworth himself has experienced a gap between the two kinds of experience and two kinds of language, the language of his 'former heart' and that of his 'purer mind'; and it was his loosening grip on the simple, and as it were pictogrammatic language that made him unable to 'paint' what once he was. There had seemed to be a problem of how to connect lofty cliffs and lofty thoughts, and the language of the sense seemed so far removed from the mature language of propositional syntax and fiduciary symbols that the first had seemed to function as an interruption of the other. But this gap he can now experience, on Dorothy's and so also on his own behalf, as a regular, and above all as a natural process of growth.

## IV

But where does all this leave Dorothy? It is a fact that we should never lose sight of, in eighteenth-century Britain, that women were excluded from what was called the 'republic of letters', for the qualification for citizenship in that republic was the ability to reduce the data of experience to abstract categories, and women, it was commonly assumed, could think in terms only of the particular and the concrete. It was a common assumption among men, at least, that the language of women, whether educated or not, was thus relatively concrete and pictogrammatic as compared with that of educated men; because though they could recall, and arrange facts and images, to the degree necessary to use concrete nouns, they could not grasp the principles in terms of which such nouns were produced; they could not deploy with confidence an abstract language either far removed or entirely sundered from the world of things and of sensible ideas; and so they could not achieve that transcendent identity which is evinced in the production of an abstract and highly articulated language. One of the most popular English grammars of the early eighteenth century – a grammar based on the epistemological and linguistic theories of Locke – is divided (as were many contemporary grammars) between a large-print text which lays down the rules of grammar, and small-print notes which explain the principles from which the rules are derived. The text, the author explains, is all that need concern, as he puts it, 'children, women, and the ignorant of both sexes'[21] – the last category seeming to concede an ability to grasp principles, which has already been denied them by the inclusion of all women, whether educated or not, in the list of those who need not consult the notes.

We can be reasonably sure that Wordsworth would not openly or even privately have endorsed such an account of the intellectual 'imbecility' of women: in the late eighteenth century, and especially in the radical circles within which Wordsworth had moved in the 1790s, the *potential* of women to achieve the levels of rationality and transcendence which educated men achieved was being firmly asserted, most firmly by Mary Wollstonecraft. But we can also say with reasonable confidence that it was important for Wordsworth that the ability of women to grasp the principles of abstraction should be conceded only at the level of a potential, not an actual ability to do so. Thus in 'Tintern Abbey' Dorothy is promised future membership among the company of the intellectual, only for Wordsworth to withhold it for the time being, and perhaps indefinitely. I have said – for this is what the poem officially invites us to believe – that the transition from signs to propositions was made unproblematic, in the poem, by reference to the growth to intellectual maturity that Dorothy would surely accomplish: in 'after years' she will sober up, and her mind will become 'a mansion for all lovely forms' – I take it for general forms, for it is already a mansion for particular images of loveliness. How long a time is implied in the phrase 'after years' is not clear, but more, it seems, than the one-and-a-half years by which Dorothy was William's junior. Nevertheless, Dorothy will, it is promised or threatened, one day grow up, and learn to perceive nature in the quiet and intellectual terms which will indicate that her wild appetitive passions are now spent, and she has finally become a subject as fully differentiated from sense and nature as her brother, able to reflect upon her relations with nature, and not simply to respond to it.

In making this promise, however, Wordsworth is a victim of a conflict of his own interests, a conflict which requires Dorothy to perform a double function in the ratification of his achievement of a transcendent subjectivity. First, he needs to believe that Dorothy will grow up and sober up, for by doing so she will naturalise and legitimate his own loss of immediate pleasure in nature. The transition she makes, from the language of the sense to that of the intellect, will be an observable process, one which will recapitulate and historicise the transition Wordsworth has already made. But in the second place, the language of the sense, as presently employed by Dorothy, stands as a present and audible guarantee of the meanings in his own language of the intellect; it assures him of the secure foundation of his language in the language of the sense. Dorothy can perform these two functions, only if her potential for intellectual growth is acknowledged, but only if, also, that potential is never actualised. Wordsworth is quite explicit about this: the 'prayer' he begins to utter at line 120 –

> Oh! yet a little while
> May I behold in thee what I was once

– is no more or less than a prayer to nature to arrest Dorothy's development, and for his benefit. The danger, if nature does not answer his prayer, is not just that a mature and a fully autonomous Dorothy will drag the anchor by which Wordsworth's own language is secured to the language of the sense. For if, as I have suggested, Dorothy belongs for Wordsworth in a category which includes childhood, including his own, the language of the sense, and nature as something directly responded to, she also belongs in a category by which she becomes, child though she is, the 'nurse' of Wordsworth's heart. Her growth to autonomous subjectivity will not, as it turns out, simply recapitulate Wordsworth's own; it will precipitate, in him, a less comfortable subject-position than he now claims to occupy, in which he will be unguarded, unguided, un-nursed, where he will be without an audible guarantor of the fiduciary symbols that compose his own language, no longer able to appeal to Dorothy as the Bank of England, underwriting the value and meaning of the coins and banknotes he issues.

The paradoxes generated by Wordsworth's need are complicated, but not unfamiliar. Dorothy must be acknowledged as capable of growing up. But she must also remain a child, if she is to remain a nurse;. and she must remain Wordsworth's nurse if Wordsworth himself is to remain a man. The point is reinforced if we glance back to the passages from The Prelude, and Hartley's Observations, which represent the nurse, not just as the guardian and guide of the male-child, but as the object of his perception, the material from which he produces complex ideas. From these in turn he will go on to produce the 'decomplex' ideas which the nurse is, at best, always only about to produce herself.

## V

So much, then, by way of an account of one of the conditions for the taking on trust of Wordsworth's abstract vocabulary. I still need to say something about the other, which seems to contradict this first condition entirely. It was – for by now it has probably been forgotten – that we should believe that the power of the poem depends upon the very indefinability of Wordsworth's lofty thoughts, and that they occupy a vertiginous eminence, wrapped in a thick cloud which conceals any visible means of descent to, or ascent from, the world of nature and of sense. However securely those thoughts can be argued as deriving from the language of the sense, as being guaranteed by being reducible to that language, that does not mean to say that we can often, if ever, perform the act of analysis and reduction. And, more importantly, it was certainly not always believed at the end of the eighteenth century that we should even wish to be able to perform it. For while there was an intellectual satisfaction to be derived from the process of closing the gap between signs and propositions, by proposing a historical continuum between them, there was also an aesthetic pleasure to be derived from leaving open the gap between simple linguistic signs and those words, fiduciary symbols, whose meaning resisted analysis and definition. The nature of this pleasure was particularly the concern of theorists of the aesthetic category known as 'the sublime'; and it was as a poem which offered the pleasures and excitements of sublimity that 'Tintern Abbey' was recognised by a number of its early reviewers.

For most English readers contemporary with Wordsworth, the pleasure to be derived from the sublime of language had been defined largely by Edmund Burke, in his *Philosophical Enquiry into the Origins of our Ideas of the Sublime and the Beautiful*, first published in 1757. In his remarks on language, Burke made an important contribution to the process of qualifying the semantic account of language proposed by Locke. To put Burke's position as shortly as possible, he argued that we do not need to understand words by referring to the ideas they signified; and that in most uses of language it was impossible to do so. We do not understand the sentence, 'I shall go to Italy next summer', by referring the words to pictorial images. How many means of conveyance – foot, horse, coach, boat – would we need to conjure up the idea signified by 'going'; how many images are necessary to provide a referent for 'summer'? and how many summers do we need to try to visualize to understand the notion 'next summer'? How many images of landscape and climate must be called up, to represent the sensible idea of 'Italy'? But more to the point, Burke argues that among the words which have the most affective power over us are what he called *compounded abstract* words – such words as 'virtue', 'liberty', 'honour' – which are almost impossible, in a connected train of conversation or reading, even to conceive of as being reducible to ideas of sense.[22]

We learn to use such words by attending to the contexts and occasions of their use, not by analysing them; and we can therefore generate contexts in which to use them without any clear understanding of their meaning, even within particular contexts. Most important of all, the affective power of such compounded abstract words as are used to express the passions is crucially dependent, Burke suggests, on their obscurity and indefinability, on the fact that their connotative aura spreads beyond our ability to grasp its limits.[23] It is this sense of the limitless, of the infinite, of the *frisson* of the indefinable, of the sense of something too deeply interfused in our being to be fully illuminated by the light of analysis, that is the cause of our experience of the sublime of language. Wordsworth's use of the word 'sublime', in the context of passages of his most evidently passionate exaltation – the 'blessed mood', a gift of 'aspect more sublime' than the landscape; the sublime 'something' that dwells everywhere and so cannot be limited by being defined – is what justifies, or would have justified in 1798, his use of that vocabulary which so engaged Davie, no less than would the counter-claim, that this vocabulary is rooted in the language of the sense.

Only the last few pages of Burke's *Enquiry* are concerned with language: the bulk of it is a natural history of our experience of the sublime of vision. He argues, in brief, that obscure objects of vision are more affecting, more 'terrible', and so more sublime, than objects perceived with clarity. Darkness, extreme distance, extreme height, extreme depth – mountains, cliffs, abysses – these are objects the sight of which gives rise to sublime experience. And it seems to him to follow from this that language is a medium more capable of communicating sublime experience than the visual arts, just because language, which uses arbitrary signs, is necessarily more obscure, in that it cannot represent objects with the same clarity as can the natural signs which even the most obscure painting employs, as well as because it is often not concerned to conjure up ideas, in the sense of images, at all.

This argument also may offer a crucial context for an understanding of the language and development of 'Tintern Abbey'. Wordsworth begins the poem with the description of a landscape which evidently partakes of the sublime: it includes steep and lofty cliffs, which appeal to the vertiginous pleasure we take in whatever prompts our fear and our concern for self-preservation; it is 'wild', a crucial term in the sublime of landscape; it is observed with wild eyes, and it prompts wild ecstasies. Yet the first movement of the poem is to turn away from these merely visual experiences, and from what seemed to many in the eighteenth century to be an almost directly referential language of naming, towards an obscure and abstract language which, by virtue of its inability to find things to name, may be all the more affective. And only after that initial turning is the attempt made to connect the sublime of landscape and the sublime of language within a historical continuum from childhood to maturity, from determination by nature to freedom from determination.

Within the discourse of the sublime, 'the language of the sense' functioned as a marker of difference; in the historical discourse, it could function also as a marker of relation. For the sublime discourse invited the polite male to experience a peculiar satisfaction in contemplating the vast gap which separated him from those others, the uneducated rustic and the impressionable female, who could perform no very elaborate operations on the impressions they received. The historical discourse, concerned with how languages develop, in a people or in the individual, could drop a ladder down to those who remained 'merged in sense', apparently to invite them to ascend to share the autonomous subject-position at its top. But the two discourses could be knotted together, as they are in this poem, because both acknowledged that the gap between the language of the sense and what Coleridge called 'the best part of human language' was one of the most crucial issues which the theory of language was obliged to address. Thus both agreed that children, the vulgar, women, could be trusted to use such a word as 'table' with as much accuracy as the educated male, and could be expected to construct such sentences as 'table' might occur in with tolerable success. With words such as 'liberty' or 'virtue' – or 'restoration, or 'moral being', or 'sublime' itself – the case was evidently very different: such words could be well used only by the highly educated, in the highly-articulated syntax which only they could deploy.

The knotting together of these two discourses within 'Tintern Abbey' ensures that the invitation extended to Dorothy, to climb the ladder to the language of reflection, would not sound too sincere, and that the power to be derived from this knotting would not be put at risk. The polite needed the uneducated and impressionable to know and to keep their place, if they themselves were to remain in exclusive possession of the top spot. Dorothy may climb, one day she will, but for the moment . . . – this strategy reveals that the ladder is really an anchor chain, to provide the polite male with the private reassurance that his own articulate and artificial language is still securely tethered to the nature which he has escaped from and transcended, but which he must still appeal to, if he is to talk, not nonsense but 'sense'.

# Notes

1 First published in Wordsworth and Coleridge, *Lyrical Ballads* (1798); quoted from the edition of Brett and Jones, see above, p. 136, n. 12.

2 Davie, *Articulate Energy* (London: Routledge and Kegan Paul, 1955), pp. 106–7.

3 Herbert Lindenberger, *On Wordsworth's 'Prelude'* (Princeton: Princeton University Press, 1963), p. 44.

4 *Biographia Literaria* (see above, p. 77, n. 11), vol. 2, pp. 52–3, but here quoted from Davie, pp. 108–9.

5 Davie, p. 109.

6 Davie, pp. 110–11.

7 *Lyrical Ballads*, p. 247.

8 Coleridge, *Aids to Reflection*, ed. Thomas Fenby (Edinburgh: John Grant, 1905), p. 199n, and see *Biographia Literaria*, vol. 1, p. 141n.; *Logic*, ed. J. R. de J. Jackson (London and Princeton: Routledge and Kegan Paul and Princeton University Press, 1981), p. 226; *Lay Sermons* (see above, p. 78, n. 14), p. 69.

9 In a famous essay on the meaning of 'sense' in *The Prelude*, in *The Structure of Complex Words* (London: Chatto and Windus, 1951), pp. 289–305, William Empson identified Wordsworth's 'the sense' in the phrase we are considering as a new form, 'and the new form,' he argued, 'must be supposed to imply some new meaning'. Thus 'the sense' could not mean simply 'the senses': 'even Wordsworth could not have got away with saying that the language of the senses was the soul of all his moral being.' It would take too many pages to take issue with the complex meaning Empson attributes to 'the sense' as Wordsworth uses it, in 'Tintern Abbey' and *The Prelude*; and it will have to be sufficient here to say that in none of the examples of the phrase Empson discusses does it seem to me that we need attribute any more complex meaning to 'the sense' than the one the OED attributes to

'sense' or 'the senses'; and that (as I hope this essay will demonstrate) Wordsworth could certainly 'have got away' with attributing to 'the language of the sense' (or 'of sense' or 'of the senses') exactly the moral function that Empson says he could not.

10  Robert Southey and Coleridge, *Omniana*, ed. Robert Gittings (Fontwell, Sussex: Centaur Press), p. 347; Coleridge, *Confessions of an Inquiring Spirit* (London: Cassell, 1886), p. 17; *Aids*, pp. 75–6.

11  *Lay Sermons*, p. 60n.; *Aids*, p. 202.

12  Wordsworth, *The Prelude*, 1799, 1805, 1850, eds Jonathan Wordsworth, M. H. Abrams and Stephen Gill (New York and London: Norton, 1979). I quote from the 1799 version, Part 2, lines 278–80, 303.

13  Hartley, *Observations on Man, His Frame, His Duty, and His Expectations* (London and Bath, 1749), Part 1, pp. 270–3, 292, 298.

14  Hartley, Part 2, p. 245; Part 1, pp. 422, 275, 277.

15  Hartley, Part 1, pp. 278, 76.

16  *Lyrical Ballads*, p. 246.

17  Hartley, Part 1, p. 292.

18  Locke, *Essay*, III, vii, 4.

19  Stephen K. Land, *From Signs to Propositions: the Concept of Form in Eighteenth-Century Semantic Theory* (London: Longman, 1974), p. 8.

20  Land, p. 189.

21  Anon., *A Grammar of the English Language* (London, 1711), 'Preface' (pages unnumbered). The division of eighteenth-century grammars into text and notes, each aimed at different kinds of readers, is discussed by Murray Cohen in *Sensible Words: Linguistic Practice in England 1640–1785* (Baltimore, Md.: The Johns Hopkins University Press, 1977), chapter 2.

22  Burke, *A Philosophical Enquiry into the Origin of our Ideas of the Sublime and Beautiful*, ed. James T. Boulton (Notre Dame and London: University of Notre Dame Press, 1968), pp. 170, 164, 166.

23  Burke, p. 175.

# Further reading

**Introduction**   Many recent critical studies have made brief attempts to describe the politics of the discourse of practical criticism, though we still lack any full length study of the topic. The most useful short discussions are probably Terry Eagleton's *Literary Theory* (Oxford: Basil Blackwell, 1983), chapter one, and Raymond Williams, *Writing in Society* (London: Verso, 1983), pp. 177–91. For a more general account of the politics of English studies as defined by F. R. Leavis and the *Scrutiny*-group, see Francis Mulhern, *The Moment of Scrutiny* (London: New Left Books, 1979).

**Chapter One**   The secondary literature on Shakespeare's sonnets is enormous: the most recent attempt to describe it critically will be found in John Kerrigan's edition, *The Sonnets and A Lover's Complaint* (Harmondsworth: Penguin Books, 1986), pp. 65–74. One essay Kerrigan does not mention, in which the presence of the 'discourse of patronage' in sonnet 29 is briefly suggested, is Thomas M. Greene's 'Pitiful Thrivers: Failed Husbandry in the Sonnets', in *Shakespeare and the Question of Theory*, eds. Patricia Parker and Geoffrey Hartman, (New York and London: Methuen, 1985), and the whole essay, though probably closer to Booth's approach than to mine, is a serious attempt to read the sonnets in a theoretical perspective, though hardly in the 'economic' perspective claimed for it in the introduction to the volume. More useful still, though it is mainly concerned with Sidney's *Astrophel and Stella*, is Arthur F. Marotti's essay ' "Love is not love": Elizabethan sonnet sequences and the social order', *English Literary History*, vol. 49 (1982), pp. 396–428.

**Chapter Two**   For a general account of grammar and syntax in Milton, see R. D. Emma, *Milton's Grammar* (The Hague: Mouton, 1964); also useful is Colin Mac-Cabe's essay, ' "So truth be in the field": Milton's use of Language', in *Teaching the Text*, eds Susanne Kappeler and Norman Bryson (London: Routledge and Kegan Paul, 1983). The syntax of Milton's sonnet on his blindness is very usefully discussed in Stanley Fish's essay 'Interpreting the *Variorum*', in *Is There A Text in This Class? The Authority of Interpretive Communities* (Cambridge, Ma., and London: Harvard University Presss, 1980, pp. 154–8). Since my own manuscript was delivered to the publishers, there has appeared an excellent essay by Janel Mueller, 'The mastery of decorum: politics as poetry in Milton's sonnets' (*Critical Inquiry*, vol. 13, no. 3, Spring 1987, pp. 475–508). Mueller discusses more sonnets than I do, and relates them more closely to the political history of the mid-century. She also discusses, as I have tried to do, the politics of their syntax.

**Chapter Three**  Laura Brown, *Alexander Pope* (Oxford: Basil Blackwell, 1985), offers a reading of the politics of Pope's poetry which goes beyond the normal party-political approach, and is particularly acute on the presence of imperialist ideology in the poetry. For a discussion and exemplification of eighteenth-century economic discourse, see Stephen Copley, *Literature and the Social Order* (London: Croom Helm, 1984).

**Chaper Four**  The best detailed study of the language of Clare's poetry is Barbara Strang's 'John Clare's Language', in John Clare, *The Rural Muse*, ed. R. K. R. Thornton (Ashington and Manchester: Mid Northumberland Arts Group and Carcanet New Press, 1982). For a fuller discussion of the issues raised by this essay, see my *The Idea of Landscape and the Sense of Place, 1730–1840: an Approach to the Poetry of John Clare* (Cambridge: Cambridge University Press, 1972); Raymond Williams, 'The Green Language', in *The Country and the City* (London: Chatto and Windus, 1973); Roger Sales, 'John Clare and the politics of pastoral', in *English Literature in History, 1780–1830: Pastoral and Politics* (London: Hutchinson, 1983); and Elizabeth Helsinger, 'Clare and the place of the peasant poet', *Critical Inquiry*, vol. 13, no. 3 (Spring 1987), pp. 509–31.

**Chapter Five**  Of numerous studies of 'Tintern Abbey', those that I find most useful – especially in that they do not regard the poem as one of unqualified affirmation – are Marjorie Levinson's attempt to return the poem to the political moment of its composition, 'Insight and Oversight: Reading "Tintern Abbey" ', in *Wordsworth's Great Period Poems* (Cambridge: Cambridge University Press, 1986), and some pages by David Simpson, in *Wordsworth's Historical Imagination: The Poetry of Displacement* (New York and London: Methuen, 1987), pp. 109–13. For another view of Wordsworth's use of Dorothy, see Gayatri Spivak, 'Sex and History in *The Prelude* (1805): Books Nine to Thirteen', in *In Other Worlds: Essays in Cultural Politics* (New York and London: Methuen, 1987).

# Index